The Eternal Covenant
God, El, Allah, The West, The Jews and the Land of Israel

Written and Edited: Albert Talker

The USA is the only true leader of the free world

The book relies on factual and historical information, and its content is sourced from Wikipedia, Research Articles and through the use of AI.

CONTENTS

Recently I find myself contemplating the origins of animosity toward the people who introduced the concept of the monotheistic God on one hand and, on the other, created the atomic bomb, which has the potential to bring about the end of our world. One might wonder if this is all part of a larger plan, perhaps ordained by a higher power.

Many individuals in the Western world may not grasp the intricacies of Middle East politics and the daily challenges confronting Israel. There is a proclivity to align with one side without a comprehensive comprehension of the situation. It is crucial to acknowledge that the Jewish people have left an indelible mark on the world, offering foundational concepts for common legal systems, advocating strict monotheism that has shaped both Islam and Christianity, and making strides in diverse domains such as science, psychology, and technology. Nevertheless, it is also a historical truth that the Jewish community has endured profound adversities, encompassing persecution, massacres, the Inquisition, confinement to ghettos, and allegations of various misdeeds, culminating in the Holocaust. Despite these tribulations, the response has not been one of seeking retribution but rather one of contributing to society, fostering creativity, and participating across various disciplines, leading to a notable number of Nobel Prizes being conferred upon Jewish individuals.

In the aftermath of Hamas's attack on October 7, this book underscores the need for a nuanced understanding of intricate issues, discouraging the formation of hasty conclusions based on limited or prejudiced information. Israel serves as the most convenient focal point for channeling the vigor of pan-Arab nationalism and anti-West sentiments. It operates as a unifying subject among Arabs, perceived as a Western entity firmly implanted in the Middle East with significant Western backing. The Arab perspective views Israel not merely as a geographical presence but as a manifestation of a Western scheme, an interpretation that essentially embodies anti-West sentiment redirected specifically toward Israel. However, it is essential to recognize that 55% of Israel's population comprises descendants of Jewish refugees from Middle Eastern countries, and approximately 18% are Arabs, Druze, and Christians, enjoying full citizens' rights alongside the Jewish population.

The Demonstration for Hamas and Palestinians started even before Israel entered Gaza. No demonstration for the Palestinians had any reference to the 240 hostages release or the abolition of Hamas that could resolve the need to invade Gaza by the Israeli forces. Amidst the streets and campuses of European and American cities, the rallying cry of tens of thousands of Middle East immigrants, students, and radical leftists echoes incessantly: "Free Palestine from the River to the Sea." A more recent addition to their repertoire is the chant, "Israel, you can't hide, we caught you in genocide."

The Day Music Died
Nova Music Festival in Southern Israel

The glaring hypocrisy of this dual messaging becomes apparent upon closer inspection. While Hamas and its supporters openly advocate for the genocidal obliteration of Israel from the Jordan River to the Mediterranean Sea, they paradoxically accuse Israel of committing genocide—a current self-proclaimed objective of Hamas and its expatriate followers. Hamas and its global allies consistently denounce Israel for retaliatory actions following the Oct. 7 massacre, where around 1,400 Israeli infants, children, women, and the elderly fell victim. There hasn't been a single global protest advocating for the release of hostages during pro-Palestinian demonstrations. However, calls for a ceasefire and the provision of essential supplies such as oil and food persist. Strikingly, there has been no demands to provide assistance to areas controlled by terrorist groups like ISIS or Al-Kaida, despite the fact that 240 individuals, including children and women, remain kidnapped.

Puzzlingly, Western nations seem inclined to restrain those defending against the murderers of Israelis and Americans, indirectly aligning with the perpetrators. This prompts the question of why the global community appears to side with the aggressors rather than those seeking justice for the murdered.

The New Western World Hero

Considering the demographic landscape, with 500 million Arabs and nearly 2 billion Muslims worldwide, the Israeli population amounts to a mere 9 million. Despite the substantial oil reserves concentrated in the Muslim Middle East, the Western perspective often perceives Westerners, like Israel, as excessively rich and pow-erful, while non-Westerners are romanticized as blameless, victimized under-dogs. The crux of this convoluted conflict seems to be rooted in a resurgent wave of antisemitism, harking back to the ancient plague that is once again sweeping the globe.

IMAGINE THEY CAME FOR
YOUR KIDS

DIPLOACT

Internationally, within Western nations, there was an abrupt realization of the terrors involving kidnapping, beheading, rape, and the mutilation of infants and wounded individuals. These gruesome acts, depicted vividly through images and videos, symbolize the collision of civilizations and Radical Islam, underscoring the profound ideological differences and the ruthless implementtation of these ideologies.

The shocking scenes, such as the beheading and rape of a German-Israeli woman by cheering crowds, reminiscent of ISIS savagery, resonated profoundly in the Western world.

Notably, similar brutality occurred on October 2000 in the West Bank when two Israeli reserve soldiers, who had lost their way, were mutilated while alive, cheered on by onlooking crowds. When individuals claim that Israel is an apartheid state, a notion deemed baseless by any rational observer, the image above illustrates the consequences when Jews enter Palestinian areas. In contrast, the image on the right depicts Arab people freely walking in Jerusalem, mirroring the situation in every other place within the state of Israel.

The Islamist ideology champions "martyrdom" as a guaranteed path to heaven, with its adherents believing they act in accordance with Allah's will. Should current trends persist, there is a looming possibility of Islamists dominating Europe, exerting influence over parts of Russia, and establishing an Islamist bloc with far-reaching power from North Africa and Europe to the Arabian Peninsula, central Asia, and Pakistan, along with sympathetic networks worldwide. The projection suggests that Islam could become the dominant religion globally within 50 years. Regrettably, the millions of moderate and modern Muslims often respond in silence, leading the global community to assume complicity from the entire Muslim world. Those Muslims living in the Western world should actively demonstrate to unequivocally condemn the repugnancy of terror attacks perpetrated by groups like Hamas.

One can engage with an idea through the presentation of an alternative concept or through the application of force. Should the Islamic world recognize, in accordance with the Quran, that the divine will sanctions the Jewish presence in the land of Israel, the fundamental tensions underlying the conflict may naturally ease, obviating the necessity for exerting force to safeguard and uphold the State of Israel. In the face of malevolent forces perpetrating heinous acts like beheadings, rape, and the killing of innocent babies, the enduring forces of truth and love inevitably triumph. While these sinister actors may momentarily seem formidable, history consistently demonstrates their ultimate downfall.

Concerning Arabs in Israel, they possess full rights, and many express a preference to remain in Israel even if a Palestinian state were established. Arabs in Israel actively participate in the democratic process, holding positions in parliament, serving as diplomats, and contributing to the armed forces. Notably, the Druze community, descendants of Yitro, proudly serves as valued citizens. The absence of a comparable democratic process with a strong commitment to human rights in the immediate region surrounding Israel is a noteworthy observation.

Commonalities in the cultures of US and Israel

The United States and Israel have distinct cultural backgrounds, however additionally they percentage some commonalities due to historical, political, and social connections. Here are some cultural aspects and values that are commonplace in each the U.S. And Israel:

1. Democracy: Both nations have democratic systems of presidency, with elected representatives, political freedoms, and a dedication to the guideline of regulation.

2. Entrepreneurship: The U.S. And Israel has sturdy entrepreneurial cultures. They are known for his or her innovation, startup ecosystems, and technology hubs.

3. Cultural Diversity: Both international locations are culturally diverse, with humans from various backgrounds, religions, and ethnicities living aspect by way of side.

4. Religious Freedom: Both the U.S. And Israel upholds the ideas of spiritual freedom, allowing individuals to exercise their faith without persecution.

5. Higher Education: Both nations have well-advanced better education structures, which includes prestigious universities and studies institutions.

6. Strong Military Traditions: Both the U.S. and Israel have strong army traditions and fairly trained defense force.

7. Philanthropy: Both countries have a way of life of philanthropy and charitable giving, with many people and agencies assisting diverse reasons.

8. Innovation and Technology: Both the U.S. and Israel are acknowledged for his or her contributions to technological know-how, generation, and innovation. They have sturdy research and improvement sectors.

9. Food Culture: Both the U.S. and Israel have diverse culinary traditions, and meals is a critical part of their cultures. Each us of a has its precise dishes and flavors.

10. Civic Engagement: Both international locations inspire civic engagement, with a strong way of life of participation in elections, volunteerism, and network companies.

11. Patriotic Values: Patriotism and a sturdy feel of countrywide identity are crucial in both the U.S. And Israel.

12. Commitment to Security: Both international locations prioritize country wide protection because of their geopolitical conditions, which has caused a shared understanding of the importance of defense.

It's critical to apprehend that at the same time as those commonalities exist, there also are extensive cultural differences between the two nations. Each nation has its specific history, traditions, and cultural impacts. Additionally, individual experiences and perspectives inside every country can vary widely.

Why the U.S. Supports Israel

Sources: Wikipedia and essays written by Dr. Stephen Zunes (Chair of the Peace & Justice Studies Program at the University of San Francisco and Foreign Policy in Focus Advisory Committee Member)

Note: In his essays, Dr. Stephen Zunes discusses the term "occupation." In this context, it's not a straightforward term to apply because historically, there hasn't been a recognized state of Palestine. Nevertheless, the presence of Arab communities in the West Bank, which are subject to varying degrees of Israeli control, may lead some to more readily use the term "occupation."

Why the U.S. Supports Israel

In both the United States and on the global stage, there is a growing chorus of voices questioning the rationale behind Washington's unwavering commitment, encompassing military, financial, and diplomatic backing, to the Israeli temporally occupation of the West Bank. The key inquiry here revolves around the remarkably robust bipartisan support for the policies of Israel's right-wing prime minister, Benjamin Netanyahu, in the occupied Palestinian territories.

The enduring and deeply entrenched connection between the United States and Israel has been a defining aspect of U.S. foreign policy for more than three decades. The annual allocation of well over $3.3 billion in military and economic aid from Washington to Israel largely escapes rigorous scrutiny within Congress. This is remarkable, as it contradicts the typical positions taken by liberals who often challenge U.S. assistance to governments implicated in widespread human rights violations and conservatives who typically oppose foreign aid across the board. While most Western nations affirm Israel's legitimate right to coexist in peace and security, they remain unwilling to provide arms and aid while the occupation of lands seized during the 1967 war continues. None of these nations come close to matching the level of unwavering diplomatic support Washington extends to Israel. In many instances, the United States finds itself standing shoulder to shoulder with Israel in international forums, even when concerns are raised over ongoing Israeli violations of international law.

While U.S. support for successive Israeli administrations is often couched in moral justifications, the evidence suggests that moral imperatives play no greater role in shaping U.S. policy in the Middle East than in other regions. While the majority of Americans do share a moral commitment to Israel's preservation as a Jewish state, this sentiment alone does not account for the substantial financial, military, and diplomatic backing

3

provided by the United States. American assistance to Israel transcends the boundaries of safeguarding Israel's security interests within its internationally recognized borders. It encompasses support for policies in militarily occupied territories that frequently contravene established legal and ethical norms of international conduct.

If Israel's security concerns truly took precedence in the minds of American policymakers, one would expect U.S. aid to Israel to have been most substantial during the early years of the nation's existence. This was a period when Israel's democratic institutions were at their zenith, and its strategic circumstances were notably precarious. As Israel's military might grew significantly and its actions against Palestinians in the occupied territories intensified, one would anticipate a decrease in U.S. support. However, the reality has unfolded in the opposite direction: the bulk of major U.S. military and economic aid to Israel commenced only after the conclusion of the 1967 war. In fact, an astounding 99% of U.S. military assistance to Israel has been provided since Israel demonstrated its supremacy over any combination of Arab armies and assumed control over a substantial Palestinian populace.

Moreover, U.S. aid to Israel is more substantial today than it was a quarter of a century ago. This is the case even though, at that time, Egypt possessed massive and well-equipped armed forces that posed a threat of conflict. In the contemporary context, Israel enjoys a longstanding peace treaty with Egypt and benefits from a significant demilitarized buffer zone, subject to international monitoring, which keeps Egyptian military forces at a safe distance. In the past, Syria was engaged in a rapid expansion of its military capabilities, supported by advanced Soviet weaponry. Presently, Syria has demonstrated a willingness to coexist peacefully with Israel, contingent upon the return of the occupied Golan Heights, while its military capabilities have diminished due to the disintegration of its Soviet benefactor.

Similarly, in the mid-1970s, Jordan asserted its claim over the West Bank, deploying substantial troops along its extensive border and the demarcation line with Israel. Nowadays, Jordan has forged a peace treaty and

4

established fully normalized relations with Israel. Back then, Iraq was embarking on a massive program of militarization, but its armed forces have since been decimated as a result of the Gulf War, subsequent international sanctions, and ongoing monitoring. Given these circumstances, one might legitimately question the rationale behind the sustained or increased annual U.S. aid to Israel.

In a hypothetical scenario where all U.S. aid to Israel were abruptly terminated, many years would transpire before Israel faced a substantially greater military threat than it does presently. Israel possesses a robust domestic arms industry and an armed force that surpasses any foreseeable combination of opposing forces in terms of capability and power. There would be no immediate concern for Israel's military survival in the foreseeable future. The surge in terrorist attacks within Israel, while prompting widespread apprehension about the security of the Israeli populace, bears little correlation to the overwhelming majority of U.S. military aid.

In summary, the burgeoning U.S. backing of the Israeli government, akin to U.S. support for allies across the globe, cannot be primarily ascribed to security imperatives or an unwavering moral commitment to the nation. Instead, akin to its approach elsewhere, U.S. foreign policy is fundamentally propelled by the pursuit of its own perceived strategic interests.

Strategic Reasons for Continuing U.S. Support

A sweeping consensus, transcending partisan lines, prevails among policymakers, affirming that Israel has been an instrumental asset in advancing U.S. interests across the Middle East and on a global scale. Israel's multifaceted contributions include thwarting the ascendancy of radical nationalist movements in Lebanon, Jordan, and Palestine, effectively ensuring regional stability. In addition, Israel has adeptly restrained Syria, a longstanding ally of the Soviet Union, from exerting undue influence.

Israel's preeminence extends to its air force, which reigns supreme within the region and has served as a crucible for assessing American weaponry's performance, often in direct competition with Soviet armaments. This dynamic has furnished invaluable insights for the U.S. military apparatus. Israel's unique role encompasses facilitating the discreet dissemination of U.S. arms to regimes and factions deemed unfavorable for overt American military support. Recipients have ranged from apartheid-era South Africa to the Islamic Republic of Iran, the military junta in Guatemala, and the Nicaraguan Contras.

Furthermore, Israeli military advisers have provided guidance to the Contras, the Salvadoran junta, and foreign occupation forces operating in regions like Namibia and Western Sahara. Israel's intelligence service has collaborated closely with U.S. counterparts, enhancing intelligence gathering capabilities and supporting covert operations of mutual concern. Notably, Israel boasts a missile capability reaching far into the former Soviet Union, maintains a substantial nuclear arsenal comprising hundreds of warheads, and actively collaborates with the U.S. military-industrial complex in the realm of research and development, particularly in the domains of advanced jet fighters and anti-missile defense systems. This multifaceted partnership between the United States and Israel stands as a testament to their aligned strategic interests and shared objectives.

U.S. Aid Increases as Israel Grows Stronger

The trajectory of U.S. assistance to Israel unveils a compelling narrative. In the wake of Israel's resounding triumph in the 1967 war, a conspicuous demonstration of its regional military preeminence, U.S. aid surged by a staggering 450%. A significant facet of this escalation, as reported by the New York Times, appears to be linked to Israel's willingness to supply the U.S. with valuable insights into newly acquired Soviet weaponry seized during the conflict. In the aftermath of the Jordanian civil war of 1970-71, which highlighted Israel's potential to curtail revolutionary movements extending beyond its borders, U.S. aid experienced a sevenfold augmentation.

Subsequently, following the 1973 war, where Israel's military actions against Arab armies met formidable resistance, the largest U.S. airlift in history demonstrated Israel's capacity to prevail over surprisingly robust Soviet-supported adversaries, leading to an additional 800% increase in military aid. These increments coincided with the British decision to withdraw its forces from "east of the Suez," heralding a period of substantial arms sales and logistical collaboration with the Shah's Iran—an integral component of the Nixon Doctrine.

Furthermore, in 1979, U.S. aid quadrupled shortly after the Shah's fall, the emergence of the right-wing Likud government, and the ratification of the Camp David Treaty. This treaty, characterized by enhanced military assistance provisions, more closely resembled a tripartite military accord than a conventional peace agreement. Notably, despite the Begin government's refusal to adhere to Palestinian autonomy provisions, the additional aid continued.

In the aftermath of Israel's 1982 incursion into Lebanon, another uptick in aid transpired. The years 1983 and 1984 marked the signing of memoranda of understanding on strategic cooperation and military planning between the United States and Israel, coupled with their inaugural joint naval and aerial military exercises. Israel's cooperation did not go unnoticed, as it was rewarded with an additional $1.5 billion in economic aid, along with half a million dollars for the development of a novel jet fighter.

During and immediately following the Gulf War, U.S. aid swelled by an extra $650 million. Moreover, when Israel notably intensified its repression in the occupied territories—a repression that included incursions into areas designated as autonomous Palestinian territories, a designation guaranteed by the U.S. government—U.S. aid experienced yet another ascent. This ascension was further accentuated following the terrorist attacks on September 11, where Israel's close alignment with U.S. interests was rewarded with amplified support.

The correlation remains unmistakable: Israel's strengthening and its willingness to cooperate with U.S. interests directly parallel the reinforcement of support.

Ensuring Israel's Military Superiority

Henceforth, the enduringly generous U.S. assistance to Israel does not stem from an apprehension for Israel's mere survival. Instead, it is the manifestation of the United States' aspiration for Israel to maintain its political hegemony over the Palestinians and its military supremacy in the region. Notably, leaders from both of America's political factions have not advocated for the U.S. to ensure a military equilibrium between Israel and its neighboring states but rather to guarantee Israeli military preeminence.

In the wake of the tragic terrorist attacks that befell the United States on September 11, there has been renewed internal deliberation concerning the extent of support the United States should provide to Israeli policies, presently overseen by the right-wing political luminary, Ariel Sharon. Pragmatic conservatives hailing from the senior Bush administration, including Secretary of State Colin Powell, have offered words of caution. They contend that wholehearted endorsement of Sharon's government, particularly during a period characterized by an unparalleled clampdown in the occupied territories, could potentially obstruct the cultivation of full cooperation from Arab governments in the pursuit of a campaign against terrorist cells affiliated with the al Qaeda network. Conversely, the more conservative segments, as embodied by figures like Paul Wolfowitz from the Defense Department, have articulated the indispensable role Sharon plays as an ally in the global war on terrorism. They argue that the Palestinian resistance is inherently intertwined with an international terrorist conspiracy targeting democratic societies.

Other Contributing Factors

Backing Israel's ongoing occupation (see above note about this misused term) and suppression bears a resemblance to U.S. support for Indonesia's 24-year occupation of and oppression in East Timor, or Morocco's persistent occupation and oppression in Western Sahara. If deemed to serve the strategic interests of the United States, Washington exhibits readiness to endorse the most blatant infringements of international law and human rights by its allies, effectively blocking the United Nations and other entities from raising objections. This commitment to maintaining realpolitik remains largely unmoved by ethnic advocacy or ideological alignments.

Some of the most egregious instances of U.S. support for oppression have not gone unopposed, leading to shifts in U.S. policies related to Vietnam, Central America, South Africa, and East Timor. In these cases, grassroots movements advocating for peace and justice reached a critical mass, prompting liberal members of Congress, as well as media figures and others, to call for an end to U.S. complicity in oppression. Yet, in other cases, such as U.S. support for Morocco's invasion and occupation of Western Sahara, the situation remains obscured from the view of most Americans, preventing a substantial challenge from lawmakers and pundits.

The scenario surrounding Israel and Palestine, however, diverges from these dynamics. While significant segments of the population question U.S. policy, there exists a widespread consensus among elite sectors of government and the media in support of U.S. backing for the Israeli occupation. Indeed, many liberal Democrats in Congress, who typically align with progressive movements on other foreign policy issues, align with President George W. Bush or, in some instances, adopt positions even further to the right on the issue of Israel and Palestine. Hence, although perceived strategic necessity underlies U.S. support for Israel, additional factors have made this issue more challenging for advocates of peace and human rights. These factors encompass:

1. The sentimental attachment held by many liberals, particularly among the post-war generation in influential positions within government and the media, to Israel. Numerous Americans identify with Israel's internal democracy, progressive social institutions such as kibbutzim, a relatively high level of social equality, and its role as a sanctuary for a historically oppressed minority that endured centuries in diaspora. A blend of guilt over historical Western anti-Semitism, personal friendships with Jewish Americans deeply connected to Israel, and apprehension about inadvertently fueling anti-Semitism by criticizing Israel collectively contributes to substantial reluctance to acknowledge the gravity of Israeli violations of human rights and international law.

2. The involvement of the Christian Right, boasting tens of millions of adherents and serving as a significant base of support for the Republican Party. Their substantial media and political influence align firmly with right-wing Israeli leaders, driven partly by a messianic theology that views the gathering of Jews in the Holy Land as a precursor to the second coming of Christ. In their perspective, the conflict between Israelis and Palestinians extends the historical battle between the Israelites and the Philistines, with God as the cosmic real estate agent designating the land exclusively to Israel, regardless of secular notions concerning international law and the right to self-determination.

3. Mainstream and conservative Jewish organizations have marshaled considerable lobbying resources, financial contributions from the Jewish community, and citizen pressure on the news media and other platforms for public discourse in support of the Israeli government. While the role of the pro-Israel lobby is occasionally exaggerated, with some asserting that it constitutes the primary factor shaping U.S. policy, it has played a pivotal role in select congressional races and in fostering an atmosphere of intimidation for those striving to moderate U.S. policy, including an increasing number of progressive Jews.

4. The arms industry, which channels five times the financial contributions to congressional campaigns and lobbying initiatives compared to AIPAC and other pro-Israel groups, possesses a substantial stake in endorsing massive arms deliveries to Israel and other Middle Eastern allies of the United States. It is significantly easier for a member of Congress to contest a $60 million arms deal with a nation like Indonesia than the more than $2 billion in arms shipments to Israel, particularly when numerous congressional districts house factories producing such military hardware.

5. Pervasive racism towards Arabs and Muslims within American society, often perpetuated by the media. This bias is compounded by the tendency of many Americans to draw parallels between Zionism in the

Middle East and the historical American experience of pioneering in North America, building a nation based on lofty, idealistic principles while concurrently subduing and displacing the indigenous population.

6. The shortcomings of progressive movements in the United States in effectively challenging U.S. policy towards Israel and Palestine. For many years, most mainstream peace and human rights organizations sidestepped the issue, reluctant to alienate a significant number of their Jewish and other liberal constituents supportive of the Israeli government. They also feared that criticism of Israeli policies might inadvertently stimulate anti-Semitism. In the absence of any counterbalancing pressure, liberal members of Congress had little incentive to resist the pressure exerted by supporters of the Israeli government. Simultaneously, certain far-left groups and individuals adopted a fiercely anti-Israel stance, which not only critiqued Israeli policies but also questioned Israel's fundamental right to exist, damaging their credibility significantly. In some cases, especially among those more conservative individuals and groups critical of Israel, latent anti-Semitism surfaced, with exaggerated claims of Jewish economic and political influence, further distancing potential critics of U.S. policy.

Conclusion

While U.S. backing for Israeli policies, much like U.S. support for its allies in other regions, predominantly hinges on the nation's alignment with perceived U.S. security interests, there exist additional complexities that hinder the efforts of peace and human rights advocacy groups to alter U.S. policy. Nevertheless, the imperative to contest U.S. support for the Israeli occupation (see note above) has never been more critical. This steadfast support has resulted not only in immense suffering among Palestinians and other Arabs but, over time, has also worked against the long-term interests of both Israel and the United States, giving rise to increasingly militant and extremist elements in response from the Arab and Islamic world.

In essence, there is no inherent contradiction between endorsing Israel and supporting Palestine, as Israeli security and Palestinian rights are not mutually exclusive; they are intricately interdependent. U.S. support for the Israeli government has consistently hindered the efforts of peace activists within Israel striving to alter Israeli policy. As the late Israeli General and Knesset member, Matti Peled, aptly described it, such support has pushed Israel toward an unyielding stance marked by callousness.

Perhaps the most beneficial type of support that the United States can offer Israel is akin to "tough love": it involves an unwavering commitment to Israel's right to exist in peace and security within its internationally recognized borders, coupled with a resolute determination to bring an end to the occupation. This is the formidable challenge confronting those who genuinely uphold fundamental values such as freedom, democracy, and the rule of law.

The Concept of God: An Exploration of Divine Perspectives

Introduction

The biggest and the most crucial question has always been, what kind of God is it or who is this god? Different peoples, religions, and philosophies have tried to determine what exactly God is and what is true about him. God is a complicated yet multi-faceted concept which has its origins in spiritual and philosophical backgrounds. The aim of this essay is to examine different opinions regarding what God is and highlight the fact that there is absolutely no final word about it.

Defining God

However, before we proceed to different notions of God, let's first define what "God" stands for generally. Generally, God is perceived as an omnipotent, omniscient, and benevolent creator of the world which is subjected to his power in Judaism, Christianity, and Islam. Many times, this type of God refers to a person who can respond to petitions, show guidance as well as distribute justice.

On contrary, in the case of polytheist view of the world like ancient Greek, Roman or Hindu mythology, there are numerous gods, each representing some aspect of existence or natural phenomenon. They have different levels of power, intelligence, and ethics. In addition, some philosophical beliefs such as pantheism and panentheism argue that God is identical with the cosmos (universal self) or that the deity lies within the natural as well as supernatural worlds.

Theistic Perspectives

Monotheism

Monotheistic religions, like Judaism, Christianity, and Islam, affirm the existence of a single, all-powerful God. This God is seen as the creator of the universe, a moral lawgiver, and a source of guidance and salvation. In

13

these traditions, God is often understood as a personal deity who interacts with believers and responds to their prayers.

Judaism: Judaism refers to God as Yahweh and stresses the bond between God and Jews. Jewish theology deals with Jewish thought on complex facets of theological issues such as the divine attributes and the relationship between God and man.

Christianity: The Holy Trinity in Christianity is made up of three parts — God the Father, God the Son - Jesus Christ and God the Holy Spirit. The trinity of God, which in turn complicates the Christian perception of the divine.

Islam: The name for God in Islam is Allah. Theology in Islam is based on the concept of tawhid and the Qur'an as the foundation. Islamic thought emphasizes on God's mercies and justice.

Deism

Deism is a perception system that posits the existence of and non-intervening God who created the universe however does no longer actively participate in human affairs. Deists reject the belief of divine revelation or miracles, relying on purpose and observation to apprehend the sector.

Polytheism

Polytheistic religions, together with historical Greek mythology or Hinduism, contain belief in more than one God, each chargeable for unique factors of existence or nature. These gods could have distinct personalities, powers, and relationships with human beings.

Pantheism and Panentheism

Pantheism holds that God and the universe are one and the equal, blurring the difference among the divine and the fabric global. Panentheism, however, asserts that God is each immanent within the universe and transcends it. These views spotlight a deeply interconnected and interdependent courting among God and advent.

14

Atheistic and Agnostic Perspectives

Atheism: Atheism is the rejection of perception within the lifestyles of God or gods. Atheists argue that the load of proof lies with folks who declare the existence of a divine being and that, without compelling proof, there may be no reason to simply accept this sort of notion. Atheists frequently floor their worldview in naturalism, maintaining that the natural world can be explained without invoking the supernatural.

Agnosticism: Agnosticism takes a more impartial stance, suggesting that the life of God is unknowable or beyond human comprehension. Agnostics chorus from making definitive claims approximately the lifestyles or non-existence of God and frequently advocate for open-minded inquiry.

Philosophical Perspectives

Philosophical Theism: Philosophical theism explores the concept of God through rational inquiry and philosophical arguments. Figures like Thomas Aquinas, René Descartes, and Immanuel Kant have offered various philosophical proofs for the existence of God, such as the cosmological argument, the teleological argument, and the moral argument.

Process Theology: Process theology offers a dynamic understanding of God, suggesting that the divine is continually evolving and interacting with the world. God, in this view, is not an unchanging, all-powerful entity but a dynamic and relational force.

Theodicy: Theodicy addresses the problem of evil and suffering in the context of a benevolent and all-powerful God. Philosophers and theologians have grappled with the question of how to reconcile the existence of evil with the concept of a loving and omnipotent God, offering various theodicies and explanations.

The Nature of the Monotheistic God: A Philosophical Exploration

Introduction

Monotheism, the belief in the existence of a single, all-encompassing God, is a fundamental tenet of several major world religions, including Judaism, Christianity, and Islam. The nature of the monotheistic God is a deeply profound and intricate subject that has been debated, contemplated, and expounded upon for centuries. In this essay, we will delve into the multifaceted nature of the monotheistic God, examining key attributes, philosophical interpretations, and the implications of monotheism in understanding the divine.

Attributes of the Monotheistic God

1. **Transcendence:** The monotheistic God is typically viewed as transcendent, existing beyond the limitations of the material world. This transcendence means that God is not confined by time, space, or the physical laws of the universe. God's existence is often described as being "beyond" or "above" the created world, emphasizing a clear separation between the divine and the mundane.

2. **Omnipotence:** The monotheistic God is believed to be all-powerful. This attribute implies that God possesses unlimited, unrivaled power and can accomplish anything that is logically possible. The concept of omnipotence is a source of philosophical inquiry and debate, especially regarding the compatibility of divine omnipotence with the existence of evil and suffering in the world.

3. **Omniscience:** God is considered all-knowing in monotheistic faiths. This omniscience extends to a perfect understanding of the past, present, and future, including the thoughts, actions, and intentions of all beings. God's omniscience raises questions about free will, predestination, and the problem of evil.

16

4. **Omnibenevolence:** The monotheistic God is often described as perfectly good, just, and loving. This attribute underpins the moral framework of monotheistic religions and provides a foundation for ethical guidelines and divine guidance. The idea of an all-loving God can be challenged by the existence of suffering and evil, leading to discussions on theodicy (the justification of God's goodness in the face of evil).

5. **Immanence:** While emphasizing transcendence, monotheistic faiths also acknowledge God's immanence, which means that God is present and active within the created world. This immanence enables believers to experience a personal connection with the divine and sense God's influence in their lives.

Philosophical Interpretations of the Monotheistic God

1. **Classical Theism:** Classical theism is a philosophical interpretation of monotheism that emphasizes the attributes of God mentioned earlier. It posits a God who is transcendent, omnipotent, omniscient, omnibenevolent, and immutable. Philosophers like Thomas Aquinas and Augustine of Hippo have made significant contributions to classical theistic thought.

2. **Process Theology:** In contrast to classical theism, process theology offers a more dynamic perspective on the monotheistic God. Process theologians argue that God is not unchanging but rather experiences a continuous process of growth and development. God is viewed as engaged in a relationship with the world and influenced by the actions and experiences of creatures.

3. **Deism:** Deism is a philosophical interpretation of monotheism that emphasizes God's role as a distant Creator who does not intervene in the world's affairs. Deists reject the idea of divine revelation and miracles, favoring reason and natural philosophy to understand the universe.

4. **Open Theism:** Open theism challenges the traditional view of divine omniscience. It suggests that God, while having perfect knowledge of the past and present, does not possess exhaustive foreknowledge of future events. This interpretation is often seen as a response to the theological tensions related to human free will and divine fore-knowledge.

Implications of Monotheism

Morality and Ethics: The monotheism's moral framework is premised on the attributes of an all-loving, just and infinitely good God. The divine commandments and ethical principles that are brought forth by the nature of God, form a guide for believers. The framework is reflected in personal and societal moral codes, which have had far-reaching implications on laws and ethics in monotheistic societies.

Worship and Rituals: These involve worship and other rituals that connect them to the powers-in-preeminence. Typically, these rituals focus on prayer, community meet-ups, and religious traditions aimed at making individuals feel close to God.

Theology and Philosophy: The book of Wisdom was centered on the nature of monotheistic God that formed subject central to theological and philosophical inquiry. Throughout history scholars and thinkers have explored theological arguments including theodicy (explaining how a good God allows evil in his world) and divine attributes.

Interfaith Relations: Interfaith relations and conflicts have been influenced by monotheism to a great extent. This shared belief in one God who controls many aspects of life has paved way for interfaith dialogue and attempts to foster understanding between the monotheistic religions. It has also proved to be a source of tension and conflict, with controversial differences in religious doctrine and interpretation leading to disputes.

God and Antimatter: Exploring the Cosmic Duality

Introduction

The issue of correlation between God and antimatter refers to the sphere of theology, philosophy and science all at once. Whereas, on the one hand, theology delves into understanding what is divine and in turn godly; on the other side science has been trying to know more about antimatter and its position in this universe. Within the context of this essay, the cosmic connection between God and antimatter is examined from theological, philosophical and scientific perspectives.

Antimatter: A Brief Overview

Antimatter is a subject that has kept scientists and sci-fi addicts interested for many years. It is simply the opposite of normal matter, made up antiparticles of charges exactly opposite to those on their corresponding particles. For instance, the antiparticle of an electron is called a positron and it has positive charge.

When they mix together, matter and antimatter particles cancel each other out to exist as energy. The same has been a matter of study and experiment due to the potential use in space travel and energy production. Nonetheless, it is very uncommon in the universe and its question of being rare still perplexes scientists.

Antimatter in the Story Concerning the Deity

Theological Reflections on Antimatter: The concept of antimatter does not play a major role in the holy books or religious discussions because ancient religious texts were written before the discovery of matter. However, theologians and philosophers have considered why antimatter is included in their conceptions of God and universe.

a. Creation and Design: For instance, some theologians suggest that the existence of antimatter is a manifestation of God's creativity and complexity in making the universe. It explains that the creation process in God is both within and beyond what humans perceive, which includes among other things antimatter.

b. Theological Parallels: The notion of antimatter following duality, including particles and antiparticles, could be considered as a theological equivalent to such things as good and evil or light and darkness. Such dualities are sometimes used in theological discussions to present some complex philosophical reasoning about God and the universe.

Philosophical Considerations

From a related broad metaphysical viewpoint, philosophers have tried to reason out the implications of what antimatter would mean in respect to God.

a. Duality and Complementarity: This existence of antimatter seems to imply a certain kind of duality or complementarity in the natural world that philosophers might associate with wider range metaphysical issues. Others are of the view that this duality is actually a manifestation of an underlying unity or dependence and they associate it with philosophical ideas of divinity.

b. The Problem of Rareness: Thus, the scarcity of antimatter raises queries of why anti-matter is there or what it does. Philosophers might wonder what it says about the divine's purposes or reality itself, that the universe shows such an asymmetry between matter and antimatter.

Scientific Explorations of Antimatter

Antimatter in Modern Physics: Modern physics is an important field that relies on antimatter. Paul Dirac had predicted it http://en.wikipedia.org/wiki/Antiparticle#Antimatter to exist in 1928 and its first particle of antimatter, positron was discovered from cosmic rays in the year 1932. This has enabled scientists to produce and experiment on antimatter in the laboratory setting since that time, helping reveal much more about our physics.

Antimatter and the Big Bang: Scientists have found the link between antimatter and the beginning of everything interesting. The theory most often mentioned states that the Big Bang should produce equal amounts of matter and antimatter. But this symmetry is not observed and the Universe is matter dominated. This is the problem of matter-antimatter asymmetry in cosmology and particle physics.

Antimatter's Potential Applications: The special properties of the antimatter have increased its potential for application. The best-known practical application is probably in spacecraft propulsion, where matter and antimatter annihilations would give way to an efficient energy source. Positron emission tomography (PET) is also an example of a medical imaging technique that uses positron annihilation to help in the identification of cancer among other diseases.

Bridging the Gap: God, Antimatter, and the Universe

Unity and Duality: Most of the time, people view God as a unifying phenomenon, transcendent being and omnipotent. Antimatter presents a dual or complimentary aspect of the physical universe. Indeed a few schools of philosophical thought hold that this duality is compatible with divine unity, and interpret it as an expression of the divine's infinite power to create.

Harmony and Order: The concept of a harmonious and ordered universe is usually emphasized in religious and philosophical traditions. The complexity of the cosmos, which can be considered as God's divine will is one way in which emptiness or antimatter has to be found and pursued. The rarity of the antimatter raises questions about a design that might be an intricate one and which we are just coming to comprehend.

Mysteries and Inquiries: The reality that antimatter exists poses provocative questions not only to science but also theology. It is an inquiry about the pursuit of knowledge, which will in turn result with a deep understanding of the universe; and it interweaves theological inquiries into the theologian's mind on significance of Antimatter and scientist's quest to understating matter-antimatter asymmetry.

21

Cross-sectional dialogues among theology, philosophy and science on antimatter. theological reflections on the nature of God can serve as a source for new perspectives in scientific research, while new scientific discoveries themselves can challenge and take further theological or philosophical discourse.

Conclusion

God and antimatter are symbols for a complex space where theology, philosophy, and science come together. Just as that related to monotheistic God, this has been a point of deep reflection and inquiry —that was created by the human minds- while antimatter is something imaginative even in science. While no religion or scripture makes specific mention of antimatter, these traditions do provide a foundation for discussing the connection between divinity and cosmic mysteries.

Theologically, the existence of antimatter mirrors God's creation entity, dualism and mechanical complexity. Philosophers study the philosophical implications of antimatter's distinctiveness and ambivalence for general metaphysical issues. The scientific inquiries into the properties of antimatter illuminate its cosmic significance and possible use, thereby creating a fresh perspective concerning our knowledge about matter.

In the end, investigating God and antimatter reaffirms humankind's continuous search for truth, awareness and an intimate bond with cosmic uncertainties. It shows that theology, philosophy and science are interconnected and support a richer understanding of the cosmos and the divine.

Challenges and Questions

The Problem of Evil: One major problem with this view of God is the fact that evil and suffering exist in the world. Theodicy is an endeavor of reconciling the nature of God with evil, which is however a perennial philosophic and theological dilemma.

Divine Foreknowledge and Free Will: Divine omniscience plus knowing the future versus free will of course everything has effect largely on human beings' agency and responsibility. If God already knows individual's choices and actions, how can they have genuine free will?

The Nature of Divine Interaction: The fact that monotheism poses questions regarding the process of God's interaction with the world. Does God Act in Human Affairs, Answer Prayers, or Operate on a Plan? The meaning of divine providence and God's interaction with creation is still a matter that theologians and philosophers continue to explore.

Conclusion

This question is thus very philosophical, theological and personal one that has no simple or universally accepted answer of who or what God is. The idea of God is rather complex and inseparable from the cultural, religious and philosophical heritages. Monotheistic faiths perceive God as one all-powerful god, who is personal. In the polytheistic belief systems, multiple gods are invoked each with distinctive features and functions. Deism, on the other hand, presents a far-off Creator without any intervention with His creation; and pantheism as well as panentheism stress on the divine and something worldly being interconnected.

Atheists argue that there is not enough proof to support the existence of God, while agnostics are more hesitant in their position concerning God. Theistic philosophy and process theology are some of the philosophical perspectives that offer reasonable and philosophic backbones in understanding God.

In the end, God is a matter of belief and faith that cannot be verified empirically. This is a topic that has spawned many such discussions and debates, speaking of the pluralism in human thinking regarding the nature of divine essence.

The speculative monotheistic God is very deeply profound and complex subject of study that has influenced beliefs, ethics, and philosophical quests for millions of individuals over the years. In the monotheistic religions, the divine is understood based on God's attributes: transcendence, omnipotence, omniscience, omnibenevolence and immanence. Available philosophical interpretations include classical theism, process theology, deism and open theism with respect to this monotheistic God.

The implications of monotheism are felt in morality, ethics, worship, theology and interfaith relations; with believers living it daily and scholars engaging discussions about the same. Yet some challenges and questions like the issue of evil, divine foreknowledge and manner in which God interacts with His creatures still remain relevant to contemplations and debates.

Ultimately, the character of monotheistic God still forms a matter of high importance and continuous fascination since it is both relevant to theologians' inquiries and makes them more or less acquainted with those who want to comprehend divinity in monotheistic faiths.Individual's religious or philosophical beliefs

Ultimately, the nature of God is a profound and often deeply personal matter, and it can vary widely based on an individual's religious or philosophical beliefs. Different cultures and religious traditions have diverse interpretations of the divine, and these interpretations influence how God is understood as a spiritual or metaphysical being.

ANTI-SEMITISM: A HISTORICAL AND CONTEMPORARY ANALYSIS

Introduction

Anti-Semitism, prejudice and discrimination against Jews, is a deeply ingrained and complex social issue that has persisted for centuries. This essay seeks to provide a comprehensive analysis of anti-Semitism, delving into its historical roots, its various manifestations throughout history, and its persistence in contemporary society. By examining the historical context and tracing the evolution of anti-Semitism, we can better understand its impact on individuals and societies and work towards its eradication.

While the global Jewish population constitutes a mere 0.0025% of the world's total, their significant contributions to various facets of society, including literature, jurisprudence, and scientific advancements, often go underappreciated. Their foundational principles have influenced the development of common legal systems and the propagation of monotheistic beliefs, which have profoundly impacted both Islam and Christianity. Additionally, they have made substantial contributions to fields such as relativity, socialism, psychology, and even the creation of cell phones. Paradoxically, they have also borne the brunt of unfounded blame for various societal ills, enduring massacres, Inquisitions, confinement to ghettos, expulsions, accusations of blood guilt, and the horrors of the Holocaust. Astonishingly, in the face of these adversities, they have refrained from seeking vengeance or implicating an entire continent in their suffering. Instead, Jewish individuals continue to excel, engaging in productive activities, shaping legal systems, and pioneering innovations.

Nevertheless, anti-Semitism remains a pervasive and enduring problem. It differs significantly from other forms of hatred, such as racism or xenophobia, and stands as the oldest and most persistently obsessive form of hatred. Negative stereotypes about Jews have deeply penetrated societal consciousness, fueled by fantastical notions, and this particular form of hatred frequently escalates into physical violence.

Dr Wafa Sultan: "The Jews have come from the tragedy (of the Holocaust), and forced the world to respect them, with their knowledge, not with their terror, with their work, not their crying and yelling. Humanity owes most of the discoveries and science of the 19th and 20th centuries to Jewish scientists. 15 million people, scattered throughout the world, united and won their rights through work and knowledge. We have not seen a single Jew blow himself up in a German restaurant. We have not seen a single Jew destroy a church. We have not seen a single Jew protest by killing people."

Mark Twain wrote this passage in the 19th Century: If the statistics are right, the Jews constitute but one per cent of the human race. It suggests a nebulous dim puff of star dust lost in the blaze of the Milky Way. Properly the Jew ought hardly to be heard of; but he is heard of. He is as prominent on the planet as any other people, and his commercial importance is extravagantly out of proportion to the smallness of his bulk. His contributions to the world's list of great names in literature, science, art, music, finance, medicine...are also way out of proportion to the weakness of his numbers. He has made a marvelous fight in this world, in all the ages; and has done it with his hands tied behind him. He could be vain of himself, and be excused for it. The Egyptian, the Babylonian and the Persian rose, filled the planet with sound and splendor, then faded to dream-stuff and passed away; the Greek and the Roman followed, and made a vast noise, and they are gone; other peoples have sprung up and held their torch high for a time, but it burned out, and they sit in twilight now, or have vanished. The Jew saw them all beat them all, and is now what he always was, exhibiting no decadence, no infirmities of age, no weakening of parts, no slowing of his energies, no dulling of his alert and aggressive mind. All things are mortal but the Jew; all other forces pass, but he remains. What is the secret of his immortality?

In contemplation of the preceding discourse, we discern the historical emergence of anti-Semitism alongside the advent of Christianity. As early as the 1920s, the Hungarian nobleman Joseph Eötvösz acutely observed that an "anti-Semite is one who hates the Jews... more than necessary." It is imperative to recognize that such sentiments were not pervasive in the pre-Christian pagan world, which, for the most part, exhibited tolerance toward the Jewish people. However, with the ascendancy of Christianity, anti-Semitism assumed theological legitimacy, codifying itself through laws, disparagement, calumnies, animosity, segregation, forced baptisms, child appropriation, unjust trials, pogroms, exiles, systematic persecution, rapine, and social degradation.

Albert Einstein contributed a profound allegory to elucidate the scapegoat theory of anti-Semitism: "The shepherd boy said to the horse..." In this analogy, the horse symbolizes a people, the lad embodies a class or clique seeking absolute dominion over the masses, and the stag represents the Jews. The narrative illustrates the horse's thirst for water and its vexation at the nimble stag's swiftness. This allegory essentially encapsulates the scapegoat theory of anti-Semitism, wherein leaders, seeking to divert public discontent, identify a minority group as "the Other" and hold it responsible for societal disquiet. Throughout European history, Jews have consistently been designated as this "Other." Nevertheless, the scapegoat theory alone is inadequate, as it only describes how anti-Semitism is employed, failing to explain its underlying causes. To operationalize this theory, anti-Semites must already exist, and once anti-Semitism becomes ingrained in European culture, it perpetuates independently, passed from one generation to the next.

Einstein expands upon the scapegoat explanation, observing that Jews are targeted due to their defenselessness. Furthermore, Jews often occupied positions that projected them as the public face of ruling elites, even though their actual power was nominal. This feature made them susceptible to becoming focal points for public ire during periods of economic turmoil or political conflict. The Jews' distinctiveness lay in their adherence to norms that appeared subversive to the established order, their unwillingness to acquiesce to imperial authority, which disconcerted ruling elites fearing that the Jewish ideals of an egalitarian society would be embraced by the populace.

Contemporary Jews have integrated into their respective societies while retaining their religious practices. Some have adapted their religious principles with new ideas and reformed modes of worship, constituting reformed Judaism. It is crucial for Christianity to acknowledge the historical underpinnings of the rise of anti-Semitism, rooted in Judaism as the progenitor of monotheistic religions and in the shared geographical origins with Jesus in modern-day Israel. By acknowledging these historical realities, Christianity can better grasp the notion that the resurgence of Israel is also part of God's divine plan. In condemning Israel, Jews, or perpetuating anti-Semitism, Christians inadvertently condemn their own faith's origins. All monotheistic religions anticipate Judgment Day, with the foreboding possibility that this momentous event could transpire in the near future, potentially utilizing yet another Jewish invention—the nuclear bomb.

Historical Roots of Anti-Semitism

Religious Roots

The beginnings of anti-Semitism lie in ancient religious differences and antagonisms. During the formative years of Christianity, anti-Semitism was pioneered by accusations of deicide where Jews were believed to have had Jesus crucified. This continued for centuries with religiously motivated anti-Semitism.

Medieval Persecutions

Throughout the medieval period, many incidences of anti-Semitism were reported such as the notorious blood libel charges and massive evacuations of Jewish societies from different countries in Europe. Jews were rarely to be found in favor, being accused of all societal ills and facing physical attacks.

The Spanish Inquisition

In the late 15th century, Jews were converted to Christianity by force during the Spanish Inquisition and this created what became known as "crypto-Jews", who even after conversion they still remained under suspicion and were persecuted); clearly indicating how historical anti-Semitism affected social attitudes and policies widely.

Modern Anti-Semitism

During the 19th and early 20th centuries, anti-Semitism changed to be more contemporary and less religious. Various conspiracy theories and stereotypes regarding Jewish control of finance, media, and politics were disseminated by popular anti-Semitic anti-heroes like Karl Lueger in addition to publications such as "The Protocols of the Elders of Zion" and the Rothschilds Conspiracy.

Manifestations of Anti-Semitism

Stereotypes and Conspiracy Theories

This anti-Semitism has been supported through damaging stereotypes and conspiracies that propose Jews as controlling or having an influence on different aspects of life. These are the belief in the Jewish world conspiracy, financial dominance and control of media.

Violence and Persecution

Violent pogroms, mass expulsions and genocide have characterized anti-Semitism throughout history. The worst incidence of antisemitism was during the Holocaust where six million Jews were ruthlessly killed by Nazis.

Discrimination and Exclusion

In different societies, Anti-Semitism has resulted into systematized discrimination, marginalization, and isolation of Jewish communities. This has resulted to discrimination in things such as education, job opportunities, social and accommodation.

Online and Contemporary Anti-Semitism

With advent of the internet, anti-Semitism has now a new face on the digital landscape. Anti-Semitic hate speech, Holocaust denial and harassment of Jews are common on online spaces. As such, the social media has become a depraved place where anti-Semites congregate.

The Holocaust: A Dark Chapter in History

The result of such level of Anti -Semitism where by it led to Holocaust. Nazi Germany had a calculated scheme of exterminating Jewry in Europe, during the Second World War. The Holocaust led to the murdering of six million Jews in gas chambers, concentration camps, as well as mass shootings. Although the occurrence of this unprecedented act of cruelty goes down in history as a major setback, it is an important lesson that purely epitomizes how far anti-Semitism can go.

Contemporary Anti-Semitism

Challenges to Define

Modern anti-Semitism is a tricky phenomenon to describe because it involves many elements. It commonly disguises as criticism over the policies of the State of Israel, and it is hard to differentiate valid critic from hate speech.

Anti-Semitism on the Political Stage

This form of anti-Semitism has taken this vice to the political arena, and in several instances, politicians have deployed anti-Semitic stands or expressed them. Concerns arise over these cases legitimizing and normalizing anti-Semitism impacting Jewish insights worldwide.

Online Hate Speech

The Internet's Rise as a Breeding Ground for Anti-Semitism. Holocaust denial, anti-Jewish conspiracies and harassment of Jews has increased in social media platforms and online forums. Perpetrators are often empowered by the anonymity, provided in online spaces.

It is one of the flashpoints over anti-Semitism and Israeli-Palestinian conflict. At times, in the past, criticisms of Israeli policies have led to anti-Semitism. This intricate connection of anti-Semitism with international conflict adds complexity to attempts at dealing with the problem.

Jewish Future in the United States

Arguments according to Daniel Pipes

Mr. Pipes posits a future scenario where American Jews may encounter less favorable prospects. His argument centers on the notion that the "Golden Age" for Jews in the United States, which commenced in 1950 with the relaxation of social constraints within universities, financial institutions, corporations, and social clubs, may be drawing to a close. This transition, he asserts, will be propelled by the burgeoning American Muslim population, within which influential factions identify American Jews as their adversaries, attributing to them the role of the perceived oppressors of Muslims.

Mr. Pipes elaborates on the strategy employed by the American Muslim community to project itself as a marginalized group, a narrative he deems unfounded. Nonetheless, it's worth noting that President Bill Clinton, in a significant proclamation, has acknowledged the existence of discrimination and intolerance directed towards American Muslims. Subsequently, the Senate has concurred, supporting President Clinton's statements on this matter.

Furthermore, Mr. Pipes underscores the prominence of various high-profile business magnates in the United States. He astutely observes the media's tendency to present Islam and Muslims in a positive and largely uncritical light. He also identifies a discernible trend among those he refers to as "enlightened" Americans, who conscientiously endeavor to cultivate

31

tolerance towards Islam and to convey a positive image of Muslims. Consequently, it is foreseeable that institutions of higher learning and educational establishments will be increasingly receptive to the influence of Islamic thought.

Arguments according to the author

In the United States, Jews are poised to once again assume the role of scapegoats for the impending afflictions of capitalism. There exist formidable elements with vested capitalist interests, which are inclined to designate American Jews as their adversaries, thus fabricating a delusion that implicates them as the wellspring of all forthcoming challenges in the nation. This ominous pattern, reminiscent of historical episodes in Nazi Germany and the Soviet Union, is anticipated to recur, wherein these groups endeavor to shape a narrative that identifies Jews as the supposed root cause of the perceived 'oppression' experienced by the working and middle classes.

Combating Anti-Semitism

Combating with anti-Semitism requires multiplicity of ways which include education, regulation, partnerships in communities and global cooperation. Here are several ways to combat anti-Semitism:

Education and Awareness

Establish education programs on tolerance, diversity, and understanding in schools. The effect of antisemitism on the world's population should be made a part of school curricula.

Legislation and Law Enforcement

The existence of laws against hate speech, discrimination and holocaust denial can help to alleviate anti-Semitic activities. These laws must be taken seriously by the law enforcement agencies and perpetrators held accountable.

Community Engagement

To bridge communities, foster interfaith and intercultural dialogue. Call on community leaders to denounce antisemitism and preach harmony.

Online Monitoring and Regulating

Watch out for hate speech on the internet and punish those who post hateful messages targeted at Jews.

Engage IT companies in coming up with efficient measures of reporting and taking down of the hate speech.

International Cooperation

Partnering with other states, including foreign organizations and governments in order to exchange ideas of successes and coordinating efforts together. Participate in efforts aimed at fighting global anti-Semitism.

Media Responsibility

Ensure that the media report responsibly since they should not contribute towards reinforcing myths and hatred. Promote media literacy in order to enable the public to critically assess information.

Support for Victims

Offer resources and aid to victims of anti-Semitism events. Provide helplines and counseling for survivors.

Political Leadership

Convince governments and politicians to firmly denounce anti-Semitism. Foster policies of tolerance and intolerance towards inequalities.

Holocaust Remembrance

Promote Holocaust education and remembrance programs to drive home the dangers of unrestrained intolerance. Preserve proper historical account of Holocaust.

Grassroots Initiatives

Support local groups fighting against anti-Semitism. Promote discussions that question stereotypes and prejudices between people.

THE CRUCIBLE OF MONOTHEISM: THE JEWISH CATALYST FOR CHRISTIANITY AND ISLAM

The tapestry of monotheistic religions is, indeed, a valuable and intricate one that has been woven with threads of faith and the revelation as well as the intellectual fermentations. Central to this narrative are two of the world's major religions: Christianity and Islam have individual effects on the history of humanity. However, it is important to acknowledge that the universe would possibly be idolatrous devoid of Judaism's influence, and Islam as well as Christianity could not have come about.

Monotheism as a Pioneering Concept

One needs to understand the nature of monotheism itself in order to grasp the full extent of how Judaism transformed this type of religious development. As a theological notion, monotheism refers to the belief in one God who has all powers and knowledge and is responsible for originating and preserving the universe. This is a deep idea that was different from the polytheistic beliefs of most ancient societies.

Judaism: The Birth of Monotheism

The beginning of monotheism leads back to the society of Hebrew Bible and their religious views. Israelites' covenant with Yahweh, a unique and transcendent deity was the basis for monotheism. This divine relationship was to become the framework for a new understanding of humans' place in the cosmos and their ethical obligations that arise from monotheistic faith.

The Ten Commandments: A Moral Compass for Humanity

In Judaism, the Ten Commandments form a basic moral code and are stated to have been given to Moses at Mount Sinai in Hebrew Bible. For the ages their principles of including "Thou shalt have no other gods before me" and "You shall not make for yourself an idol". This moral code

35

was centered on the one true God, not only guiding people in their religious practices but also laying foundation for monotheism.

The New Testament: Bridging Old and New

The Hebrew Bible or traditional Old Testament is valuable in the Christian religion and creates a link from Jewish religious belief to Christianity through The New Testament. The New Testament established a deep connection between the two religions by placing Jesus as Messiah on Jewish scripture's backdrop. This linkage, basing on Jewish monotheism is a pivot of Christian belief.

Islam: A Continuation of Monotheistic Tradition

Islam, which its religion based on the Judeo-Christian tradition, similarly emerged around 7th century CE in Arabian Peninsula. The holy book of Islam, the Quran accepts that Judaism and Christianity have had earlier monotheistic revelations. It acknowledges the Prophet Muhammad as "Seal of the prophets" who came to recover and finalize basic monotheistic message originally expressed through Judaism and Christianity.

A Shared Monotheistic Heritage

That is the Abrahamic lineage that Judaism, Christianity and Islam claim connection with to support this Jewish monotheism having impacted these religions. But in fact, all three religions of monotheism accept the Abrahamic covenant and worship Abraham, Moses and other prophets who were shared among them.

Idolatry and the Dismantling of False Powers

Both Christianity and Islam echo Judaism's vehement rejection of idolatry. Later monotheistic faiths emulate the Israelites' unwavering refusal to bow down to idols. First Commandment's announcement, "You shall have no other gods before me," strongly expostulates idolatry.

An Unceasing Moral Imperative

Monotheism's ethical implications have been passed down through the generations as well. For Christians, the Ten Commandments which originate from Judaism have remained moral forces that echo deeply in Islam ethics. This moral continuity collapsed in monotheistic tradition what became a truly indelible mark of the human civilization.

Monotheism's Unifying Vision

The Jewish notion of monotheism focused on worshiping the one true God, which has contributed to a unified vision among other subsequent monotheistic religions. This vision has gone beyond geographical and cultural lines to create a common spirituality, morality and human destiny.

A Catalyst for Human Progress

The influence of monotheism developed through Judaism is wider than mere religious change. Christianity and its monotheistic beliefs have been major speculations of morality in the Western culture. They have provided the foundations for legal systems, democratic ideals and human rights. Art, literature, philosophy and the struggle for social justice in Judeo-Christian-Islamic heritage.

Monotheism in the Face of Idolatry

It was a major departure from the polytheistic and idolatrous beliefs held in many ancient civilizations. Judaism, Christianity and Islam broke the trend of worshipping many deities that prevailed in many societies.

Monotheism's Moral Imperative

The doctrine of a just and merciful God, the ethical obligation which monotheism engenders in human conduct. Monotheistic faiths had this transcendental morality as a key socially unifying, empathic and ethically oriented element.

In order to comprehend these monumental changes, the historical framework of monotheism's genesis is highly important. Monotheism came about as a radical departure from the norms of idol and god worship in a world that believed in multiple gods. It served as a light for those who hoped and abode by the abandonment of false gods to acknowledge one inclusive God.

In Closing: The Jewish Crucible

Christianity and Islam could therefore not have arisen, neither would their moral and ethical frameworks developed without the presence of Jews as the basic contributors to monotheism. Jewish monotheism, with its everlasting morality laws and antigod-worship moralizes, has been a powerful force in making the spirituality and governing of mankind. As perceived, they all profess the great monotheism of worshipping one living God, which gives Judaism an integral role in their crucible as a very fact. Reflecting on such a lasting legacy, we can see how profound Jewish monotheism has been in the world and understand that without Jews Christianity and Islam might never have come to pass as moral lights of civilization.

Is the United States descending into a realm of spiritual desolation? When the visionary architects of this magnificent nation proclaimed, "In God we trust," their affirmation was an unequivocal testament to the Holy Trinity, for they, in their majority, were devout Christians, with a substantial number among them being of Puritan conviction. The prevailing faith among the European settlers who migrated to these shores was fundamentally steeped in the tenets of Christianity.

The perennial contest between creation and evolution, an issue often referred to as the creation-evolution controversy or the origins debate, unfolds as a recurring cultural, political, and theological skirmish, revolving around the enigma of Earth's beginnings, the emergence of humanity, the origins of life, and the vast universe itself. This fervent dialogue has found its most pronounced stage in the United States, although traces of it can also be discerned in Europe and elsewhere, often painted as a fragment of the broader culture war.

Creationists, steadfast in their convictions, challenge the body of evidence supporting the concept of shared ancestry between humans and other living creatures, as disclosed by modern paleontology. They also raise objections to the well-established conclusions of contemporary evolutionary biology, geology, cosmology, and other allied disciplines. In their quest, they champion the narratives of creation elucidated in the Abrahamic religious texts, endeavoring to position it within the domain of credible science, encapsulated under the label of 'creation science.' While the roots of this debate delve deep into history, its current iterations predominantly revolve around the contours of quality science education, with the political arena of creationism predominantly engaged in the discourse surrounding the teaching of creation and evolution in the public educational domain.

This dispute extends its tendrils into a multitude of interconnected issues, encompassing the very definition of science, the determination of what qualifies as scientific research and evidence, the contours of science education, the principles of free speech, the separation of Church and State, and the realms of theology.

Within the scientific realm and the academic sphere, the theory of evolution reigns supreme as an undisputed fact, with resounding consensus among scholars. The scientific community, in essence, unites in support of the theory of evolution. In stark contrast, the allegiance to the Abrahamic accounts or any other creationist alternatives is a rarity, with a profound scarcity of adherents, particularly within the precincts of the pertinent scientific disciplines.

Curiously, a Gallup survey from 2012 reveals a dissonance between the scientific consensus and public sentiment in the United States. It reports that forty-six percent of Americans endorse the creationist viewpoint, upholding the belief that God created humans in their present form within the last 10,000 years. Remarkably, this inclination remains virtually unchanged from thirty years prior, when Gallup first broached the question. About a third of Americans avow their belief in the notion that humans evolved, albeit with the guidance of a divine hand. An additional fifteen percent posit that humans evolved through a process devoid of divine intervention.

The prevailing narrative oftentimes characterizes this discourse as a clash between the domains of science and religion. Nevertheless, the United States National Academy of Sciences, in its wisdom, provides a perspective that merits our contemplation:

In our contemporary milieu, numerous religious denominations have come to acknowledge the validity of biological evolution as the force behind the magnificent tapestry of life, unfurled over countless eons in the annals of Earth's history. Many among them have issued declarations affirming the concordance of evolution with the tenets of their faith, emphasizing that there exists no inherent conflict between their profound reverence for the Divine and the compelling evidence that substantiates the concept of evolution.

Within this fertile terrain, one encounters the harmonious articulations of scientists and theologians who, in their eloquent narratives, convey a

40

profound sense of wonder and awe at the unfolding chronicle of the cosmos and life on our terrestrial abode. These individuals poignantly convey that, in their discernment, no chasm exists between their abiding faith in a higher power and the compelling substantiation of evolutionary principles.

It is worth noting that the religious denominations that remain resolute in their rejection of the concept of evolution are typically those that cleave to a stringent and literal interpretation of their sacred texts.

"I want to know how God created the universe. I am not interested in this or that phenomenon. I want to know His thoughts; the rest are details." —Albert Einstein

Our Physical World

Our universe is a tapestry woven from matter and the void of space. Within this cosmic fabric, all matter possesses mass and consists of atoms as its elemental building blocks. These atoms, in turn, are composed of protons, neutrons, and electrons, and it's the quantity and arrangement of these fundamental particles that bestows each element with its distinctive chemical and physical properties.

As we embark upon experiments and delve deeper into the mysteries of the atom, we unearth a startling revelation—that the subatomic constituents and their associated fields of force might embody self-sustaining manifestations of wave-like motions. Furthermore, in the realm of light, we encounter the intriguing duality of wave-like particles, fundamentally challenging our classical, mechanistic understanding of the physical world.

Amidst this labyrinth of scientific inquiry, we, as sentient beings, can discern a profound truth: all matter is, at its core, a manifestation of fundamental forces and wave-like particles. The colors that grace our vision are, in essence, vibrant waves of photon-like particles, each bearing a distinct wavelength, gracefully interpreted by our eyes as a spectrum of colors.

Contemplating the chair on which I now rest, it becomes evident that this seemingly tangible matter is, in truth, a composite of empty space interwoven with wave-like particles, interconnected through the unifying agency of fundamental forces. These particles emanate photons of diverse wavelengths, giving rise to the kaleidoscope of colors that we perceive. In essence, all that we perceive in the physical world may not be as "physical" as it first appears; our comprehension of the universe is profoundly bound to the intricacies of perception.

With this philosophical backdrop, let us pose a series of inquiries concerning the essence of our physical world: Why does the electric energy coursing through our brains drive the machinery of our thoughts and consciousness? Can we liken the brain to the hardware of a vast, intricate computer, with the software representing the very soul of our being, with its operations executed through the intricate choreography of electrical signals within the neurons of our cerebral domain? Might time, in all its enigmatic dimensions, hold the key to the universe's most profound mysteries? What new vistas of understanding might we uncover if time were not constrained to the linear path that we have long held as an immutable truth?

Creation

The vast expanse of the universe unfolds before us as an intricate series of events, intertwined across the tapestry of time, linked together in an unbroken causal chain. Each event emerges as both the offspring of its predecessor and the progenitor of its successor, creating a continuous procession of cause and effect. The world, as we perceive it today, stands as the culmination of an evolving narrative, emerging from the world as it once existed, itself a product of the world before that. As we journey backward along this trail of events, we confront a pivotal question: What lies at the origin of this causal continuum?

At first glance, it appears that there exist two potential answers. We might ultimately encounter the inaugural event, the prime catalyst at the genesis of the universe, the spark that ignited this grand cosmic symphony. Alternatively, the past may extend endlessly, with no initial event and no temporal boundary—an infinite regression of causation. The prevailing Big Bang theory, championed by the majority of physicists and substantiated through meticulous observation, posits our universe as an expanding entity that commenced from a singular point. However, within the realm of science, we find no established laws that dictate the spontaneous generation or annihilation of matter, requiring a radical reconsideration of the conservation of matter and energy, and thus, the bedrock principles of science.

43

In contrast, matter and energy, although not eternal, exhibit a dynamic interchangeability, encapsulated within Einstein's iconic equation ($E=MC^2$). Matter, under certain circumstances, can metamorphose into energy, which can in turn dissipate, whether in the form of the sun's radiant energy or the detonation of an atomic bomb. Contemplating these intricacies, one is compelled to query the genesis of the primal matter and energy that set the cosmos into motion.

Moreover, if we entertain the notion that matter can be self-existent, never created but simply enduring, we face a logical conundrum. To propose the inception of something from nothing, emerging from the void devoid of force, matter, energy, or intelligence, challenges the very fabric of scientific understanding. When we circumvent the concept of creation, this scenario can only unfold through a novel and enigmatic process that has thus far eluded the purview of science, or through the realm of the miraculous, a return to the idea of creation.

The mysteries of the cosmos beckon us to contemplate the enigma of our existence, and as we delve deeper into the fabric of reality, we encounter profound questions about the origin and nature of the universe.

God's Image

When we entertain the notion of God, it is essential to shatter the confines of an anthropomorphic and physically bound deity, as such a conception not only strays from the biblical and common-sense understanding but also leads us into the quagmire of questioning God's origin—a dilemma that is alien to genuine theological inquiry.

The Old Testament, the ancient wellspring of Judeo-Christian wisdom, offers a portrayal of God as a spiritual entity, transcending the finite bounds of our three-dimensional, physical realm. God's existence is something that resides beyond the tangible, in the ethereal realm of human consciousness. It beckons us to ponder the genesis of this universal idea, to grapple with the enigma of its inception, and to question its compatibility with the framework of evolution—a question that finds no simple resolution within the confines of evolutionary discourse.

44

Throughout the annals of history, across the diverse tapestry of human cultures and civilizations, a consistent thread weaves its way through the fabric of our collective consciousness: the unwavering conviction in a divine Creator, a God worthy of reverence and worship. It is incumbent upon us to recognize that the sheer magnitude of adherents to this belief, representing a kaleidoscope of sociological, intellectual, emotional, and educational backgrounds, does not, in and of itself, render a belief as absolute truth. Nevertheless, the prevalence of this belief, manifesting independently across societies, compels us to seek understanding.

The question arises: Is this widespread phenomenon a mere fortuity, a serendipitous collision of human thought, or does it serve as a profound psychological defense mechanism, shielding us from life's adversities? If it is indeed a psychological defense, then why is it unique to humanity? Animals, traversing a harsher terrain, display no inclination toward religious belief. While a faithful dog may regard its owner with an air of godliness, this reflects a master-slave relationship, rooted in the immediate physical surroundings. Only in the human psyche does the innate propensity to transcend the confines of the physical world persist.

The burning query lingers: What drives this intrinsic belief in a spiritual God, firmly etched into the human consciousness, inviting us to traverse the realms of theology and philosophy in search of answers?

Intelligent Design

The exploration of intelligent design has taken on a multitude of facets and inquiries. For many of us, the simple act of gazing upon our newborn offspring suffices to dispel any notion of random chance. In the intricate tapestry of molecular biology, we uncover an abundance of encoded information within each living cell—a revelation that beckons our contemplation. Molecular biologists, in their tireless pursuits, unveil the presence of innumerable exquisitely crafted molecular machines, testaments to the artistry at the most minuscule level of existence. It becomes evident that information necessitates an intelligent source, and design is inseparable from the notion of a designer.

The sheer complexity of our world points our gaze toward an intentional designer, one who not only ushered our universe into existence but sustains its delicate equilibrium to this very day. Humans have long gravitated towards dualities in their thinking—cold juxtaposed with heat, light in contrast to darkness, good locked in an eternal struggle with evil, and our terrestrial realm set against the backdrop of the infinite cosmos. These dualistic paradigms, however, unveil deeper layers of interpretation. Cold finds its foil in the abyss of infinite heat, darkness is but the absence of light, and evil emerges as the consequence of a world devoid of the Divine presence. Our world is irrevocably intertwined with the vast expanse of the universe, transcending the confines of duality.

In matters of faith, the simplicity of dualistic thinking wanes. Faith, at its essence, entails the recognition of God, yet it does not necessarily secure God's reciprocal acknowledgment. The human brain stands as a testament to the marvels of simultaneous processing—a symphony of colors, sensory perceptions, temperature discernment, tactile sensations, auditory revelations, and the nuanced pleasures of music and culinary experiences. It also bears the weight of emotional responses, the labyrinth of feelings, and the repository of our thoughts and memories. Concurrently, it meticulously oversees the intricate workings of our physical being, monitoring the rhythmic cadence of breath, the flutter of eyelids, the pangs of hunger, and the orchestration of muscular movements. Astoundingly, the human brain grapples with over a million messages each second.

In this intricate tapestry of human existence, we are compelled to ponder whether the human brain, with its grandeur, complexity, and multifaceted functions, could emerge as a product of pure evolution—from a humble virus to a fully realized, sentient organ. Charles Darwin, the luminary of evolutionary theory, once postulated that "numberless intermediate varieties" should exist if his theory held true, bridging the chasm between species. However, the fossil record, despite its richness, has yet to yield evidence linking viruses to the emergence of thinking, sentient mammals with evolved brains.

Within the wondrous tapestry of our world, we are compelled to marvel at the intricacies and marvels that grace our existence: the Earth's precise alignment with the sun, the extraordinary properties of water, or the sheer sophistication of a single organ in the human body. Could any of these phenomena be the mere result of happenstance? The theory of evolution, though it strives to elucidate the intricate dance of life, remains incapable of furnishing a comprehensive explanation for the profound fine-tuning of our universe, as it is the laws of nature that establish a limited framework for evolution, yet cannot address the enigmatic genesis of life. In essence, the grand design of creation stands as the genesis, upon which God has permitted evolution to operate and fine-tune His initial blueprint to finite degrees. Evolution, in its essence, finds itself incapable of shedding light on the bewildering journey from a simple virus to the fully cognizant human being. It is intelligent design that bears the torch of understanding in this regard.

Contained within the genetic code, akin to all messages and information, we encounter a form of existence that transcends the boundaries of matter. The meaning infused within the genetic code does not arise from the physical or chemical properties that govern the arrangement of its symbols and alphabets; rather, it is an ethereal entity that defies reduction to the material realm. Only through the lens of intelligent design can we unlock the mysteries enshrined within DNA's enigmatic script. Biochemists and mathematicians, driven by meticulous calculation, have unveiled the astronomical odds stacked against life's emergence from non-life through unintelligent processes. In fact, the scientific community remains uncertain whether life could naturally evolve from such processes devoid of intelligent influence.

The prevailing evolutionary assumption, which posits that the labyrinthine linguistic structures woven into the blueprints and operational manuals governing the intricate nano-machinery and sophisticated feedback control mechanisms found within even the simplest life forms must have a materialistic explanation, stands on shaky ground. In the grand narrative of the origins of living entities, two archetypal explanations emerge:

47

creation and evolution. These paradigms exhaust the spectrum of potential explanations. Living species either emerged upon the Earth's stage in a fully developed state as original, originating species, or they did not. It is within the realm of this logic that creation and evolution find harmonious coexistence. The originating species, if they appeared in a fully developed form, must have been the handiwork of a supreme intelligence.

Even the simplest single-cell organism remains a profound enigma, defying the notion that a sequence of serendipitous events could bestow it with the intricate architecture of DNA and the mechanisms to replicate and propagate. The prospect of a series of evolutionary steps yielding a fully formed, cognizant human being remains a statistical improbability. Thus, the domain of evolution is circumscribed to the transformation of species into their present states from an earlier, created state, an arena where creation and evolution coalesce, each playing a distinct role in the unfolding drama of life's narrative.

Time, Space and Relativity

Within the scope of our human comprehension, we've long regarded our existence as tethered to a four-dimensional universe. Our perceptual faculties are bound to a coordinate system that embraces the dimensions of length, width, height, and the inexorable passage of time. Yet, the epochal year of 1916 bore witness to a profound transformation, as Albert Einstein unveiled his theory of General Relativity, later followed by his Special Relativity, forever reshaping the landscape of cosmology and redefining the very essence of our known dimensions.

Intriguingly, the theory of Special Relativity ushered in a paradigm shift, challenging our hitherto steadfast belief in time as an immutable and absolute construct. It proffered the disconcerting notion that time, a bedrock of our understanding, could metamorphose, accelerating or decelerating contingent on one's velocity through the cosmos. Moreover, this groundbreaking theory cast the birth of creation to within a span of less than 20 billion years—a temporal canvas that modern data now revises to a more refined estimate of 12 to 13 billion years, while the Earth coalesced approximately 4.5 billion years in the past. This compact timeframe, we soon realized, left precious little room to accommodate the emergence of life through the whims of random chance processes, a notion most saliently captured by the theory of evolution.

At the outset, Biblical literalists, steadfast in their belief that the cosmos came into being over the course of six 24-hour days, around 6,000 years in the past, found themselves in direct conflict with this emerging theory. Nevertheless, a distinct perspective emerges when we venture into the realm of alternative coordinate systems. It is possible that the time of creation referenced in the Bible might not precisely align with the time coordinate we customarily adhere to.

Should we embark on a journey through the biblical account of creation, an intriguing alignment surfaces—one that approximates the sequence of creation when we factor in the nuanced interplay of Special Relativity and the Evolution theory. Notably, the evolution theory diverges from the creation theory in terms of the sequencing of sun-earth and fish-plant-bird creations. The days of creation, which serve as our temporal reference points, may unveil a different dimension of time altogether, a dimension delineated in the Bible through simplistic temporal markers, readily grasped by our understanding.

Consciousness, Mentality and Morality

The deeply ingrained sense of right and wrong that courses through the veins of humankind defies facile biological or evolutionary explication. It is a shared experience, transcending cultural boundaries, as universal as the very air we breathe. In our collective human journey, we encounter a tapestry woven with threads of courage, self-sacrifice for noble causes, love, dignity, duty, and compassion. Yet, one is compelled to ponder: from whence do these noble virtues spring? In a world governed solely by the ruthless dictate of "survival of the fittest," one might question the source of our innate proclivity to assist one another. What foments this inner moral compass?

Morality, at its core, emerges as a commanding authority—an edifice of moral imperatives that shape our lives. The moral argument, rooted in the existence of moral laws, finds its foothold in the evidence of God's existence. According to this argument, the very concept of morality finds itself inextricably linked with the divine; to echo the sentiments attributed to Dostoyevsky by Sartre, "If there is no God, then everything is permissible." Where moral laws exist, the realm of possibility is circumscribed, not everything is admissible, and the domain of civilized order prevails. Herein lies the contradiction with the dogma of evolution—a doctrine anchored in the concept of "survival of the fittest," a paradigm that stands bereft of the explanatory power to illuminate the origins and underpinnings of morality.

The realms of consciousness and sub-consciousness have long been explored and scrutinized by luminaries such as Freud, Adler, Jung, and other renowned psychologists. As human beings, we transcend mere physical systems, bearing the weight of rich and intricate mental lives. Natural selection, the guiding hand of evolution, has consistently sifted through organisms, singling out those whose behavior ensures their survival. It is imperative to recognize that an organism mirroring our actions but devoid of the accompanying mental states enjoys an identical degree of survival value.

In essence, mentality stands not as a prerequisite for behavior, and mere behavior suffices for the imperative of survival. As far as evolution is concerned, the survival drive, epitomized by Freud's id, is the crux of the matter. Consciousness and sub-consciousness serve as gateways to the inner workings of our mind, unveiling the intricate tapestry of thought, spirituality, intellectual yearnings, personality, self-awareness, the imperatives of survival, and our innate sexuality—each an integral facet of our mental landscape.

However, within this intricate mosaic, the evolutionary narrative accords value solely to the id, which encapsulates our fundamental drives, the impetus for survival, and our primordial sexuality. The ego and super-ego, integral constituents of our minds, find themselves bereft of direct evolutionary significance, prompting us to ponder the enigmatic facets of evolution theory and their bearing on this intricate psychological tableau.

History

The annals of archaeology persistently reinforce, rather than undermine, the veracity of the Bible. A notable illustration arises from an archaeological discovery in northern Israel back in August 1993, which lent credence to the existence of King David—an iconic figure, and the prolific author of many Psalms in the Bible. The hallowed troves of the Dead Sea Scrolls, alongside a panoply of other archaeological revelations, serve as compelling testaments to the historical precision of the Bible.

Archaeological excavations on Egyptian soil affirm the presence of Hebrews in the land, coinciding with the reign of Ramses, an epoch firmly documented in the Bible. Notably, the Bible offers mention of the cities of Pittum and Ramses. What adds to the remarkable tapestry of biblical narratives is the astonishing fact that this sacred text, composed over an expanse of countless years, by diverse authors, each with their distinct geographical and temporal settings, and employing three distinct languages, unfurls a remarkable consistency that transcends the boundaries of time and space.

Philosophical Arguments

The realm of philosophical discourse on the existence of God is an avenue that cannot be bypassed, especially after the compelling reasons presented above. Here, I shall provide a succinct overview of these philosophical arguments, an arena where distinguished philosophers spanning the past four centuries have dedicated their intellectual energies to scrutinizing God's existence, deploying reason as their guiding beacon.

Renowned thinkers like Descartes (1596-1650) and Leibniz (1646-1716) embarked on a journey wherein they perceived God's existence as a rational verity—an intrinsic component of their philosophical tapestry. Among their ranks, the French mathematician Blaise Pascal (1623-62) proffered an argument tailored to resonate with agnostics. His line of reasoning unfolds thus: God's existence, or lack thereof, stands as a binary proposition. Should we hold belief in God, and He indeed exists, we shall be bestowed with the promise of eternal heavenly bliss. Conversely, should we believe in God, and He exists not, our cost is no greater than the forfeiture of a smattering of fleeting, sinful pleasures. Yet, if we shun belief in God, and He does exist, we may relish transitory pleasures, but incurring the peril of eternal damnation. Lastly, in the absence of belief in God and His nonexistence, our sins shall remain unpunished. Can any judicious gambler conclude that a modicum of sinful pleasures is worth the gamble of eternal perdition?

Hegel (1770-1831), in his philosophical odyssey, conceived of the God of religion as an intuitive manifestation of Absolute Spirit—or, as he elegantly phrased it: Geist. It is essential to discern that Hegel's Geist stands apart from the transcendent God of conventional Christianity, as it subsists within the realm of immanence. As we embrace the insight that history unfolds as the narrative of Geist's self-cognition, we glimpse the profound realization that we, as sentient beings, are integral components of this transcendent, immanent Godhead—indelibly intertwined with Geist, or God, as Hegel envisioned it.

veritable nature of reality lies beyond the precincts of our experiential realm. Even if God's existence is acknowledged, our understanding of God remains forever veiled, preventing us from grasping the essence of His being. In Kant's intricate tapestry of thought, the Christian's faith in God assumes a pivotal role—one that harmonizes seamlessly with reason and the categorical imperative. Human autonomy, which empowers us to craft moral values, endows us with the capacity to entertain the belief in a God who bestows purpose upon the moral realm.

Albert Einstein (1879-1955), in his eloquent declaration that "God does not play dice," conveyed a profound message—namely, that the universe's order is not contingent on random chance. Einstein's intellectual odyssey was anchored in the conviction that the laws of physics embodied a manifestation of the divine. This profound belief guided his pursuit of a universe describable through the elegance of simple mathematics. Armed with the knowledge of these laws, the universe's intricate tapestry could be unraveled with unwavering precision. However, Einstein's deep-seated aversion to the perplexing implications of quantum mechanics ignited a fierce ideological clash, with quantum enthusiasts admonishing him, "Einstein, cease instructing God on the use of His dice."

Søren Kierkegaard (1813-1855), in alignment with Kant, concurred that the realm of reason could not furnish conclusive proof of God's existence. Nonetheless, Kierkegaard diverged in his perspective, asserting that rationality ought not to serve as the lodestar guiding one's faith in God. Rather, he advocated for the primacy of faith even in the face of what reason might deem absurd. In this theological landscape, reason finds no place; God transcends its confines and resides in a realm that eludes the grip of rational inquiry.

There are three main philosophical arguments for the existence of God: The argument from design, the ontological argument and the cosmological argument.

1. The Argument from Design: Imagine stumbling upon a meticulously crafted timepiece, carefully examining its intricate inner workings. The notion that such a sophisticated mechanism could have materialized purely by happenstance appears implausible. You would likely conclude that this marvel was intentionally designed. Now, direct your gaze to the cosmos—a tapestry of complexity that extends from the celestial dance of planets around the sun to the intricate cellular structures within your own fingernails. Can we reasonably attribute the existence of this immensely intricate mechanism to mere chance? It seems inconceivable. Instead, it stands to reason that a grand designer fashioned this intricate cosmos, and this supreme designer we identify as God.

2. The Ontological Argument: God epitomizes the zenith of perfection. Possessing all conceivable perfections, He cannot be lacking in any aspect, including existence itself. In essence, the very fact that God embodies perfection necessitates His existence.

3. The Cosmological Argument (God as the "First Cause"): The principle that underlies this argument is simple: every effect is traceable back to a cause. However, within this chain of causality, there must exist an inaugural cause—a "prime mover" or first cause that predates all others. This prime mover is indispensable in elucidating the existence of the universe. Within this framework, this first cause is none other than God.

Creation vs. Evolution - Conclusion

Throughout the annals of history, mankind's awareness of a Supreme Being, the Master and Creator of all, has remained unwavering. Numerous individuals profess to have encountered the divine directly, an experience distinct in nature from the realms of sensory perception or intellectual revelation. But is belief in God merely a product of wishful thinking or an emotional imperative? Are we the outcomes of evolutionary processes, or the result of a purposeful and intelligent design? Julian Huxley once asserted, "We are as much a product of blind forces as is the falling of a stone to earth or the ebb and flow of the tides. We have simply emerged through a sequence of remarkably fortuitous occurrences."

Christianity, deriving its name from the Ancient Greek "Christianos" and the Latin "-itas" suffix, stands as a monotheistic and Abrahamic faith rooted in the life and teachings of Jesus, as presented in canonical gospels and New Testament writings. It equally holds the Hebrew Bible, known as the Old Testament, in high canonical regard, encapsulating a comprehensive spiritual tradition. Its adherents bear the title of Christians.

The central tenet of mainstream Christian belief asserts that Jesus is both fully divine and fully human, serving as the savior of humanity. In light of this, Christians commonly designate him as Christ or Messiah. His ministry, self-sacrifice, and subsequent resurrection are encapsulated by the term "Gospel," signifying the "Good News" (from the Greek "euangélion"). In essence, the Gospel heralds the victory of God the Father over the forces of evil, promising salvation and eternal life to all through divine grace.

Globally, Christianity is marked by three principal branches: the Roman Catholic Church, the Eastern Orthodox Church, and various Protestant denominations. The schism between the Roman Catholic and Eastern Orthodox patriarchates in 1054 AD and the emergence of Protestantism during the 16th-century Reformation marked pivotal historical moments in the faith's evolution.

Christianity's origins trace back to a Jewish sect in the mid-1st century, taking root in the Levant region of the Middle East. Swiftly, it spread to encompass Syria, Mesopotamia, Asia Minor, and Egypt. Over the course of a few centuries, it grew in size and influence, ultimately becoming the official state religion of the Roman Empire by the late 4th century, supplanting other forms of worship prevalent under Roman governance. Throughout the Middle Ages, the majority of Europe underwent Christianization, and Christians became substantial religious minorities in the Middle East, North Africa, Ethiopia, and pockets of India. In the wake of the Age of Discovery, Christianity reached across the globe, propelled by missionary endeavors and colonization, establishing its presence in the Americas, Australasia, sub-Saharan Africa, and beyond.

The Christian belief centers on Jesus as the long-foretold Messiah, as prophesied in the Hebrew Bible, also known as the 'Old Testament' in Christian tradition. The theological bedrock of Christianity finds its articulation in the early Christian ecumenical creeds, containing affirmations widely embraced by Christian faithful. These declarations proclaim that Jesus endured suffering, death, burial, and ultimately triumphed over death through resurrection. His purpose was to bestow eternal life upon those who place their faith in him and rely on his grace for the forgiveness of their sins, a concept integral to the notion of salvation. Furthermore, it is held that Jesus ascended bodily into heaven, where he rules and reigns alongside God, the Father. The majority of Christian denominations teach that Jesus will return, presiding over the judgment of all humanity, both living and deceased, and ushering his followers into eternal life. He serves as a paragon of virtuous living and embodies the divine revelation, serving as the tangible incarnation of God.

As we traverse into the early 21st century, Christianity boasts approximately 2.5 billion adherents worldwide. It represents approximately one-third of the global populace, securing its status as the world's largest religion. Several nations have enshrined Christianity as their state religion. A demographic distribution reveals that among the Christian community, 37.5% reside in the Americas, 25.7% in Europe, 22.5% in Africa, 13.1% in Asia, 1.2% in Oceania, and 0.9% in the Middle East. Notably, Christianity has played a pivotal role in shaping both sub-Saharan African and Western civilizations.

Who Is Jesus?

The central figure of the Christian faith, Jesus of Nazareth (c.4 BC — c. 30 AD/CE). In different Christian denominations, he is regarded as the Son of God and God himself in human form. He is also regarded as the anticipated savior in the Old Testament. Nonetheless, it is important to note that these claims are rejected in Judaism. On the other hand, Islam views Jesus as a prophet and also accepts him as the Messiah, while other religions revere him differently.

The primary source from whence knowledge of Jesus' life and teaching is relayed, is found in the four canonical gospels especially the Synoptic Gospels. However, some scholars argue other texts like the Gospel of Thomas are as important as canonical gospels in making a historical portrayal of Jesus. Many scholars in the fields of history and biblical studies concur that the New Testament provides useful insights to building a summary of Jesus' life. The mainstream view is that he was a religious Jewish teacher and healer. Furthermore, it is widely agreed that he was baptized by John the Baptist and crucified in Jerusalem after being accused of insurrection against the Roman Empire by Pontius Pilate who was a Roman Prefect at Judaea.

Apart from such basic concerns, academic debates seem to have little agreement on the timing of Jesus' life, the central theme of his ministership as well as his socio-economic status, culture and background. Jesus has had various interpretations in academic circles including the awaited Messiah, self-proclaimed Messiah, apocalyptic movement leader, wandering sage and charismatic healer among others.

Christian understanding of Jesus is based on the belief that he was a deity, Old Testament Messiah and rose again from the dead after being crucified. In essence, for Christians Jesus is the 'Son of God' indicating that he has a divine nature as the second person in Trinity-God the Son. Christian dogma has it that he came to make possible man's salvation and bringing back of good relationship with God through his death for their sins. In addition, this doctrine develops additional thoughts of Jesus' supernatural conception; his astral activities; ascension to Heaven and his prospective return. While the Trinity concept is well received by a majority of Christians, there is some slight resistance within minority groups who consider it non-biblical.

Jesus is described in historical reports as a healer who announced the coming back of God's kingdom. Based on most historical accounts, it was generally agreed that he was baptized by John the Baptist and eventually lost his life at the hands of Roman powers. Concerning Jerusalem, the Galilean nationalists were equally dreaded by Jewish and Roman authorities; most of those nationalists would promote or participate in violent revolt against the Romans. The gospels indicate that Jesus was incarnated, on political related offenses as a charismatic ungovernable leader. Another unique aspect of Jesus' teachings was His focus in addressing God as a father above.

Was Jesus Aramaic a Hebrew, primarily resident in Galilee? His name 'Yehoshua', which in Greek it translates to 'God delivers.'

Major Denominations Within Christianity

Christianity divides into three major branches: Catholicism, Eastern Orthodoxy, and Protestantism. Additionally, various Christian denominations exist outside these core categories. The Nicene Creed holds authoritative status in the Roman Catholic, Eastern Orthodox, Anglican, and significant Protestant traditions. Within the realm of self-proclaimed Christians, one encounters a spectrum of doctrines and rituals. Some groupings are commonly referred to as denominations, yet theological nuances can lead to resistance to such categorization. Another line of demarcation frequently emerges between Eastern Christianity and its Western counterpart.

Catholic

The Catholic Church consists of particular ecclesiastical bodies that are under the unwavering guidance of bishops, in conjunction with the Pope, who is commonly stated as Bishop of Rome. The Pope is the highest authority in the Catholic Church and delves into faith, morals, as well as overall governance. Like the Eastern Orthodox tradition, the lineage of Roman Catholic Church dates can be dated back to a community created by Jesus Christ for they hold that Jesus "one, holy, catholic and apostolic church" fully resides in it. However, it acknowledges the other Christian denominations also and tries to bring about reconciliation among all Christian communities.

The valid knowledge of the Catholic faith is contained in the Catechism of the Catholic Church.

There are 2,834 dioceses in total under the mantle of the 23 specific rites with Latin Rite being the majority. There are distinctive liturgical practices as well as sacramental methodologies of each rite. At 1.1 billion baptized members, the Catholic Church is the world's largest Christian denomination and constitutes more than half of total Christianity worldwide and about one-sixth of all people on earth.

Other smaller ecclesiastic groups, such as the Old Catholic and Independent Catholic Churches, use "Catholic" in their names and have a lot in common with Roman Catholicism. Nevertheless, these groups have broken their relations with the See of Rome. Anglican Communion has retained its union with the Old Catholic Church.

Orthodox

Eastern Orthodoxy consists of the churches in communion with the Eastern Patriarchal Sees such as Patriarch, who are based in the church and Episcopal complex. Similar to the Roman Catholic Church, the Eastern Orthodox church also traces its origins to early Christianity through Apostolic succession and operates under a bishop-led hierarchy. Nevertheless, it lays stress on the self-government of separate national churches. Lastly, the Great Schism followed a number of theological and authoritative contests with Western Christendom. Being the second largest single Christian denomination, Eastern Orthodoxy has a followership exceeding 200 million people.

On the other hand, Oriental Orthodox Churches go by Old Oriental Churches and acknowledge Nicaea, Constantinople and Ephesus as the first three ecumenical council. However, they differ in that they reject doctrinal definitions advanced by the Council of Chalcedon and adopt a Miaphysite Christology. The Oriental Orthodox communion is provided by six independent entities which are the Syriac Orthodox, Coptic Orthodox,

Ethiopian and Eritrean Orthodox, Malankara Orthodox Syrian church in India as well as Armenian Apostolic. These six churches remain in communion. However, they have some isolation within the structural hierarchy. Of particular note is the fact that these churches have typically not shared communion with the Eastern Orthodox Churches although they involve themselves in dialogues for fellowship.

Protestant

The protestant movement that came to be known as Protestantism was first introduced during the 16th century through Martin Luther, Huldrych Zwingli and John Calvin. Lutherans refer to Luther's principal theological successors while the legacy of Zwingli and Calvin brings together a wider variety denomination generally referred as Reformed Tradition. The Reformed tradition is the source of many Protestant traditions in some form.

In addition, Anglicanism developed as a unique denomination of Protestantism following the English Reformation. While the Anabaptist tradition suffered marginalization from other Protestant factions by then, it has emerged over time and earned recognition. However, some Baptists do not consider themselves as Protestants since they claim to have a direct line of descent back to the apostles in the 1st century; though not all Baptist hold this view.

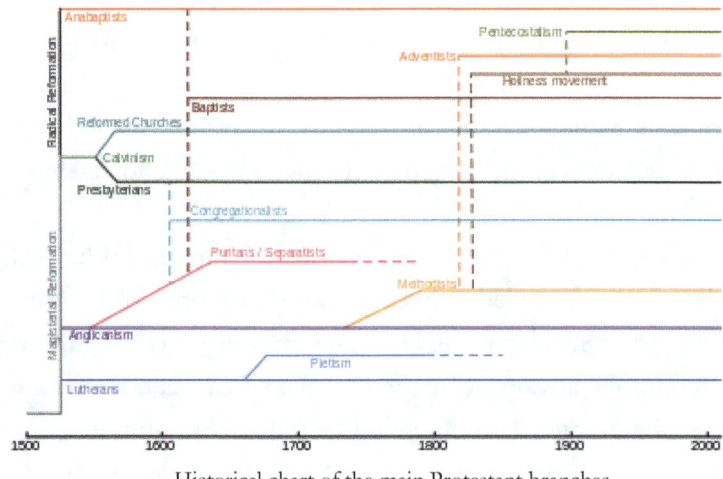

Historical chart of the main Protestant branches

The first Protestant denominations originated during the 16th-century Protestant Reformation, which was the inaugural split from Catholicism. As a result, Protestantism moved further resulting to the development of different divisions. The Methodist Church, however, originated from the evangelical and revival movement popularized by Anglican minister John Wesley. The transformative power of the Holy Spirit was emphasized in a number Pentecostal and non-denominational congregations that had emerged from this tradition. As a result, these groups often preach the need of "accepting Jesus as your personal Lord and Savior," a concept that originates from John Wesley's focus on the New Birth, leading them to identify themselves as "born-again."

It is difficult to estimate the total number of Protestants because of problems associated with categorizing denominations. However, in the same vein it is worthy to note that Protestantism is undoubtedly the second largest Christian group amongst believers after Catholicism though smaller than any of its single denominations when compared with Orthodox Church. Usually, the number of Protestant is estimated to be approximately 850 million. Protestantism forms part of the 2.4 billion Christian community that also incorporates orthodox church with about 240 million adherents and Catholic Church having about 1.2 billion followers across the globe.

Amidst this heterogeneity, Anglican churches emerge as a unique class, whose association with the Church of England and organization in Anglican Communion. There are those Anglican Churches that identify themselves as members of the two affiliations comprising Protestant and Catholic, while others view their church as a constituent party of the larger 'One Holy Catholic Church'-a position not acceptable by Roman catholic Church and other factions in Eastern Orthodox.

Additionally, there exist those that share in main Protestant principles but mainly identify themselves as 'Christians' or 'born-again Christians.' Their separation from the confessional and creedal components of other Christian families makes them allude to such terms as being non-denominational. These groups are mostly founded by singular pastors and have superficial linkages with recognized denominations.Other Branches

Esoteric Christianity refers to a range of spiritual movements that consider Christianity as a secretive religion. Such traditions assert to have certain hidden esoteric teachings or practices, unknown by common people, and available only for few illuminated, initiated or educated persons. Connection in between, is belief in reincarnation among one of these mystical denominations. The Rosicrucian Fellowship, the Anthroposophical Society, and Martinism are some of the institutions related to esoteric Christianity.

The early 1800s in the United States saw a time of religious renewal, with Second Great Awakening contributing to development of unrelated churches. These groups generally perceived their role as that of rejuvenating Christ's church and not reforming existing ones. The Restorationists believed that other branches of Christianity had brought doctrinal flaws into the faith, called the Great Apostasy.

There are churches established during this period that have historical connections to the early nineteenth century camp meetings in Midwest and Upstate New York America. Emerging from Evangelical Protestantism were American Millennialism and Adventism, which contributed to the establishment of Jehovah's Witnesses movement with a membership of about 7 million. Furthermore, the Seventh-day Adventists came up directly due to the William Miller's response. Other churches, like the Christian Church (Disciples of Christ), Evangelical Christian Church in Canada, Churches of Christ, and the Christian churches and churches of Christ come from a parallel movement—the Stone-Campbell Restoration Movement that mostly developed in Kentucky and Tennessee at about the same time. Denominations such as the Christadelphians and The Church of Jesus Christ of Latter-day Saints, whose largest faction is the Latter-Day Saint movement with more than 14 million followers today, abounds from this historical period. The churches of the Second Great Awakening are similar in some external ways but are different by their doctrines and practices.

Source: Islamic Affairs Department, Royal Embassy of Saudi Arabia

"This day have I perfected your religion for you and completed My favor unto you, and have chosen for you as your religion Islam." (Quran, Surah V:3)

Introduction

Islam is a faith founded on the act of surrendering to the One God. The very essence of the religion, known as ALISLAM in Arabic, encapsulates both submission and peace. By submitting to God's Will, individuals find peace in their lives, both in this world and the hereafter. Islam's message revolves around God, referred to as Allah in Arabic, and it delves into the deepest aspects of human nature. It addresses humanity as originally created by God, without considering them as fallen beings. Consequently, Islam sees itself not as an innovation but as a reaffirmation of the timeless truth found in all revelations: the Oneness of God.

This truth has been proclaimed by the prophets of old, particularly Abraham, the forefather of monotheism. Islam holds profound respect for these prophets, including not only Abraham, the father of both Arabs and Jews, but also Moses and Christ. The Prophet and Messenger of God, Muhammad, upon him be peace and blessings, stands as the last in this noble line of prophets, and Islam represents the ultimate religion, continuing until the Day of Judgment. It serves as the final embodiment of the Abrahamic tradition, and it is more accurately described as the Judeo-Christian-Islamic tradition. Islam shares with other Abrahamic faiths a common sacred history, the fundamental ethical teachings of the Ten Commandments, and, above all, a belief in the Oneness of God. It reaffirms the authentic tenets of Judaism and Christianity, referencing the scriptures of these religions as divinely revealed texts in its own sacred book, the Quran.

In the Islamic faith, the Quran stands as the tangible Word of God, unveiled through the archangel Gabriel to the Prophet of Islam over a span of twenty-three years during his prophetic mission. These revelations were delivered in the Arabic language as a sonic message, orally transmitted by the Prophet to his companions. Consequently, Arabic became the language of Islam, even for non-Arab Muslims. Guided by the Prophet, the verses and chapters of the Quran were organized in the sequence familiar to Muslims today. A singular Quranic text is universally accepted among all branches of Islamic thought, devoid of any variations.

The Quran holds the utmost sacred significance in Islam. It serves as the initial and final audible presence in a Muslim's life. Revered as the direct Word of God and a manifestation of His Will, the Quran stands as the ultimate guide for Muslims, encompassing all aspects of their lives. It is the wellspring of all Islamic doctrines and ethical principles. Islamic scholarship and jurisprudence draw their essence from the Quran. It is arguably unparalleled in the depth of veneration it commands from any collective human tradition, particularly within the context of a religion centered around sacred texts. Islam, fundamentally a religion of the book, acknowledges the association of authentic religions with divine scriptures. This is the reason why Muslims often refer to Jews as the 'people of the book'.

Throughout its chapters and verses, the Quran underscores the paramount importance of knowledge. It urges Muslims to learn and acquire knowledge, extending beyond comprehension of God's laws and religious decrees. The Quran's rich and multifaceted language underscores the significance of observation, contemplation, and rational inquiry into the diverse natural world. It assigns the acquisition of knowledge the highest status among religious pursuits, deeming it most pleasing in the eyes of God. Thus, wherever the message of the Quran was embraced and comprehended, the pursuit of knowledge thrived.The Prophet of Islam

Muslims hold the Prophet of Islam in such high respect because this was a divine choice made by God to use him and reveal His word to humanity. For instance, Muhammad, may the peace and blessings of God be upon him, is not considered to be divine but an exceptional human being. He was as a gem most bright on earth among things darker. He was born in 570 A.D. into one of the influential tribes in Arabia specifically the tribe that was given custody to look after Ka'bah and later he became an orphan raised by his granddad before being picked up by his uncle. In his early ages, Muhammad was recognized for his great amount of honesty whereby people requested him to handle their tribal arguments.

In that period, the Arabs were idol-worshippers and each tribe used to worship its own idols in Ka'ba which was a cubical shaped structure Abraham had built for elevating God. However, the monotheistic message of Abraham had been forgotten in the conscious of Arabian Peninsula. Yet young Muhammad on his part, never lost a faith in the same one God and he always abstained from idolatrous practices of his tribe.

Muhammad reported first seeing the archangel Gabriel, while he was forty and hitherto characteristically indwelled in a mountain yardstick retreat outside Makkah. During this experience God revealed to him his Word (the Quran) and that he was the messenger of God. For the following thirteen years, he propagated this Word of God to the people of Makkah where he told them to abandon idolatry and follow faith in One God. Some Makkans embraced his call but the majority especially those from his tribe was violent against this perception of new religion, which posed a big threat to their economic and social dictatorship since it all revolved around the Ka'bah. However, the Prophet continued to preach Islam calling for more and more men and women into the faith. As a result, the persecution against Muslims intensified and ultimately forced the Prophet to send some of his companions to Abyssinia, where he sought audience with a Christian King who accorded them support.

It was during this Makkan period that the Prophet and noble companions, who formed the backbone of a soon to be established worldly religion, went through profound experiences on their path of spirituality. In the course of this, God commanded change of Qibla from Jerusalem to

Makkah. Up to date, there are only three holy cities in Islam including Makkah, Madinah and Jerusalem.

In 622 A.D., God directed the Prophet to migrate to Yathrib, a city located north of Makkah. Complying with the divine order, the Prophet embarked on this journey, and henceforth, the city came to be known as "The City of the Prophet" (Madinat al-nabi) or simply Madinah. This event holds such significance that the Islamic calendar commences with this migration (hijrah).

In Madinah, the Prophet established the first Islamic society, serving as a model for all subsequent Islamic communities. A series of battles unfolded against the invading Makkans, with the Muslims prevailing against daunting odds. Soon, additional tribes embraced Islam, leading to the conversion of most of Arabia in a matter of years.

After enduring numerous tribulations and successive victories, the Prophet triumphantly returned to Makkah, where the people finally embraced Islam. He extended his forgiveness to all former adversaries and proceeded to the Ka'bah. Here, he instructed his cousin 'Ali to assist him in dismantling the idols, ultimately restoring the ritual of pilgrimage as originally founded by Abraham. Subsequently, the Prophet made another pilgrimage to Makkah upon returning from the initial pilgrimage, where he delivered his farewell address. Shortly thereafter, he fell ill and, after three days, passed away in 632 A.D. in Madinah, where he was interred in the chamber of his house adjacent to the first mosque of Islam.

The practices and traditions of the Prophet, encompassing his sayings (Hadith), became the guiding light for Muslims in comprehending the Quran and in the practice of their faith. The Quran itself acknowledges the Prophet as an exemplar for Muslims to follow. In addition to emulating the Prophet in all aspects of life and thought, his teachings were compiled by various scholars and subsequently codified in books of Hadith, meticulously separating the authentic from the spurious. The Sunnah has consistently remained, following the Quran, the second most profound source of Islamic knowledge.What Is the Islamic Religion?

As per a renowned saying of the Prophet, Islam is built upon five pillars, which stand as follows: First, Shahadah which simply states that "La ilaha illa 'Llah," (There is no divinity but Allah) and "Muhammadun rasul Allah" (Muhammad is the messenger of Allah). The second is the five daily prayers (al-salat) where Muslims face Makkah. Fasting (al-sawm) is the third principle of worship, which involves abstinence from dawn until sunset daily during Ramadan. The fourth obligation involves making a pilgrimage to Makkah (al-hajj) at least once in one's lifetime, given the person is financially and physically capable of doing so. Fifth, payment of a 2 1/2% tax (al-zakat) on one's capital for the benefit of the community. Also, Muslims are ordered to enjoin good and forbid vice). Ethics is a key feature in Islamic teachings and demands that individuals should constantly conduct themselves ethically towards each other. The Prophet has put it most descriptively, "None of you truly believes until he wishes for his brother what he wishes for himself."

With respect to faith, for a person to be considered as of Islamic one ought to believe in God, His Books, His kittn messengers, the Day of Judgment and Divine determination of human destiny. It cannot be overstated that the definition of al-iman refers to books and prophets in plural form, highlighting a sense of universality surrounding revelation and the deep respect for other religions as strongly emphasized in Quran. Equally noteworthy is the concept of al-ihsan, or virtue; which means worshiping God as though seeing Him and recognizing that He watches us even when we cannot see him. It requires a consistent awareness of God and is the climax of one's practice of Islam.Islamic Law (Al-Shari'ah)

Islam possesses a religious law called al-Shari'ah in Arabic which governs the life of Muslims and which Muslims consider to be the embodiment of the Will of God. The Shari'ah is contained in principle in the Quran as elaborated and complemented by the Sunnah. On the basis of these principles the schools of this day were developed early in Islamic history. This Law, while being rooted in the sources of the Islamic revelation, is a living body of law that caters to the needs of Islamic society.

Islamic laws are essentially preventative and are not based on harsh punishment, except as a last measure. The faith of the Muslim causes him to have respect for the rights of others and Islamic Law is such that it prevents transgression from taking place in most instances. That is why what people deem as harsh punishments are so rarely in need of being applied.

The Spread of Islam

The message of Islam emanated from the arid oasis cities of Makkah and Madinah in the Arabian desert and surged forth with astonishing rapidity. In the span of just half a century following the Prophet's passing, Islam had extended its reach across three continents. Contrary to certain Western misconceptions, Islam is not a faith of the sword, nor was its primary expansion driven by warfare. In the heart of Arabia, where a primitive form of idolatry prevailed, Islam was promulgated through conflict with tribes that resisted God's message. However, Christianity and Judaism were not compelled conversions, and people were not forced into accepting Islam.

Beyond Arabia's borders, the vast territories conquered by Arab armies in a relatively brief period did not succumb to the sword's coercion but rather to the allure of this new faith. It was the belief in the One God and the emphasis on His Mercy that beckoned countless souls into the embrace of Islam. The new religion did not impose conversion upon the masses, allowing many to persist in their Jewish and Christian beliefs. To this day, substantial Jewish and Christian communities coexist within Muslim lands.

Furthermore, the dissemination of Islam extended far beyond its remarkable early expansion beyond Arabia. In subsequent centuries, peaceful acceptance of Islam unfolded, as the Turks, along with a considerable portion of the Indian subcontinent and the Malay-speaking regions, embraced the faith. Even in Africa, Islam found fertile ground over the past two centuries, despite the overpowering presence of European colonial powers. Presently, Islam continues its growth not only in Africa but also in Europe and America, where Muslim communities have become significant minorities.

General Characteristics of Islamic Civilization

Islam was preordained to transcend the confines of a regional faith, giving rise to a global religion and forging a civilization that extended its influence from one end of the earth to the other. Early on, during the reign of the Muslim caliphs, the Arabs initiated the foundation of classical Islamic civilization, which was later enriched by the contributions of the Persians and, subsequently, the Turks. By the 13th century, both Africa and India evolved into grand epicenters of Islamic civilization. Moreover, Muslim realms sprouted throughout the Malay-Indonesian world, and Chinese Muslims thrived in various parts of China.

In its essence, Islam stands as a faith for all people, irrespective of their racial or cultural backgrounds. Islamic civilization is grounded in a unity that staunchly opposes any form of racial or ethnic discrimination. Major racial and ethnic groups such as the Arabs, Persians, Turks, Africans, Indians, Chinese, Malays, and numerous smaller units all embraced Islam and played a pivotal role in shaping the edifice of Islamic civilization. Furthermore, Islam did not disdain the wisdom of earlier civilizations, readily assimilating their scientific knowledge, scholarship, and culture as long as these did not conflict with Islamic principles. Each ethnic and racial group that embraced Islam brought its unique contributions to the overarching Islamic civilization, in which everyone was regarded as part of a universal brotherhood and sisterhood transcending local affiliations with particular tribes, races, or languages.

The resultant global civilization created by Islam fostered collaboration among individuals of diverse ethnic backgrounds, as they collectively cultivated various arts and sciences. Although the civilization was deeply rooted in Islamic traditions, even non-Muslim "people of the book" were active participants in the intellectual pursuits, and the fruits of this labor were accessible to all. The environment mirrored the contemporary scientific climate of America, where scholars and intellectuals from every corner of the world actively engage in advancing knowledge that belongs to humanity as a whole.

Furthermore, the global civilization forged by Islam successfully invigorated the intellect and cognition of those who embraced its tenets. As a consequence of Islam's influence, the nomadic Arabs emerged as champions of science and learning. The Persians, renowned for their great civilization even prior to the advent of Islam, flourished in the domain of science and knowledge during the Islamic era more than ever before. The same can be said for the Turks and other peoples who embraced Islam. The religion of Islam not only catalyzed the creation of a worldwide civilization in which people from diverse ethnic backgrounds participated, but it also played a central role in nurturing intellectual and cultural life on an unprecedented scale. For nearly eight centuries, Arabic served as the predominant intellectual and scientific language worldwide. In the centuries following the rise of Islam, Muslim dynasties governing various regions of the Islamic world bore witness to the flourishing of Islamic culture and intellectual achievement. It is worth noting that this tradition of intellectual activity experienced a temporary decline at the onset of modern times due to a combination of waning faith among Muslims and external dominion. Nonetheless, today, this intellectual activity is rekindling in many parts of the Islamic world.

The Aftermath of the Colonial Period

Towards the close of 19th century, during the height of European colonization, most of Islamic world was under colonialism. A few exceptions to this included some parts of Middle-Ottoman Empire, Persia, Afghanistan, Yemen and certain areas in Arabia. However, these regions were not also immune to tribal contacts and Ottoman in the was frequently faced by persistent danger from outside. After the end of World War I, the Ottoman Empire crumbled leading to birth of self-sufficient Arab countries like Iraq, formation of new entities such Jordan and mandate or colonization to regions sunch as Palestine, Syria and Lebanon by French. During this period, Saudi Arabia was eventually consolidated. Regarding other parts of the Islamic world, Egypt, which gained more independence. Dismantling of Ottomans saw the conversion of Turkey into a secular republic by Ataturk while Pahlavi dynasty opened new chapter for Persia renaming it to Iran. But the colonialism held the larger part of the Islamic world.

Actually, the rest of Islamic world has just recently managed to free themselves from their national vows only after the Second World War when British, French, Dutch and Spanish Empires were dissolved. By the 1960s, Syria, Lebanon, Libya and a number of sheikhdoms around the Gulf and Arabian Sea won their independence in Arab world. On the other hand, their northwestern counterparts such as Tunisia, Morocco and Algeria had to fight long wars of independence with that of Algeria being eventually concluded twenty years later. Palestine was however an exception as it did not realize independence in 1948 but rather became partitioned when the state of Israel was established.

Muslims joined the Hindus in the fight for independence from British rule in India. Eventually, independence was achieved in 1947 whereby Muslims established their own country known as Pakistan and founded on the basis of Islam to become the Muslim most populous state although many Muslims remained part of India. But in 1971 it split up when East Pakistan became Bangladesh. Indonesians became independent of the Dutch colonizer eastwards while Malays bow out from British colonialism. At first, Singapore was part of Malaysia that later seceded in 1963 to become an independent state. Pockets of small colonies still persisted in the region, and they laid claims for independence until as recent as 1984 when the Kingdom of Brunei officially gained its independence.

In Africa, large Muslim-populated countries like Nigeria, Senegal and Tanzania were just gaining independence in the 1950s and 1960s. As a result, by the late 1960s almost every part of the Islamic world was transformed into independent states. Nevertheless, there were still exemptions within this tendency. The Muslim Soviet Union could not gain autonomy or independence. This was also the case in Eastern Turkestan, referred to by Muslim geographers as Sinkiang. Also, Eritrea and the southern Philippines are still being faced by independence movements.

From the time when Islam in third of twentieth century entered into modern era under national states, attempts were made to increase co-operation and unity within Islamic world. Such appetite was not just displayed in meetings of heads of state and the formation of OIC with its secretariat, but also in the creation of institutions targeted at serving the whole Islamic world. The Muslim World League (Rabitat al-Alam Al-Islami) based in Makkah; Saudi Arabia is one of the most notable. It is this organization that has been instrumental in their establishment and sustainability.

The Revival and Reassertion of Islam

Muslims aspired not only to attain political independence but also to reaffirm their religious and cultural identity. Beginning in the 18th century, a cadre of Muslim reformers emerged, seeking to reassert the tenets of Islam and reform society based on Islamic principles. Among the earliest figures was Muhammad ibn 'Abd al-Wahhab, hailing from the Arabian Peninsula, who passed away in 1792. Supported by Muhammad ibn al-Sa'ud, the founder of the first Saudi State, al-Wahhab's reformist ideas transcended the borders of Arabia, exerting a lasting influence on other Islamic lands.

Throughout the 19th century, the resurgence of Islam took on various forms, encompassing movements like the Mahdi movement in Sudan and the Sanusiyyah in North Africa, which engaged in conflicts against European colonizers. Educational endeavors, exemplified by the Aligarh movement in India, aimed to reeducate Muslims. In Egypt, Al-Azhar University remained a central hub of Islamic learning. A multitude of reformers addressed distinct facets of Islamic thought, some emphasizing law, others economics, and still others the challenges posed by Western civilization with its formidable scientific and technological advancements.

Jamal al-Din al-Afghani, originally from Persia but settled in Cairo, emerged as a prominent proponent of Pan-Islamism, advocating the political and religious unification of the Islamic world. His student, Muhammad 'Abduh, who later served as the rector of al-Azhar, left a considerable imprint on Islamic theology and thought. Another influential figure, Rashid Rida, a Syrian student of 'Abduh, held positions more closely aligned with 'Abd al-Wahhab, advocating for the stringent application of the Shari'ah.

Among these luminaries, Muhammad Iqbal, a renowned poet and philosopher, is celebrated as the progenitor of Pakistan.

As Western influence permeated deeper into Islamic society, organizations emerged with the objective of reshaping society along Islamic lines and preserving it from secularization. Examples include the Muslim Brotherhood (Ikhwan al-Muslimin), founded in Egypt with branches in many Muslim countries, and Pakistan's Jama'at-I Islami, founded by the influential Mawlana Mawdudi. These organizations typically pursued peaceful means and aimed to reestablish an Islamic order through educational initiatives. Nevertheless, over the last two decades, in response to the mounting frustrations of many Muslims facing pressures from a secularized external world, some have sought to reject the adverse facets of Western thought and culture, striving to return to an Islamic society grounded in the comprehensive application of the Shari'ah.

Today, strong movements dedicated to preserving and disseminating Islamic teachings are present in every Muslim country. In places such as Saudi Arabia, Islamic Law is actively practiced, serving as the bedrock for the country's prosperity, development, and stability. In nations where the Shari'ah is not yet fully implemented, the endeavors of Islamic movements predominantly revolve around facilitating its complete application, thereby enabling the nation to prosper while upholding the faith of its people. It is imperative to discern the widespread aspiration of Muslims to apply Islamic religious law and reaffirm their religious values and identity from isolated instances of violent eruptions, which, although existing, are frequently sensationalized by Western mass media.Conclusion

Today, the Islamic world sprawls across vast territories, extending from the Atlantic to the Pacific, while also maintaining a significant presence in Europe and America. It is characterized by the influence of Islamic teachings and a resolute commitment to asserting its distinct identity. Amid the presence of nationalism and various secular ideologies, Muslims are resolute in their aspiration to coexist within the modern world. Nevertheless, they are determined not to merely replicate Western practices blindly.

The Islamic world earnestly seeks peaceful coexistence with both the East and the West. It aims to avoid subjugation while directing its resources and efforts toward crafting an improved life for its people. This endeavor is rooted in the teachings of Islam and seeks to prevent the wasteful dissipation of resources in both internal and external conflicts. Ultimately, the goal is to foster greater mutual understanding between the Islamic world and the West. Through this enhanced comprehension, both can better serve their respective populations and contribute to the advancement of human welfare on a global scale.

Source: Islamic Affairs Department, Royal Embassy of Saudi Arabia

Radical Islam

Islamic fundamentalism, often referred to by its Arabic term "usul," denotes a collection of religious ideologies that emphasize a return to the foundational principles of Islam, namely the Quran and the Sunnah. The precise definitions of Islamic fundamentalism may vary, sparking debates among scholars and observers.

There are differing viewpoints regarding the term's usage. Some contend that it is problematic, suggesting that it implies that all Muslims must be fundamentalists, while others see it as a label employed by outsiders to characterize perceived trends within Islam. Prominent figures associated with Islamic fundamentalism, often referred to as Islamists, include individuals like Sayyid Qutb, Ruhollah Khomeini, Abul Ala Mawdudi, and Israr Ahmad. Western scholars often point to the 1979 Islamic Revolution in Iran as a significant political success for Islamic fundamentalism.

Economist Eli Berman presents the alternative term "Radical Islam" to describe various movements emerging post-1920s, beginning with the Muslim Brotherhood. This distinction is made because these movements are believed to practice "unprecedented extremism," which sets them apart from a straightforward return to historical fundamentals.

(Source: Wikipedia, the free encyclopedia)

Social and Political Goals

In alignment with followers of various other fundamentalist movements, Islamic fundamentalists posit that the world's predicaments find their roots in secular influences. However, scholars like Bassam Tibi challenge the self-proclaimed traditionalist stance of Islamic fundamentalists. Tibi, highlighting the incongruity in their message, points to fatwas issued by fundamentalists proclaiming that "every Muslim who pleads for the suspension of the shari'a is an apostate and can be killed." Importantly, the killing of these apostates, according to Tibi, stands beyond the bounds of justification within Islamic law, as it goes unsupported by the Qur'an. He unequivocally states, "The command to slay reasoning Muslims is un-Islamic, an invention of Islamic fundamentalists." This critique underscores the nuanced nature of Islamic fundamentalism, revealing internal contradictions within its theological and ideological foundations.

(Source: Wikipedia, the free encyclopedia)

Conflicts with the Secular State

The aspirations of Islamic fundamentalism, advocating for the implementation of Sharia and the establishment of an Islamic State, find themselves in direct opposition to the principles of a secular, democratic state, as articulated in globally endorsed documents like the Universal Declaration of Human Rights. Anthony J. Dennis astutely observes that the Western and Islamic conceptualizations of the state, the individual, and society not only diverge but often stand in complete contradiction.

Within the realm of human rights, there exists contention between fundamentalist Muslims and internationally recognized norms. Areas of dispute include:

1. Freedom from religious police

2. Gender equality

3. Separation of religion and state

4. Freedom of speech

5. Freedom of religion

6. The right of non-Muslims (known as 'Murtad') to convert to Islam is celebrated.

This clash highlights the profound divergence in the foundational principles shaping the vision of the state and the role of individuals within society, revealing a fundamental discord between the ideals of Islamic fundamentalism and the principles embedded in the Universal Declaration of Human Rights.

(Source: Wikipedia, the free encyclopedia)

Controversy

The designation "Islamic fundamentalism" is a term that often faces critique. Notably, Bernard Lewis, a distinguished scholar of Islam, expresses reservations about its application, asserting that while its use is established and must be accepted, it remains unfortunate and can lead to misconceptions. He points out that "fundamentalist" is rooted in Christian terminology, particularly referring to certain Protestant churches and organizations that uphold the literal divine origin and inerrancy of the Bible, opposing liberal and modernist theologians advocating a more critical, historical view of Scripture.

Lewis underscores the absence of a liberal or modernist approach to the Qur'an among Muslim theologians. He contends that, in principle, all

Muslims are fundamentalists in their reverence for the text of the Qur'an. The distinguishing features of so-called Muslim fundamentalists, according to Lewis, lie in their scholasticism and legalism. Unlike Christian fundamentalists, Islamic counterparts draw not only from the Qur'an but also from the Traditions of the Prophet and the body of transmitted theological and legal knowledge.

John Esposito challenges the term due to its associations with political activism, extremism, fanaticism, terrorism, and anti-Americanism. He prefers the terms "Islamic revivalism" and "Islamic activism." On the contrary, Anthony J. Dennis acknowledges the term's widespread use, deeming Islamic fundamentalism as more than a religion but a global revolutionary movement. He highlights the convergence of social, religious, and political objectives within the movement, emphasizing its significance for secular analysis as a revolutionary ideology.

In 1988, the University of Chicago, with the backing of the American Academy of Arts and Sciences, initiated The Fundamentalism Project, an extensive study of fundamentalism across major world religions. The project defined fundamentalism as an approach or set of strategies employed by beleaguered believers to preserve their distinctive identity through selective retrieval of doctrines, beliefs, and practices from a sacred past.

While some, like John Esposito, express reservations about the term, at least two Muslim scholars, Sadiq Jalal al-Azm and Hassan Hanafi, defend its use. Al-Azm finds the phrase suitable for new Islamic movements, characterizing them as an immediate return to Islamic basics and fundamentals. Hanafi similarly supports the term "fundamentalism," asserting its adequacy, accuracy, and correctness in capturing the essence of what is termed Islamic awakening or revival in the West.

Atheism might be over-or under—represented in particular countries because of its differently evaluated acceptability by governments. The accuracy of such estimations would be questioned mainly because there can be cases of intentional or non- intentional reporting, especially for those who are never organized under any formal institutions. This is compounded by surveys using "agnostics" and "atheist-agnostic" not specifying what is meant by these terms, while others refer to themselves as Ag-Atheists.

In addition, research often involves non-religious identification putting together agnostics and atheist together with believers (theists) under the heading "no religion." For example, in American studies it was demonstrated that "no religion" status grows more rapidly than any other type of religious affiliation thus

A 2004 BBC poll showed that about 9-10% of the Americans did not believe in God. The same year saw a smaller proportion—6% of the American populace who believe in no God or a universal spirit in a survey conducted by Gallup. Another report by the ARIS in March 2009 noted that over 34 million American were non-religious, and 1.6 percent explicitly stated their atheistic stance as agnostic. Such numbers reveal how fast religious views are changing in the US and how it is tricky to determine that many people don't believe in God anymore.

(Source: Wikipedia, the free encyclopedia)

Judaism is among the oldest religion and it is very significant due to its long history and different teachings and customs. Over years, through its history Judaism has seen different sects where each of them interprets the religion differently. The role of these sects in defining the Jewish community and its interaction with the outside world cannot be overestimated.

Orthodox Judaism

Halakhic orthodoxy is the observance of Jewish law according to the traditional interpretation as practiced in Orthodox Judaism. This focuses on the significance of respecting the commandments and traditions found in the Torah. According to orthodox Jews, the Torah is the exact words of God that should be followed by all Jews. They worship on Saturday, maintain kashrut, eat kosher food as well as dress modestly. Study of Jewish texts and observance of Jewish customs are essential for Orthodox Judaism. First, it is built on a high level of community spirit while also striving to keep the flow of Jewish lifestyle.

Conservative Judaism

To answer the modern challenges of Orthodox Judaism, a new religious movement known as Conservative Judaism started to emerge at the end of the 19th century. It attempts to be traditional yet modern at the same time. The conservative Jews acknowledge that the Torah came from God, and this is why it must be interpreted using human understanding to understand its teachings. They obey the commandments and participate in ceremonies with discretion. Therefore, conservative Judaism attaches much importance to learning and Jewish textual studies. It also appreciates women and lesbian, gay, bisexual, transsexuals, and queer persons (LGBTQ+) in religion so that they can play different roles in the society.

Reform Judaism

A new religious movement known as Reform Judaism occurred in the 19th century due to the enlightenment and the need to be incorporated fully into the surrounding community. The reform Jews are not very keen on following most of the rituals and have belief in Jewish ethics only. The second group regards the Torah as the work of man for morality and ethics, and not a true history. According to reform Judaism, Jews need restructuring of rituals and traditions in order to make them compatible with modernity. Its focus is largely on social equity and social justice. In the reformed synagogues, women are allowed to actively participate in religious services and dress freely.

Other Jewish Sects

Apart from the three major sects, there are also other small sects in Jewish faith. Hasidic Judaism was born out of Eastern Europe in the 1700s. These Jews are known as the Hasidic Jews, who put much emphasis on spiritual aspects and Mysticism. The followership believes that their leaders can communicate and reach God for them. Most Hasidic Jews will form their own tight knit communities, and are of course very traditional and orthodox. They wear unique clothes, have prayers and studies as their way of life.

Another one of such sects that can be noted is Reconstructionist Judaism. Reconstructionist Judaism came up on the scene in the 20th century and it originated from Mordecai Kaplan. It denies the notion of a personal God and sees Judaism as an evolving secular culture. Reconstructionist hold that Jews embrace cultural heritage, historical experiences, and customs but still give room for personal practice and opinions about religion. Community defines Jewish identity, as they promote social justice leading to an egalitarian society.

Summary

There have been different sects of Jews that played an important role in Judaism and its development throughout history. Orthodox Judaism is responsible for preserving and transmitting the Jewish traditions and practices that have been handed down since times immemorial. Conservatism in Judaism aimed at adjustment of Jewish law to contemporary problems. In particular, Reform Jew has embraced the moral principles of Judaism and social activism. In this regard, the Hassidic Jews have maintained emphasis on spirituality and mysticism, while Reconstructionist Jews have been concentrating upon cultural aspects in their practice, as well as community.

These sects in Judaism demonstrate its evolution, as well as variations in thought among individuals in their society. Despite their differences, these sects believe in one God, a commonality which is the basis of their shared heritage within the larger community of Jews. The sects of Judaism are always developing together with the needs and views of Israeli community thus guaranteeing vibrancy and relevance of the Religion into the modern period.

Finally, Judaism has a long tradition, many different tenets, and numerous practices that have shaped it as a religion. Several sects of Judaism such as Orthodox, Conservative, Reform, Hasidic, Reconstructionist and many more have contributed to formation as well as understanding among the Jews and the world at large. Every sect views Judaism in a particular way, focusing on distinct parts and reacting to the demands of the era. Notwithstanding this, they all agree with each other about some points such as being Jews, Torah and Jewish morality.

The United States undergoes a transformative shift from being a predominantly Christian nation to one characterized by religious diversity on one hand and a growing atheist/agnostic presence on the other. The Catholic Church contends that while natural law contributes to morality, religion serves as a more robust foundation. Interestingly, there was a time in the U.S. when atheists were barred from testifying in court, reflecting a distrust rooted in the belief that atheists lacked a moral compass.

Renowned atheist figures like Richard Dawkins propose an evolutionary, socio-biological origin for human morality, emphasizing the dynamic nature of moral imperatives shaped by biological and cultural factors. While natural law provides a groundwork for constructing moral rules, some argue that religious-based morality carries greater weight. Evangelical theologian Douglas Wilson asserts that belief is essential for individuals to rationally account for their moral obligations.

Critics, including Cardinal Cormac Murphy-O'Connor, view atheism as a significant societal evil, attributing war and destruction to its influence. However, the correlation between atheism and peaceful nations is complex, with historical examples like Soviet Russia, where atheism was enforced, leading to religious persecution and mass murders.

Dinesh D'Souza contends that crimes committed in the name of atheistic ideologies, as seen in Stalin's regime, highlight the dangers of secular attempts to establish utopias. He draws parallels between atheistic regimes and religious dogma, emphasizing their shared dogmatism and cult-like tendencies.

In response, Sam Harris argues that fascism and communism resemble religions in their dogmatism, emphasizing political, racial, and nationalistic dogma as the root causes of atrocities rather than a rejection of religious beliefs. The New Atheists' criticism of religion as the sole cause of conflicts is challenged by Robert Wright and Mark Chaves, who highlight the need to address deeper root causes and the evolving nature of religious beliefs.

Anthropologist Jack David Eller criticizes prominent New Atheist authors for not presenting new arguments against the existence of gods and for focusing on the dangers of theism. He notes their tendency to mischaracterize religions and highlights the evangelical nature of their movement, drawing parallels with evangelical Christianity.

Professors of philosophy and religion, Jeffrey Robbins and Christopher Rodkey, critique the evangelical nature of the new atheism, pointing out its assumption of possessing "Good News" to share at any cost, with an ultimate goal of converting as many people as possible. They draw parallels between the fervor of the new atheism and evangelical Christianity, suggesting that both contribute to endless conflict without progress. Sociologist William Stahl observes the striking frequency with which the New Atheists are depicted as mirror images of religious fundamentalists. He delves into their structural and epistemological parallels, arguing that both the New Atheism and fundamentalism attempt to reestablish authority in the face of crises of meaning in late modernity.

While atheism and agnosticism expand in the U.S., and organized religion's role diminishes, Islam has the potential to gain acceptance due to its promises. Islamic teachings emphasize ethical conduct, encouraging individuals to perform good acts and abstain from evil. Islam is portrayed as a religion for all people, fostering unity against racial or ethnic discrimination. Declarations from the Islamic Affairs Department at the Royal Embassy of Saudi Arabia envision Islam becoming a global religion, creating a civilization spanning the entire globe.

The prospect of Islam spreading rapidly in the West, including the U.S., is contemplated. The potential clash of civilizations may not originate in the U.S., but Radical Islam is envisioned as a force more likely to cause global destruction than the Communist adversaries, driven by stark differences in ideology. The Islamist ideology, with its emphasis on 'martyrdom' as a pathway to heaven, is considered more perilous. Unlike the atheistic Communist ideologues, the Islamists' spiritual convictions make them less predictable, presenting a greater challenge to influence. If ongoing trends persist, there is a conceivable scenario where Islamists dominate Europe, control parts of Russia, and establish an Islamist bloc extending from North Africa and Europe to the Arabian Peninsula, central Asia, and Pakistan, with sympathetic networks worldwide. The U.S. is seen as the prized goal for the Islamization process globally.

"Islam was destined to become a world religion and to create a civilization which stretched from one end of the globe to the other."

(Source: Islamic Affairs Department, Royal Embassy of Saudi Arabia)

Introduction

"We should not be astonished if in the cases where we see an inferiority complex, we find a superiority complex more or less hidden. On the other hand, if we inquire into a superiority complex and study its continuity, we can always find a more or less hidden inferiority complex. [Definition by Adler.]

An inferiority complex is characterized by feelings of falling short of established standards, self-doubt, and a lack of self-esteem, often manifesting subconsciously. Afflicted individuals tend to overcompensate, resulting in either remarkable achievements or extremely asocial behavior. Modern literature now favors the term "lack of covert self-esteem" to describe this condition.

The term "superiority complex" serves as the counterpart to an inferiority complex, functioning as a psychological defense mechanism where feelings of superiority mask or counteract underlying feelings of inferiority. Various causes contribute to the development of these complexes, including low socioeconomic status, fear of stereotypes and discrimination, minority status with physical and cultural differences, discouragement or failure, constant criticism, feelings of inadequacy from pursuing unattainable goals, past negative experiences, inability to fit into society or peer groups, the fear of failure, physical defects, and religious fundamentalism.

The Complex Basis of Many Ailments in Society and its Implications

Supremacy over Other Groups - Classical Racism.

Examples:

- KKK and other white-supremacy groups

- Antisemitism (one of the causes)

- In the US, black Muslim theology came about as a form of religious views in response to white supremacism and assumed a version of black supremacist. (e.g. Farrakhan)

- One immigrant group over other or Ashkenazi over Mizrahi Jews in Israel.

- Supremacy of Arab in Some Parts of the World

- Ancient Indians considered all men who were not of their castes as barbarians and despised the other casts in Asia.

- Indian caste system

- In China, the Europeans were seen as nauseating, or ghostly beings, and at worst as devils.

- Adolf Hitler led Nazi Germany which depicted an ideal image of a superior, Aryan; however Hitler was not the very model of this perfect identity.

Supremacism is an ideology that posits the superiority of a certain class of people, who are perceived as destined to rule over others. Few of these examples are Nazism, Supremacy Groups (e.g., KKK), Some Religious Fundamentalist groups...

Fundamentalism —Christian: One of the reasons for crusades in the Holy Land as well as attacks on Muslims and pagans throughout Europe was Christian supremacism. Pogroms and massacres of European Jewish minorities that continued for centuries based on the theories of European supremacism. Christian supremacism has also been blamed for the Atlantic slave trade.

Fundamentalism- Muslim: Supremacists have used the name Islam to mean, among other things, the Muslim participation in African slave trade, Abdul Hamid II's early 20th century pan-Islamism , imposition of jizya and rules on marriage observed in Muslim countries on non-Muslims , interpretation of rules pluralism into majority by Muslims in Malaysia and defending supremacism like per se some migrants from non-Western parts.

In his book The Politically Incorrect Guide to Jihad eBook Professor William Kilpatrick proposes that unlike other different, Islam is unique and its founders command its disciples to always impose the law or religious believe on all people including adherents and non-believers at will.

Fundamentalism —Jewish: Joseph Massad, Professor of Arab Studies, argues that religious and secular Zionism have had a "dominating principle" of "Jewish supremacism." Though, this is basically an erroneous assumption, it is held by many ethnic and religious groups. The political goal of Zionism was to establish a Jewish state where Jews could dominate as opposed to the minor individuals existing in all countries globally that time. Theodor Herzl, the ideologue of Zionism argued that being an eternal feature of all societies in which Jews lived as minorities, Antisemitism could allow separated seeking to save themselves from peaceful death alone in face of their seeker. In what is supposed to be a modern democratic country, Israel, some of the Ashkenazi Jews display conscious and sub-conscious supremacism over their Mizrachi and Sephardic denominations. Currently, majority of Ashkenazi Jews still hold most of the ruling posts and belong to the ruling class.

Sexism: In patriarchy, some feminists argue that the overarching standard of male supremacism is instituted using a range of cultural, political and interpersonal mechanisms. Since the nineteenth century a number of feminist movements against male supremacists have been founded targeting equal legal rights and protection for woman in all cultural, political and interpersonal relations.

Sources: Al Jazeera & Wikipedia.

Overview

Multiculturalism is characteristic of the modern secular society and large urban areas. In reference to sociology, multiculturalism is the end-state of either a natural or artificial process (for example: There exist two acceptable ways through which immigrants can enter a nation as either legally-controlled migration) from large nationals into peripheral parts of the country or to smaller communities within the same. Opponents of multiculturalism often question the viability, contradiction and with multi-cultural ideal where cultures peacefully coexist and interrelate but remain independent. According to arguments, the host nations lose their distinct culture in favor of enforced multiculturalism which previously should have been synonymous with nation states coming up and losing a distinctive cultural identity of their own.

Multiculturalism could have been successful in people of closely shared culture such as Europeans' Canadians and Americans who merged from their national bases after many generations. The discussion is if the very distinct cultures promise many-sided to interpenetrates and gradually stream into a recent developed culture or absolutely unable are isolated with each other for generations.

Ethnologist Frank Salter writes: People of relatively homogenous societies invest more in public good, reflecting a higher level of Public Altruism. For instance, government share of gross domestic product and average wealth per citizen have correlation with level of ethnic homogeneity. Illustrative examples of the United States, Africa and South-East Asia show that multi-ethnic societies are less charitable and more incapable to cooperate in public infrastructure development.

Worldwide, diverse peoples get involved in each other's hate most times or even with killing. Most historical precedents do not support a diverse, peaceful or stable society. Unchecked neoliberal economics has created an underclass of whites in the US and Europe who are either jobless or very poorly paid. The situation is conducive to the emergence of a white nationalist movement similarly delusional as those in KKK, but more destructive that could annihilate all that multiracial progressives have constructed with their blood, sweat and tears and lead to large scale conflict. For instance, others may grow destructive superiority feeling which may cause them to turn violent. While there has been little economic difference between the 'inferior' groups that much of whites belong to, whites continue regarding themselves as best and therefore distort their peripheral lives absorbing frustration. illusion to superiority complex helps the united creation of frustration and anger off whites under suppressed partners especially when such bubbles they become like effective vent. Instead, tensions are directed towards "Poorer counterparts" by origin races, ethnic or religious namely Jews or Muslims.

Summary

The triad of fatherless homes, racially and ethnically segregated into homogenous neighborhoods, and existing or inculcated ethnic and religious groups' superiority/inferiority complex will breed myriad violent behaviors among the young. Multiculturalism is an idea based on co-existing cultures which create space for plurality and understanding. It is mostly viewed as a constructive way of promoting social cohesion and comprehension. While, in most instances multiculturalism can work well with supremacy, but when these two ideas coincide on dangerous consequences that can emerge and extend to societal level.

Conversely, supremacy is a sense of belonging that an individual believes his culture/group is better than others. The idea stems on the belief that any nation or society should conquer, master and lord over others. The clash of these two ideologies is dangerous for social stability and rights of individuals.

Multiculturalism can pose a threat if it creates feelings of "them" against "us". It promotes separation and antagonism against others when a given culture thinks of itself as better than others. Such a situation promotes discrimination, prejudice, and violence as well. Multiculturalism and supremacy, however, may promote inter-ethnic rivalry and hostility rather than celebration of diversity and fostering of mutual understanding among different culture groups.

However, multiculturalism and supremacy have also been shown to result in the dilapidation of personal liberties. Marginalization and subjugation of minority cultures is often linked with situations where a powerful culture or group imposes superiority on others. This may lead into inhibition of cultural expression, restricted access to resource allocation and disrespect for human values. A genuinely diverse multi-cultural society can only be fostered where everyone is allowed to openly express their culture and faith free from oppression or victimization.

The existence of multiculturalism and supremacy also leads to the promulgation of stereotypes and prejudices. In most cases, this results into generalization while labeling other people as inferior. As a consequence, this may lead to stereotypes that perpetuate marginalization and dehumanization of a culture or group. The presence of stereotypes affects social development and equality since people tend to discriminate in employment, education, and housing because of assumptions made about individuals based on certain characteristics.

Further, multiculturalism and supremacy could inhibit social harmony. This idea about the dominance of one's culture over others tends to promote differences rather than fostering unity and common values. Segregation will likely result into segregated communities with members from various cultures failing to completely participate in their social environment. Failure to integrate can impede economic development, social progress, and social cohesion generally.

However, promoting real inclusiveness and equality to deal with the threats and consequences of multiculturalism and supremacism. It should involve educating people about different cultures, having a meaningful conversation with them, and acknowledging the worth of every culture and person. Diversity encompasses the practice of tackling biases, undermining stereotypes, and facilitating authentic interaction between cultures.

There is also a need to put in place laws, policies, and regulations that safeguard individual rights and create an atmosphere of equality. Hence, various governments and institutions should make every effort to ensure that everybody has a fair chance in life, regardless culture, to flourish and participate in societies. This involves providing accessibility to education, health care facilities, job opportunities and politics to everyone regardless of their culture background.

Finally, although multiculturalism is a concept that aims at celebrating differences and toleration, threats and adverse impacts come in where those aspects overlap with racist notions. For example, multiculturalism is a source of division, discrimination, and subversion of personal liberty. These risks should be curtailed through the development of encompassing societies where there is open-mindedness, and fair chance opportunity towards each individual. Supremacy has been among them but only through real understanding and respect for various cultures can we build a multicultural society rather than just an aggregation of people.

THE OSMOSIS PROCESS OF THE INDUSTRIALIZED NATIONS

Overview

In the realm of biology, osmosis orchestrates a silent ballet, orchestrating the spontaneous flow of solvent molecules through a selectively permeable membrane into regions of higher solute concentration. This subtle dance aims to harmonize the solute concentrations on either side of the membrane, bringing equilibrium to the stage.

When we traverse the landscape of economies, industrialized nations emerge as the shining beacons of prosperity. These nations cultivate an environment conducive to private enterprise, prioritizing the fulfillment of consumers' long-term desires and needs. They boast impressive literacy rates, cutting-edge technology, a thriving middle class, and elevated per capita incomes.

On the flip side, we encounter less-developed nations, often referred to as the least-developed countries (LDCs), wrestling with the heavy burden of poverty, meager per capita incomes, modest living standards, and insufficient literacy rates. These lands bear the weight of an absent middle class, their technological landscape remains barren, and they grapple with the absence of robust governmental, financial, and economic structures needed to nurture a thriving business community. Their economies pivot around agriculture and the extraction of raw materials, from mining to timber industries.

Then, we enter the dynamic realm of developing nations, where transformation is the order of the day. These lands are in the midst of a transition, shifting from economies deeply rooted in agricultural and raw material production toward industrialized landscapes. Education and technology are on the rise, as are per capita incomes, though the middle class is but a modest ensemble, with a handful of influential business figures often taking center stage. Governments in these nations are diligently sculpting a more enticing business environment, luring investment and nurturing economic growth.

In the context of human migration, we encounter "Osmosis Migration," a natural flow of low-skilled individuals from developing or less-developed nations across the discerning borders into the welcoming arms of industrialized nations. This migration, like osmosis in nature, seeks to create a balance in societies, economies, and social structures on both sides of the equation.

Controlled skilled migration into industrialized nations can indeed be a beneficial element, akin to a well-choreographed ballet. However, the open-border approach championed by figures like President Biden and the Democratic party may accelerate this osmotic process, potentially resulting in the erosion of the middle class and the concentration of power in the hands of a select few, a narrative reminiscent of situations observed in other developing nations.

Human Migration and Osmosis Migration: A Complex Dance of People and Borders

Introduction

Human migration is a fundamental and enduring aspect of our species' history. Since time immemorial, individuals and communities have moved across regions, countries, and continents in search of better opportunities, safety, and a brighter future. This phenomenon has been shaped by various factors, including economic, social, political, and environmental forces. One unique and thought-provoking aspect of human migration is what can be termed "Osmosis Migration." This essay explores the multifaceted nature of human migration and delves into the concept of Osmosis Migration, shedding light on its dynamics and implications.

Human Migration: An Overview

Human migration is the movement of individuals or groups of people from one place to another, either within a country or across international borders. It is a complex and multifaceted phenomenon that has been an integral part of human history. Migration can be driven by a variety of factors, including:

1. **Economic Opportunities:** Many people migrate in search of better job prospects and higher income. Economic migrants are often drawn to regions or countries with robust job markets and the promise of a higher standard of living.

2. **Political Asylum:** Political instability, conflict, and persecution in one's home country can force individuals to seek refuge in more stable and safe regions. These refugees may be fleeing war, violence, or political repression.

3. **Family Reunification:** Family ties are a significant driver of migration. Individuals often move to be with family members who have already migrated. This can lead to the formation of diaspora communities.

4. **Environmental Factors:** Climate change, natural disasters, and environmental degradation can displace communities and force them to seek new places to live. Climate refugees are becoming increasingly common.

5. **Educational and Professional Goals:** People often migrate for educational opportunities or to pursue specific careers or professions in countries with advanced educational and professional systems.

Osmosis Migration: A Unique Perspective

In the discourse of human migration, one intriguing concept is "Osmosis Migration." Osmosis, a term borrowed from biology, refers to the spontaneous movement of solvent molecules through a selectively permeable membrane from an area of lower solute concentration to an area of higher solute concentration. The concept of Osmosis Migration borrows from this biological phenomenon and applies it to human movement.

Osmosis Migration can be defined as the natural migration of individuals from less-developed or developing nations into industrialized nations, often across selective borders. It is a migration phenomenon that seeks to harmonize societies, economies, and social structures on both sides of the equation. Understanding Osmosis Migration requires exploring its unique characteristics and implications:

1. **Harmonization of Societies:** Osmosis Migration aims to bring about a balance in societies, as individuals from less-developed nations migrate to industrialized ones. This migration can help bridge cultural gaps, fostering a sense of unity and shared experiences.

2. **Economic Balancing Act:** The movement of individuals from regions with fewer economic opportunities to those with more robust economies can contribute to a leveling of economic disparities. It brings a workforce with diverse skills and backgrounds, driving economic growth.

3. **Social Structure Evolution:** Osmosis Migration can lead to changes in social structures in both the sending and receiving nations. While it may contribute to a burgeoning middle class in less-developed nations, it can also lead to economic disparities and concentration of wealth in industrialized nations.

4. **Cultural Exchange:** The cultural exchange that accompanies Osmosis Migration enriches societies with new perspectives, traditions, and ideas. This exchange can be a catalyst for societal development.

Challenges and Controversies

While Osmosis Migration holds potential benefits, it is not without its challenges and controversies. Some of the issues associated with Osmosis Migration include:

1. **Economic Disparities:** Osmosis Migration can exacerbate economic disparities in both sending and receiving nations. Industrialized nations may see a concentration of wealth and power, while less-developed nations may grapple with brain drain and a lack of skilled professionals.

2. **Social Integration:** Integrating individuals from diverse cultural backgrounds can be challenging. Receiving nations may face difficulties in fostering social cohesion and ensuring that migrants are fully integrated into society.

3. **Cultural Clashes:** Cultural differences can sometimes lead to misunderstandings and tensions. Resolving these clashes and promoting cultural acceptance can be a complex endeavor.

4. **Political Controversies:** Osmosis Migration often sparks political debates, particularly in receiving nations. Debates around border control, citizenship, and rights of migrants are common.

The Role of Government and International Cooperation

Governments play a crucial role in managing and addressing the challenges of Osmosis Migration. They must implement policies that balance the benefits of migration with the potential drawbacks. These policies should focus on:

1. **Border Control:** Ensuring secure and controlled borders is essential for managing migration. This involves both the regulation of immigration and addressing issues of human trafficking and illegal migration.

2. **Economic Integration:** Receiving nations should develop policies that facilitate the economic integration of migrants while ensuring fair labor practices and protections for all workers.

3. **Cultural and Social Integration:** Programs that promote cultural understanding, social cohesion, and integration is crucial. Governments should foster inclusive societies that value diversity.

4. **International Cooperation:** Migration is a global issue that requires international cooperation. Countries must work together to address the root causes of migration, create pathways for legal migration, and provide support to refugees.

Conclusion

Human migration, a multifaceted and deeply rooted aspect of human history, plays a significant role in shaping societies, economies, and cultures. Osmosis Migration, a unique perspective, offers a lens through which to view the complex interactions between individuals from less-developed and developing nations and industrialized ones.

While Osmosis Migration has the potential to harmonize societies, economies, and social structures, it also poses challenges, including economic disparities, social integration, cultural clashes, and political controversies. Addressing these challenges requires a multifaceted approach involving governments, international cooperation, and policies that balance the benefits and drawbacks of migration.

As the world continues to witness shifts in demographics, economic landscapes, and cultural exchanges, it is imperative to embrace the complexity of human migration and Osmosis Migration as dynamic processes that shape our global community. Recognizing and understanding these dynamics will enable us to navigate the challenges and opportunities they present, fostering a more inclusive and prosperous world for all.

Political environments of Arab nations are complicated due to the peculiarity of historical, cultural and geopolitical features typical for this region. Among these Arab countries are nations that operate under different forms of government including monarchies and republics. This paper will examine the political landscape in Arab states and shed some light on several of the political beliefs/parties prevalent in the region.

On the extreme side of the scale there are the conservative and traditionalist ideals based on the protection of customs and religious beliefs. This extends towards Islamic parties like the Muslim Brotherhood that aim at instituting Islamic nations dictated by the Sharia law. Such parties often get their support from the more religiously conservative segments of society such as Egypt or Jordan, which are known to exercise a fair share of influence on politics.

The relationship between politics and religion defines one of major components of the political space of the majority of Muslim states. Many Muslins have incorporated Islam in their lives; therefore, it is usually one of the influential factors that shape their political thoughts and actions. Nevertheless, there are differences in the interpretation of Islam upon politics depending on specific countries or areas.

Some countries have gone for a somewhat strict and classical interpretation of religion tagged to as "Islamist" or "Islamic fundamentalist" dictatorships. The objectives of these governments are to enforce sharia as a source of law. These are examples of Islamist regimes in countries such as Iran, Saudi Arabia, and Sudan. These kinds of governments have more of an authority structure where religious leaders also are influential in decision making processes.

At the other extreme, there are more liberal and progressive philosophies concerning personal liberties, human rights, and democratic governance. Several liberated parties and movements were born up in some Arabic state, where they demanded a wide change in the constitution, woman's position, and free speech. Such movements or parties are mostly confronted by conservatists, yet, maintain their significance as democracy upholders.

A cluster of nationalistic and socialist parties, which focus on economic growth, social equity and freedom from external dictation, is found in the center of the political spectrum. Many times, these parties always oppose imperialism and focus on solving the issues of poor people such as workers. Over the years the region has been governed by Arab nationalist parties. The Ba'athist Party in Syria and Iraq has contributed significantly in promoting unity among Arabs and equal distribution of opportunities across the society.

However, one should bear in mind that there is no fixed political landscape and the spectrum does not end with these three categories. In addition, there are several other political parties and movements that cannot be simply classified in terms of left-wing or right-wing categories. Moreover, the political frontline keeps changing under the influence of internal and external forces.

The events that were collectively known as "the Arab spring," which occurred in most of the Arab nations in 2011, led to notable changes in the political context of these states. These revolts sought end of corruption, political reforms and social injustice. These revolutions toppled entrenched dictatorships and gave rise to new political actors like the Islamists, liberals, and youth movements.

The Arab spring, however, has left traces of political instability, inter-conflicts in its aftermath and authoritarian assertions within some countries. For some states, this translates into the degradation of democracy, with less room for dissenting voices which is likely not only in terms of politics but also with respect to economy.

Therefore, the political spectrum in Arab countries is multifaceted as it comprises various sets of ideas and different political movements. Arab countries encompass, among others, Islamist parties; liberal movements; nationalists; and other political camps. Although the Arab Spring revolutionized the Middle East's political environment, it also showed how difficult and complicated change is in the region. It becomes important to build inclusive and democratic governments that will observe respect of both the rights and desires of each citizen as such Arab nations undergo changes in their politics.

Palestinian State that Never Existed

The Palestinian nation has not been officially declared in a way that is universally recognized. The establishment of a Palestinian nation is a complex and unresolved issue that has been a valuable awareness of the Israeli-Palestinian battle for many years.

The Palestinian Declaration of Independence, which became issued by using the Palestine National Council in Algiers on November 15, 1988, was a massive moment within the Palestinian quest for statehood. This declaration changed into a symbolic circulate and asserted the Palestinian proper to self-determination. It turned into identified by means of some of international locations, and the Palestinian Liberation Organization (PLO) subsequently sought reputation because the valid representative of the Palestinian people.

However, the status quo of a completely identified, impartial Palestinian state with defined borders has no longer came about, and the fame of the Palestinian territories, together with the West Bank and Gaza Strip, stays a subject of dispute and negotiation inside the Israeli-Palestinian peace system. The final aim of accomplishing a Palestinian state along Israel, regularly referred to as the "two-state solution," has but to be realized, and the difficulty remains a supply of ongoing battle and global diplomacy.

Who Controlled Gaza and the West Bank before 1967 War

Before 1967, the Gaza Strip was controlled by Egypt. It came under Egyptian administration after the 1948 Arab-Israeli War, which resulted in the division of the former British Mandate of Palestine into separate territories. The Gaza Strip was administered by Egypt, while the West Bank, including East Jerusalem, was controlled by Jordan. This situation lasted until the Six-Day War in June 1967 when Israel captured both the Gaza Strip and the West Bank, including East Jerusalem, and has maintained control over them since.

Before the 1967 Six-Day War, the demand for a Palestinian state was not as prominent or unified

Prior to the 1967 Six-Day War, the Palestinian national movement lacked the name and cohesion that would emerge in later years. Regional politics were complicated, and the Palestinian national movement was still in its infancy. Prior to 1967, Jordan and Egypt controlled the Palestinian territories, including the West Bank and the Gaza Strip, during the Arab-Israeli War of 1948. During this period, Palestinian expressions of will to build self-determination and nation-building often find common ground with the broader discourses of pan-Arab nationalism. Some Palestinian leaders colluded with Arab nationalist groups everywhere, complicating the situation. The establishment of the Palestine Liberation Organization (PLO) in 1964 was an important development. The organization would subsequently emerge as a key factor in advocating for and pursuing Palestinian self-determination and statehood goals. Originally, the PLO's goal was "the liberation of Palestine," without specifying a specific strategy for statehood. It was not until after the Six-Day War in 1967 that the explicit demand for a Palestinian state, including the West Bank, Gaza Strip and East Jerusalem, became prominent.

The events of the 1967 war, when Israel occupied the West Bank, the Gaza Strip, and East Jerusalem, significantly changed their dynamics and intensified Palestinian demands for statehood in those territories. The United Nations passed Resolution 242, which called for Israel to withdraw from the territories occupied during the war and recognized that all countries in the region, including Israel, have the right to live in peace and security. The idea of a Palestinian state with defined borders gained considerable momentum in the years that followed.

Founding the Palestine Liberation Organization (PLO)in 1964

The Palestine Liberation Organization (PLO) was founded by the Arab League in 1964. It was founded in response to the Arab-Israeli conflict and the desire to represent Palestinian interests on the international stage. The first task of the PLO was to unite Palestinian groups and organizations towards the goal of "the liberation of Palestine". Over time, the organization developed into the main representative of the Palestinian national movement, working to ensure the self-determination, statehood, and rights of the Palestinian people and played a central role in the Palestinian struggle for a Palestinian state and Israel and the internal settlement of the Palestinians in war. Yasser Arafat, who later became a prominent Palestinian leader, played a pivotal role in the history of the PLO, leading the organization for many years the PLO has a complex and multifaceted history, including political and militant aspects, and is milestone in the Palestinian national footprint.

HAMAS

Hamas Terrorism: A Complex Reality

Hamas, formally known as the Islamic Resistance Movement, is a Palestinian political and military organization that has been at the center of numerous debates and controversies for decades. The group's complex history and activities have led to its designation as a terrorist organization by many countries, while others view it through a different lens. In this essay, we will explore the origins, ideology, actions, and the global perception of Hamas as a terrorist group.

Origins and Ideology: Hamas was founded in 1987 during the First Intifada, a Palestinian uprising against Israeli occupation. The organization's establishment can be seen as a response to the failure of diplomatic efforts to address Palestinian grievances. Hamas's ideological roots are grounded in Islamism, and it seeks to establish an Islamic state in historic Palestine, replacing Israel.

Hamas's Charter, adopted in 1988, includes anti-Semitic rhetoric and calls for the destruction of Israel. This uncompromising stance has been a major source of controversy and has contributed to its designation as a terrorist organization by many countries. Critics argue that such positions promote violence and undermine the prospects for peace in the region.

103

Militant Activities: Hamas is perhaps best known for its militant activities, which have included suicide bombings, rocket attacks, and other forms of violence against Israeli civilians and military targets. These acts of terrorism have led to the loss of innocent lives and widespread suffering, making Hamas a highly controversial entity in the eyes of many.

The organization's armed wing, the Izz al-Din al-Qassam Brigades, is responsible for these operations. Their tactics have led to extensive condemnation and have been a significant factor in the global perception of Hamas as a terrorist group.

International Designation as a Terrorist Organization: Dozens of countries and international organizations, including the United States, Israel, Canada, the European Union, and others, have officially designated Hamas as a terrorist organization. They cite the group's violent actions, its anti-Semitic rhetoric, and its refusal to recognize Israel's right to exist as key reasons for this designation.

These countries argue that the use of indiscriminate violence against civilians and its aversion to peaceful negotiations make Hamas a destabilizing force in the Israeli-Palestinian conflict. This designation enables these nations to implement legal and financial measures against Hamas and its members.

Alternative Perspectives: While many countries label Hamas as a terrorist organization, there are alternative perspectives as well. Some nations and entities, particularly in the Arab and Muslim world, view Hamas as a legitimate resistance movement fighting against Israeli occupation. They argue that Hamas's actions should be seen in the context of a long-standing conflict and the failures of diplomatic efforts.

The Arab League, for instance, has refrained from designating Hamas as a terrorist organization and has supported the Palestinian cause. Such alternative perspectives emphasize the importance of addressing the root causes of the Israeli-Palestinian conflict and the need for a just and lasting solution.

Conclusion: The question of whether Hamas is a terrorist organization is a deeply polarized one. Its origins, ideology, and actions have led many countries to designate it as such, while others see it as a legitimate resistance movement. This complexity underscores the challenges of resolving the Israeli-Palestinian conflict.

In any case, it is essential to recognize that the situation is not black and white. While condemning acts of terrorism and violence, it is equally important to address the underlying issues, such as the occupation of Palestinian territories, the lack of a viable peace process, and the humanitarian suffering in Gaza. Ultimately, a lasting resolution to the Israeli-Palestinian conflict will require a comprehensive and inclusive approach that considers the grievances of both sides and strives for a just and peaceful coexistence.

Who Funds Hamas?

Hamas is designated as a terrorist organization by the United States and the European Union, and it is cut off from official assistance provided to the PLO in the West Bank. Historically, funding for Hamas has come from Palestinian expatriates, private donors in the Persian Gulf, and some Islamic charities in the West, leading to asset freezes by the U.S. Treasury. Gaza's economic situation, already dire before the 2023 assault on Israel, has been further worsened by the conflict, with border restrictions contributing to extreme poverty. While Israel has allowed Qatar to provide assistance through Hamas, other foreign aid typically reaches Gaza via the PA and UN agencies.

After the blockade commenced, Hamas generated revenue by taxing goods using an elaborate network of tunnels that bypassed the Egyptian crossing into Gaza. This included essential items such as food, medicine, cheap gas for electricity, as well as cash, construction materials, and arms. When Egyptian President Abdel Fatah al-Sisi assumed power in 2013, Egypt, viewing Hamas as linked to the Muslim Brotherhood, became hostile and closed down many tunnels during its counterterrorism campaign. Although Egypt allowed some commercial goods through the Salah al-Din border crossing in 2018, it significantly impacted Hamas's tunnel-based revenue. As of 2021, Hamas was reportedly collecting over $12 million monthly from taxes on Egyptian goods.

Currently, Iran is a major supporter of Hamas, providing financial aid, weaponry, and training. Despite a brief strain in relations during Syria's civil war, Iran contributes around $100 million annually to Hamas, PIJ, and other U.S.-designated terrorist Palestinian groups. Iran swiftly expressed support for Hamas's 2023 assault on Israel.

'Ali Khamenei, Ali Khamenei and Hassan Nassralah

Turkey, under President Recep Tayyip Erdogan since 2002, has been a consistent supporter of Hamas and a critic of Israel. While Ankara claims to back Hamas politically, it faces allegations of funding Hamas's terrorism, including through aid redirected from the Turkish Cooperation and Coordination Agency.

How Palestinians Perceive Hamas

How Palestinians perceive Hamas is diverse, but a June 2023 poll by the Palestinian Center for Policy and Survey Research (PCPSR) indicated that the political division between the West Bank and Gaza is widely disapproved. About one-third of Palestinians see it as the most detrimental development since Israel's establishment in 1948. The same poll revealed that over half of Palestinians in both Gaza and the West Bank would choose Hamas's Haniyeh over PA President Mahmoud Abbas in a presidential election. Only one-third of Palestinians would opt for Abbas. Notably, Abbas postponed the 2021 national elections indefinitely, citing Israel's alleged hindrance of Palestinians in East Jerusalem from voting, although there are suspicions that Abbas aimed to avert a potential Hamas victory.

Hamas Objectives

Hamas is an Islamic organization both politically and militarily in origin, Palestinian. Its objectives have evolved over time, and they include:

1. Resistance Against Israel: Historically, Hamas engages in combat against Israel with a desire to end the occupation of the Palestinian lands, such as the West bank and Gaza strip.

2. Establishment of a Palestinian State: Hamas aims at setting up an independent Palestinians State in those territories they termed "Palestinian" and consider east Jerusalem to be their capital. It denies any right accorded to Israel and demands the emancipation of all historical Palestine.

3. Islamic Governance: Hamas is an Islamist movement that seeks to enforce Sharia law in their territories. Since it took over the Gaza Strip with violence in 2007, the Islamist organization Hamas has ruled the area.

4. Resistance to Peace Agreements: Hamas, however, has criticized peace talks between PA and Israel and has rejected settlements that do not satisfy its requirements.

GAZA

Gaza's status is an intricate and controversial matter. The disengagement plan refers to the situation when Israel withdrew its troops and settlements from the Gaza strip in 2005. Since this time the Gaza strip has been administrated by Hamas, a Palestinian military organization that is called terrorist by Israel, the USA although Israel withdrew all of its military forces from the region of Gaza, it continues to block the area through enforcing control at the borders, airspaces, and maritime zones. Consequently, debates regarding whether Gaza can be considered as occupied continue until present with some scholars asserting that Israel's control over Gaza's borders and restrictions on movements of people and products constitute an occupational measure which is similar but does not equal an effective occupation.

1. Water: The region is prone to high levels of stress associated with water supply. Most of its water is derived from underground aquifers that have been over pumped resulting into salty intrusion and contamination. Secondly, most water infrastructure systems in the region have been badly affected by armed conflicts at various occasions. Some of the water sources are controlled by Israel and at times water is transferred to Gaza on limited basis. Nevertheless, the water problem in Gaza is still an important matter that causes much difficulty with water shortages.

2. Electricity: In particular, electricity in Gaza is an intricate matter. The Gaza strip has its own power station; however, it does not generate sufficient energy required by its citizens. Therefore, Gaza has depended on the supply of electricity by multiple sources including the state of Israel. There have also been incidents of power outages on and off especially due to this problem.

3. Labor and movement: During some periods of time Gazans could work in Israel—especially before the second Intifada but for an extensive period of time these restrictions are being toughened up gradually. While security issues and political troubles have made it difficult for Gazans to find employment in Israel, free travel between Gaza and Israel is very strictly controlled.

However, the question about the situation in Gaza remains an issue for discussion and a global challenge, including humanitarian and political ones. Many parties disagree with regard to the situation in Gaza; it is regarded as either occupied or not by different international actors.

The West Bank is a region, which was occupied by Israel in the course of the Six-Day War which occurred in the year 1967. After that, Israel has been holding onto the West bank and has also established settlements in the region. The West Bank's political status constitutes the basis for considerable international controversy.

While the United Nations and a majority of the international community see the Israeli Occupation of the West Bank as illegitimate, Israel considers its settlement of this territory as normal. Many efforts were directed at resolving the conflict surrounding the status of the West Bank as well as other aspects of the Israeli-Palestinian issue, however, these efforts failed to result in a final solution and the conflict thus remained an ongoing issue.

THE ORIGIN OF THE PHILISTINES AND THE EVOLUTION OF THE TERM "PALESTINE"

Introduction

Mention of the first Philistines and the word Palestine invokes a complicated story filled with layers of meaning. The ancient philistines have to do with modern **Palestine** an example of the persistence nature of this corner even in modern man's collective imagination. This paper examines their origin, the meaning behind Palestine and how it relates to today's Israel Palestinian conflict.

The Original Philistines

These are actually the same philistines, an old people that lived in the south-eastern coast of the Levant called Philistia, before that. Sometimes they are correlated with the biblical stories about the Israelites capturing Canaan. The word Philistine comes from a Hebrew word "p'lishtim" which in turn translates into modern Palestine.

Historical Context: It is assumed that the Philistines moved into this area around the year of 1200 BCE, just when the Bronze Age was collapsed. They established a confederation of five city-states: Gaza, Ashkelon, Ashdod, Gath, and Ekron. They established an independent culture as they engaged in pottery making and artistry and hence came to be known as the Philistine Cities.

Biblical Mention: Philistines are well noted in Hebrew Bible as enemies against the Hebrews. For example, famous biblical stories like that in which David fights with Goliath illustrate the conflict and interaction between these two peoples.

Decline and Disappearance: Starting from the seventh century BC, the culture of Philistines started to wane down and then, they were merged into a larger region inhabitant during the later period. The biblical texts and archaeological research findings were used as a means of preserving their history.

The Evolution of the Term "Palestine"

The term "Palestine" itself has a complex history that changed through different periods and authorities. The nature of his ideas is a reflection of the region's history and vagaries in its geopolitics.

Classical Antiquity: The name Palestine is said to have originated during the classical antiquity; Roman Empire under Emperor Hadrian named it Judea, meaning Land of Jews and Palaestina around 135CE. In fact, the renaming of Hadrian was viewed as an act to disconnect Jews from their historical and cultural attachment to this land after the Bar Kokhba Revolt.

Islamic Period: The name "Filastin" or "Filistin", linguistically related to its preceding Palaestina, lived on throughout the Islamic Caliphate happened in different Islamic caliphs including Umayyad, Abbasid, and Ottoman.

British Mandate: Following the demise of Ottoman Empire after World War I, the League of Nations gave United Kingdom a mandate over this territory which included today's Israel, West Bank and Gaza. "Palestine" in this case referred to the whole territory during the British Mandate.

Post-World War II: After the World War II, which was succeeded by the founding Israel as a state in 1948, major developments were experienced in this region. The term "Palestine" became synonymous with the territory inhabited by Jewish and Arab peoples. The phrase eventually emerged as the embodiment of Palestinian national identity.

Modern Connotations of "Palestine"

Today, the word "Palestine" is politically and culturally charged with meaning given to it largely due to Israeli-Palestinian conflict.

Israeli-Palestinian Conflict: Therefore, the use of "Palestine" in modern discourse mostly implies to the present Israeli-Palestinian conflict. It represents an underlying fight for territorial sovereignty and national self-determination.

National Identity: "Palestine" represents the national identity of Palestinians. It symbolizes the Palestinian people's desire for statehood, self-rule and recognition as an equal member of the international community.

Geopolitical Disputes: The reference to "Palestine" brings about territorial disputes, since it comprises places like the West Bank, Gaza strip and East Jerusalem. Negotiations concern these territories; peace processes are conducted there and they become the object of geopolitical tensions.

International Recognition: The issue of recognizing Palestine as a state has sparked international controversy. The diplomatic landscape is complicated with complaisance of recognition from various countries and international organizations to the State of Palestine.

Conclusion

The reference to the original Philistines and name Palestine is highly compounds for the region have ancient history, politics and culture. The ancient city-states with which the original Philistines are associated have become part of the historical and biblical narratives. Over the years, the meaning of term "Palestine" has changed with politics and cultural changes within this area.

"Palestine" as a modern term carries the meaning of local Arab nationalism, territories being disputed and a nationhood in international law. The lands surrounding Israel and Judea have seen many empires and people come to traverse or govern. They also include Canaanites, Ammonites, Moabites, Nabateans Philistines Babylonians Assyrians Persians Greeks Romans Byzantines Arabs Mamluks Ottomans. Of course, the presence of Israelites among these peoples was the most durable one in view of the Roman-driven diaspora that took place two millennia ago. The logic behind why the Arabs living in the borderlands of contemporary Israel opted to take up the name "Palestine" remains a puzzle. One might also pose a question as to whether names like Ammonites, Moabites or even Nabateans would induce more empathy from the Jewish population in Israel.

THE INTERPLAY OF NATIONALITY AND RELIGION IN THE POLITICAL PROCESS

Introduction

Throughout history, nationality and religion have acted as a combined power driving towards the fusion of the political process. In general, politics, policies and decision making is greatly influenced by the dynamics and interplay between public opinion and private judgments of the individuals. The essay discusses the complexity in the association between nationality and religion and how these sentiments of identity affect political practice in the domestic front and the external arena.

The Role of Nationality

National identity and contribution to politics among youths in Uganda. In many instances nationality which also may be associated with patriotism has been shown to be one of the major factors influencing people's involvement in political activity. Individuals love their country and therefore develop an emotional attachment towards it which pushes them partake in governance activities to ensure their interests are upheld. Belonging to a certain nationality gives one a feeling of being a part of that particular group and such feelings are utilized by political leaders to generate support for their programs.

1. National Symbols and Identity: Powerful nationalistic symbols such as flags anthems and emblems are instrumental in promoting a sense of belonging. These symbols serve to mobilize support and patriotic commitment to national political institutions.

2. National Pride and Unity: Unity amongst diversified populations is facilitated by a shared sense of nationality. It transcends barriers based on ethnicity, cultures, and regions and fosters unity among nations.

3. Nationalism and Political Movements: Generally, nationalists movements arise due to fears of threats against their national identities or countries' independence. Such movements can have substantial implications for political decision making and policy formulation.

B. Nationalism and Sovereignty

The notion of sovereignty forms the basis for nationality and it has been instrumental in structuring the political arena. These sentiments are frequently expressed through demands for autonomy, secession, and local government.

1. Secessionist Movements: Secessionist movements throughout history have pursued new nation-state creation on ethnic basis. One can cite recent developments such as the dissolution of the former Yugoslavia or the collapse of the Soviet Empire.

2. National Interests in International Relations: Nation-states are actors in international politics, pursuing national interest, motivated by a duty to preserve their being and identity. It may result in diplomatic tensions or conflict.

The Influence of Religion

A. Religion and Political Legitimacy

Over the years, religion has been an important source of authority to legitimation of political authority. Numerous political orders, especially monarchies, have used religious organizations as a means of justifying their rule.

1. The Divine Right of Kings: In the past, rulers were perceived by the people as being divinely appointed and therefore legitimate in terms of religion. The "divine right of kings" was a religious justification for political authority.

2. Religious Institutions and Governance: Religious leaders usually have great political powers in theocracy. Policymaking is under the influence of these religious institutions of a theocracy. It is a historical precedent that Vatican has administered the Papal States.

B. Political views and religious beliefs.

Political attitudes and behaviors are significantly influenced by religious beliefs and values. People frequently turn to their religion for advice on such questions of right or wrong in life affairs, which also determines their point of view concerning certain political affairs.

1. Moral and Ethical Foundations: Religious followers are guided by religious doctrines which have been developed based on morals and ethics. This framework guides them on matters relating to abortion, same-sex marriages, and social justice.

2. Religious Lobbying and Advocacy: It is important to note that religious grouping participate in lobbying. They want legislation changes and other policies in line with their creed. They argue about issues such as separation of church and state.

The Complex Interaction

It is not an easy task to describe such an interaction based on nationality and religion into the politic process since it leads to diverse results such as inclusion or separation.

A. Cultural and Religious Diversity

A lot of countries and areas have diverse culture and religion backgrounds. Political systems have the challenge of managing this diversity. Social cohesion requires recognizing various national and religious identities.

1. Cultural Pluralism: Respecting different national and cultural identity helps promote cohesion and unity in any nation. These diversities are addressed by multicultural policies.

116

2. Religious Freedom: In countries where there are multiples religions, it is very important to guarantee protection of religious freedom and separation between church and state. This curbs unfair religious discrimination as it allows coexistence with other cults and religions.

B. Identity-Based Conflict

Identities sometimes result in conflicts due to mixing up of religion with nationality. In most cases, political tension becomes strife when political processes are discriminatory towards particular citizens or religions.

1. Ethnic and Religious Conflict: There have been several instances in history where conflicts have originated from suppressing or subjecting ethnic or religious minorities. Such examples include the Balkans, Northern Ireland, and the Israeli-Palestinian conflict.

2. The Role of Political Leaders: These identity-based conflicts can be either aggravated or reduced by political leaders. The way public views about them can be influenced by their rhetoric and policy.

C. Identity and Political Mobilization

Furthermore, nationalism or religion may spark politicization. The mobilize people into political processes, cause grouping, and voting on basis of one's identity in relation with the beliefs.

1. Identity Politics: Many policy agendas are derived from identity-based political movements such as religion and nationality. These include how they can determine elections, referendums, and legislations.

2. Populism: Populist leaders use their people in this way as they exploit nationalism and religion to get support. they put political matters into question concerning national security and cultural and moral integrity.

The issue of nationalism and religion and its political ramifications in the modern age is a lot of trouble. To tackle the complexity inherent in issues such as growing populism, clash between secularism, and religious fundamentalism, as well as impacts resulting from globalization must be treated with due care.

A. Populism and Nationalism

The populist leader capitalizes on patriotism and belief in Godhood to achieve his ends. They appeal to public emotions, simplifying complicated matters to show that they are patriotic and faithful to their religions.

1. Challenges to Democratic Values: However, populism may also subvert democratically-based checks and balances, constrain free speech, and suppress minority rights.

2. Divisive Rhetoric: In some instances, populist leaders use inciting speech directed towards minorities in order to divide society politically and socially.

B. Secularism and Religious Fundamentalism

Another current challenge is the existence of secularism alongside religious fundamentalism. Finding a balance between religion and human governance is paramount.

1. Freedom of Religion: The principle of democracy provides for protection of religious freedoms. It allows people to practice the religion they deem fit, devoid of any form of stigmatization and prejudice.

2. Secular Governance: This is necessary as religious beliefs should not become a basis for enacting policies without due consideration to non-religious groups and minority religions in a secular nation.

C. Globalization and Identity

The intermingling of identities is inevitable as a result of globalization which has brought people from diverse cultures and religions together. This offers both potentials and difficulties to them.

1.   Cultural Exchange: It develops mutual understanding between various nationalities, civilizations, religions and cultures worldwide.

2.   Identity Conflicts: But at the same time, it may result in identity crises since people try to resolve issues surrounding the dual or mixed identities.

Conclusion

Nationalism and religion in politics has been an ongoing story in human history. These sentiments of identity have a great effect on political engagement, policymaking and even international relations. It should be noted that the cross currents running through nationality and religious can lead to unity or division.

Introduction

Israel stands as a unique instance of a country where the interaction of nationality and religion profoundly influences its political manner. This Middle Eastern kingdom isn't simplest a place of birth for a diverse array of ethnic and spiritual agencies however also the epicenter of world Abrahamic faiths. The complicated dynamics between nationality and faith have performed an imperative role in shaping Israel's politics, society, and global members of the family. This essay explores the intricate relationship among those two forces, delving into how they affect the political panorama of Israel.

Historical and Cultural Context

A. The Jewish Homeland

The ancient and cultural significance of Israel is deeply rooted in its fame because the ancestral place of origin of the Jewish human beings. For centuries, Jewish communities the world over maintained their connection to this area thru spiritual, cultural, and ancient ties.

1. Zionism: The late 19th and early 20th centuries witnessed the emergence of Zionism, a political motion advocating for the status quo of a Jewish hometown in Israel. This movement laid the muse for the introduction of the State of Israel in 1948.

2. Historical and Religious Sites: Israel is home to several historic and non-secular sites of great importance to Jews, together with the Western Wall, the Old City of Jerusalem, and the Masada fortress.

Israel's population is notably numerous, encompassing Jews, Arabs, Druze, Christians, and numerous other ethnic and religious organizations. This cultural tapestry presents each possibility and demanding situations.

Three Druze brothers that are pilots in the Israeli Air-Force

1. Religious Pluralism: Israel is home to a range of spiritual beliefs, from Orthodox Judaism to Islam and Christianity. Religious variety provides layers of complexity to political processes.

2. Arab-Israeli Minority: The Arab-Israeli minority constitutes a giant part of Israel's populace. Their identity and pursuits are pivotal in the political panorama.

Judge. Kabub was appointed in 2022 at the Supreme Court of Israel

The Influence of Nationality

National Identity and Zionism

National identity plays a foundational role in shaping Israel's politics. Zionism, particularly, is deeply intertwined with Jewish countrywide identification, guiding political aspirations and rules.

1. State-Building: The Zionist movement's core objective changed into the established order of a Jewish nation in the ancient place of birth of the Jewish people. This imaginative and prescient culminated within the creation of Israel in 1948.

2. Israeli Nationalism: The choice to guard and hold the Jewish identity of the state remains a effective force in Israeli politics, influencing troubles like immigration, defense, and international relations.

Nationality has profound implications for Israel's technique to country wide protection. The state's records of warfare and safety concerns deeply impacts its political choice-making.

1. Security Challenges: Israel faces unique safety challenges, together with regional conflicts, territorial disputes, and the threat of terrorism. Nationality plays a position in shaping defense strategies and rules.

2. Military Service: National identity is carefully connected to obligatory army carrier in Israel. Serving inside the Israel Defense Forces (IDF) isn't always only a duty however a ceremony of passage for lots Jewish residents.

The Influence of Religion

Religious Parties and the Knesset

Religion has an instantaneous presence in Israel's political gadget through spiritual political events that take part inside the Knesset, Israel's parliament.

1. Religious Influence: Parties along with Shas and United Torah Judaism suggest for guidelines based totally on Jewish religious law (Halakha). They wield influence on troubles related to marriage, divorce, and religious schooling.

2. Coalition Building: Israel's fragmented political landscape regularly necessitates coalition governments. Religious parties have performed pivotal roles in shaping authorities' coalitions and policies.

B. Conflict Over Religious Practices

Religious identification and practices are on the center of political disputes in Israel, mainly when it comes to issues like non-secular conversion, marriage, and get entry to holy web sites.

1. Marriage Laws: Israel does now not have civil marriage, that could create demanding situations for interfaith or non-non-secular couples. This issue has sparked debates and requires reform.

2. Access to Holy Sites: The manipulate and get right of entry to spiritual sites, which includes the Western Wall and the Al-Aqsa Mosque, had been factors of competition and diplomatic tension.

Complex Interplay

The interaction of nationality and faith in Israel's political manner is complex and multifaceted. It has each unified and divided the nation, shaping its home and foreign policies.

A. Unity and National Pride

Nationality and faith have the electricity to unite Israelis, fostering a robust experience of countrywide delight and shared identity.

1. Historical Achievements: The establishment and continued lifestyles of Israel as a Jewish state is a supply of vast delight for its residents, irrespective of their religious beliefs.

2. National Solidarity: National and spiritual holidays, together with Independence Day and Passover, provide opportunities for Israelis to return collectively and have a good time their shared heritage.

B. Divisions and Identity-Based Conflicts

While nationality and religion can unite, they also can divide. Israel grapples with complicated divisions that revolve around troubles just like the Israeli-Palestinian struggle, religious freedoms, and country wide and ethnic identities.

1. Israeli-Palestinian Conflict: The struggle among Israelis and Palestinians is driven by national, religious, and territorial factors, leading to complicated identification-primarily based tensions.

2. Religious vs. Secular Divides: Israel contends with divisions between spiritual and secular segments of society, affecting policies on troubles like Sabbath observance and non-secular education.

Contemporary Challenges

In the contemporary era, Israel confronts various contemporary demanding situations related to the interplay of nationality and religion inside the political process.

Peace and Conflict Resolution

The Israeli-Palestinian battle stays an urgent mission, deeply rooted in questions of nationality, religion, and territorial sovereignty.

1. Two-State Solution: The debate over a -country answer, which involves the creation of a Palestinian kingdom along Israel, hinges on country wide identity and safety issues.

2. Religious and Historical Ties: The spiritual and ancient importance of Jerusalem and the Temple Mount make resolving the metropolis's repute a deeply touchy trouble.

Religious Freedom and Democracy

Balancing spiritual freedoms and democratic ideas poses challenges in a state with diverse non-secular and ethnic corporations.

1. Religious Freedom: Ensuring the protection of religious freedoms for all residents is vital for fostering inclusivity and variety.

2. Democratic Values: Israel's democratic values necessitate the equitable treatment of all citizens, regardless of their religious or national identity.

Conclusion

Israel's ability to navigate this intricate interplay of nationality and religion will play a critical role in shaping its future as a democratic and inclusive nation, while addressing the complex challenges that define its political landscape. Understanding the historical and contemporary dynamics of this interplay is essential for comprehending the complexities of Israel's politics and its role on the global stage.

The Islamic countries span across the Middle East, Asia, Africa, and beyond and represent a rich and intricate patchwork of cultures, customs, and governance models. Nationalism and religion interact very much to determine how politics work in these nations. There exist different ethnicities, languages and cultures as well as the single unifying identity of Islam. However, this paper analyses the complicated inter-linkage between nationhood and religion amongst Muslims' states; it elucidates on how they impact on internal political developments, foreign policy, and identity construction.

Historical and Cultural Context

The Role of Islam

Many countries with Islamic identities claim their roots are from Islam, which is renowned worldwide for both its history and culture. This impacts the region's identity as well has influences on its politics and social set up.

1. Islamic Heritage: A lot of times, countries that are Muslim in orientation tend to use their common Islamic origins to link and establish their political identity with the earliest days of Islam. They take pride through the historical importance of the Islamic Golden Age and its achievements in matters like science, philosophy, and arts.

2. Religious and Cultural Diversity: Cultural and religious diversity is highly prevalent among Islamic countries. Although Islam remains the common element, there is a lot of different sects, traditions, ethnical identities.

Political life in Muslim-majority nations has been shaped significantly by the effects of European imperialism. Political complications have arisen from colonial borders drawn insensibly towards the region's cultural and religious realities.

1. Artificial Nation-States: The colonial powers created arbitrary "nation-states' which usually encompassed an ethno-linguistic and religious mosaic. The historical divides still impact politics and identity.

2. Post-Colonial Nationalism: Post-colonial nationalism has appeared in many Islamic states that had been colonized in order for them to identify and safeguard their nationhood.

The Influence of Nationality

National Identity and Ethnicity

As a result, nationality linked to ethnicity has been at the core of politics among Muslim countries. Ethno-nationalism is an important tool for determining the limits of a nation and its statehood.

1. Ethnic Conflicts: There have been several incidents involving ethnic tensions among different parts of Islamic nations where uniform nationalism is questioned. For instance, conflicts such as those in Kurdistan, Baluchistan, and Darfur can be used as such examples.

2. Ethnic Nationalism: Ethnic nationalism is a situation whereby ethnic groups respond to state oppression, marginalization or other social ills by creating political movements as a means of asserting their own rights.

National identity and politics are tightly bound together. Nationalistic feelings are therefore frequently used by political movements and parties to mobilize supporters toward a certain state conception.

1. Nationalism and Independence Movements: Islamist movements pursuing national self-determination as the drive force behind regional independence and sovereignty in Islamic countries. As a symbolic example, this search may be illustrated by the Palestinian case.

2. Political Parties: Political parties often associate themselves with particular nations or ethnics. One of such groupings is meant to be represented. The parties could prefer regional autonomy, preservation of cultures etc.

The Influence of Religion

The role of Islamic law (sharia)

Sharia is the main determinant of the laws and politics of majority of Islamic countries. Its purpose is mainly to provide a basis for legislation and government.

1. Islamic Jurisprudence: Different Muslim countries apply Sharia in varying ways. The diversity shows various religious and legal traditions.

2. Religious Courts: Several Muslim states have specific courts that deal with family issues, inheritances as well as religious issues. However, the way in which these Islamic courts interact with the secular legal system also differs.

Religious Parties and Movements

In Muslim countries, religious parties and movements pressure to include those Islam laws into the judicial and the state political procedures.

1. Political Islam: Muslim Brotherhood in Egypt, AKP in Turkey are political movements trying to combine religion and politics. Such are common practices among Islamic-inspired regimes.

2. Political Influence: Such a scenario can lead to the takeover of religious parties in politics, framing of legislation and shaping international relations. This is dependent on each country's politics and their levels of prominence change from state to state.

Complex Interplay

Muslim countries are diverse in terms of experience, opportunities, and challenges surrounding the complicated nature of religion and citizenship that shapes domestic and foreign policies stem from this multitude of conditions.

Unity and Identity

Citizens can be united by nationality and religion which makes it possible to form the collective consciousness leading to the feeling of national pride and unity.

1. Cultural Celebrations: People come together in the celebrations of national and religious holidays, and this strengthens family ties and fosters patriotism. They come together for Eid al-Fitr, Ramadan and National Day of Independence.

2. Religious Pilgrimages: Muslim pilgrimage is conducted in Islamic countries for example Hajj (a religious visit in Saudi Arabia). This brings people together who share one faith and gives them an opportunity to meet each other and exchange their experiences during this pilgrimage.

B. Divisions and identity-based conflicts

Nationality and religion often result in tensions and identify-driven confrontations that are hard to deal with.

1. Intersecting Conflicts: Many of the conflicts based on identity also merge with the regional & geopolitical disputes like Israeli- Palestinian, Sunni vs Shia making the scenes very complex and highly tense.

2. Ethnic and Religious Minorities: These include ethnic and religious minorities who are at the risk of social as well as political antagonism due to discrimination, marginalization and associated tensions.

Western Government Systems

The Western world has been profoundly shaped by historical movements such as the Renaissance, Ages of Discovery and Enlightenment, as well as the Industrial and Scientific Revolutions. In the United States, the foundation of American government drew inspiration from two primary sources: (1) Enlightenment philosophy and (2) the ancient world of Greece and Rome, particularly the contributions of thinkers like Socrates, Plato, and Aristotle.

The Enlightenment era, spanning the 18th century, played a pivotal role in shaping Western political thought. Influential philosophers like Montesquieu, Rousseau, John Locke, and Immanuel Kant contributed significant ideas. Kant, a Lutheran who was proficient in Hebrew, emphasized the role of reason as the source of morality, and he linked aesthetics to a faculty of disinterested judgment.

The early modern era in the West witnessed a transformation in the traditional power structure, with shifts in the balance between monarchy, nobility, and clergy. The late 18th and early 19th centuries marked a period of revolutions across much of the Western world, leading to the emergence of new ideologies and societal changes.

Adam Smith, often regarded as the father of modern capitalism, left an indelible mark on Western society. His ideas significantly influenced economic thought and policies.

The concept of the "Separation of Powers" was introduced by the 18th-century philosopher Montesquieu. This model advocates for the division of government into independent branches, each wielding distinct powers. The judiciary's authority is counterbalanced by the legislature's capacity to enact new laws and propose constitutional amendments, ensuring a system of checks and balances.

The differences

Western and Muslim government systems differ in their philosophical underpinnings, organizational structures, and sources of authority. Western democracies, rooted in Enlightenment ideals, emphasize individual liberties and secularism, while Muslim systems draw inspiration from Islamic principles, intertwining governance with religious tenets. Many Muslim-majority countries feature variations of Islamic law as a foundational element, impacting legal and political frameworks. Leadership structures also differ, with Western systems favoring elected representatives and some Muslim nations upholding monarchical or theocratic models. Both aim to provide governance and uphold societal order, but their foundations and guiding principles shape diverse political landscapes.

Contemporary Challenges

Modern problems faced by Muslim countries where personal identities between religious faiths and citizenship are played out in political processes.

Democratization and Governance

Several Islamic countries are faced with the task of balancing their religious identity while promoting democratic principles such as the grant of religious freedoms, and political pluralism.

1. Democratization: However, the quest for democracy always results in tension between people's right to religious expression and their duty to recognize the minority rights and to keep religion out of state matters.

2. Religious Freedom: It is essential that these countries protect religious liberties for their citizens to create an atmosphere of plurality.

Security and international relations in relation to many Islamic nations are considered due to their geopolitical importance and participation in intra-regional disputes.

Conflict Resolution: Diplomacy is sensitive in addressing issues such as the Syrian civil war, the Yemeni conflict, and the ongoing Israeli-Palestinian conflict which are intertwined with religion, ethnicity, and nationhood.

Foreign Policy: This results in complicated interstate relationships based on religious and national factors of their regions and abroad.

Conclusion

Religion and nationality in interaction within the Islamic countries' politics is one complex and complicated issue. These nations are reflected in it as a combination of history, culture, and religion with which they were born and live every day. The place of Islam as cohesive element, combined with diversification of ethnic and nation-origin affiliations considerably affects both internal policies and foreign policy.

How these diverse interests will impact on the future of Islamic countries as democracies, inclusive societies, and prosperous states largely depends on how well Islamic countries are able to negotiate with these conflicting forces. For one to understand the modern and historical dynamics of this relationship, we must appreciate the intricacies involved in their politics as well as their role globally. In this regard, issues surrounding nationality and religion will continue playing an instrumental part in the development of politics of the modern world.

African-Americans and Latinos display antisemitism more than average

ADL surveys reveal that around 12% of Americans harbor deeply rooted anti-Semitic sentiments. A striking contrast emerges when examining specific demographic groups, with over 30% of African Americans and Latinos holding such views. Considering their collective representation of almost 30% in the population, it suggests that approximately 9% of the 12% of Americans with deeply entrenched anti-Semitic views are African Americans or Latinos.

Consequently, among the 70% or so of the population not comprising African Americans or Latinos, only 3% maintain deeply rooted anti-Semitic beliefs. In simpler terms, less than 5% of whites, Asians, and other ethnicities, including Native Americans, collectively harbor deeply entrenched anti-Semitic views. This stands in stark contrast to the over 30% prevalence among African Americans and Latinos, or at least as indicated by those willing to express such attitudes to pollsters.

The notable aspect is that despite these statistics, concerns about predominantly hypothetical anti-Semitism from white evangelical Christians appear to preoccupy Jewish communities more than anti-Semitism within core Democratic constituencies. As previously noted, studies emphasize people's tendency to downplay or overlook information favoring their political adversaries while accentuating anything unfavorable.

ADL President Abe Foxman attributes the persistence of anti-Semitism among African Americans to a denial of the problem and a lack of black leaders addressing anti-Semitism. Within the Latino community, these attitudes are attributed to remnants from Latin America, where traditional Catholic anti-Semitism endures, resulting in higher anti-Semitic attitudes than in the United States. Interestingly, as Latinos acculturate to the U.S., anti-Semitism tends to decline. Among first-generation immigrants, approximately 40% hold anti-Semitic attitudes, while the number drops to 20% among those born in the United States.

An update to the discussion references a more recent ADL survey from 2013, indicating a lower rate of black (22%) and Latino (36% foreign-born, 14% native-born) anti-Semitism than originally asserted. While the 2011 data aligns more closely with the author's statement, the overall figure was not 12% but 15%, with 29% (not over 30%) for African Americans and 42% and 20% for foreign-born and native-born Latinos, respectively. Despite potential discrepancies in the specific figures, the fundamental point persists: "entrenched anti-Semitic views" are notably more prevalent among African Americans and Latinos compared to other demographic groups.

Why Some Individuals or Groups from Minority Communities Turn to Active Anti-Semitism and Are Critical of Israel

Why does active anti-Semitism among some individuals and groups from minority communities, and criticism of Israel are so difficult to generalize it can be termed as a complex question? This issue should be handled with care having in mind that no one solution fits all scenarios. However, there are several factors that may contribute to such attitudes among some individuals or groups:

1. Social and Economic Factors: The marginalized minority communities believe they suffer as a result of global or local power dynamics and can blame it on either the Israelis or Jews, depending on their circumstances. Frustration and resentment may arise due to economic disparities, discrimination, and other social issues.

2. Political Beliefs: People within minorities can be affiliated to political beliefs or factions which openly oppose Israel. In some cases, for example, it could encompass a certain form of a political movement or party that may be anti-Israeli or anti-Zionist, with such stance influencing its following.

3. Influence of Propaganda: Perceptions, especially those of politicians, can be shaped by propaganda and misinformation. Lack of information can lead to false beliefs through mis-informative campaigns, biased media coverage, or social media narratives that reiterate such negative perceptions about Israel and Jews.

4. Historical Narratives: Attitudes can be influenced by historical events and stories. Take, for instance, the Israeli-Palestinian conflict which is very contentious and individuals' opinion could be informed on how they perceive the subject matter.

5. Religious Beliefs: At times, such adverse views may also be derived from religious belief. The ideas might be promoted by certain religious, or even extremist groups that would consider themselves against the existence of Israel according to their understandings and beliefs.

6. Social Networks: One's peer groups can also be powerful determinants of what they believe in. A person might also acquire and strengthen these prejudices if they belong to a social group that promotes such attitudes towards Jews and Israelis.

7. Lack of Education and Awareness: At times individuals may not be aware of the intricacies of the Israeli-Palestinian dispute and this results in biased views. Education and awareness on history and complexities of conflict goes a long way for balanced understandings.

It is important to state that in majority cases we do not talk about entire ethnic groups or people from minority communities. Many people come from dissimilar ethnic groups with varying views concerning Israel and that issue. It is unethical to generalize any group of people by looking at the deeds or opinions of few individuals in it. Discussions and teaching about this subject should encourage greater openness in order to promote better understanding of these difficult questions.

Muslims often face accusations of being a primary contributor to the escalating violence against Jews and the surge of new antisemitism, blurring the lines between opposition to Israel and its policies and hostility toward Jews regardless of their global residence. This portrayal, however, oversimplifies the diverse and heterogeneous nature of Muslims. Spread across the world, not confined to the Middle East and North Africa (MENA), Muslims exhibit variations in cultures and historical experiences, distinguishing southeastern European, central and southern African Muslims from those in the MENA region.

Contrary to the prevailing notion of Muslims as predominantly anti-Semitic, the study reveals that, on average, Muslims in the U.S. exhibit a leaning positivity toward Jews, although less favorable than non-Muslims. Further exploration of Muslim attitudes unveils a spectrum ranging from highly anti-Semitic to philosemitic. Factors such as education, foreign-born status, and perceived discrimination affect both Muslim and non-Muslim attitudes toward Jews similarly. However, distinctions emerge regarding age and religion's influence, where older Muslims hold more negative attitudes toward Jews than their younger counterparts, and the importance of religion leads to positive attitudes among non-Muslims but negative attitudes among Muslims.

While shedding light on Muslim attitudes, several studies leave some questions unanswered, calling for more refined data on factors such as the length of residence for foreign-born Muslims, nation of origin, distinctions within the Muslim religion (Shiite and Sunni sects), and political orientations of native-born black Muslims. Additionally, exploring Muslim-Jewish relations and comparing Muslim and Jewish perceptions presents an intriguing avenue for future research.

A broader challenge arises from concerns about the influx of antisemitism with Muslim immigrants, underscoring the prospect of mitigating and transforming attitudes toward Jews. The American Muslim community, on the whole, does not align with antisemitism, and interactions with the broader Muslim community and society may foster greater tolerance among recent immigrants. As economic security and education levels rise, the study suggests a potential moderation of anti-Semitic tendencies among Muslim immigrants, advocating vigilance in addressing such issues while recognizing the heterogeneity within American Muslim attitudes toward Jews.

Introduction

The Jewish left refers to Jews who support left-wing or left-liberal causes, either as individuals or through organizations. They have been significant forces in various movements, including labor, settlement house, women's rights, anti-racist, anti-colonialist, and anti-fascist organizations in various countries. Jewish leftism has its roots in the Jewish Enlightenment and the support of European Jews like Ludwig Börne for republican ideals after the French Revolution and Napoleonic Wars. In the 18th and 19th centuries, a movement for Jewish Emancipation spread across Europe, strongly associated with political liberalism. Many emancipated Jews became closely associated with liberal parties, supporting the American Revolution, French Revolution, and European Revolutions.

Historical Roots of Jewish Leftism

In the late 19th century, a Jewish working class emerged in Eastern and Central Europe, and a Jewish labor movement emerged. Distinctive Jewish socialist organizations formed and spread across the Jewish Pale of Settlement in the Russian Empire. Jews also played a major role in the Social Democratic parties of Germany, Russia, Austria-Hungary, and Poland. Historian Enzo Traverso has used the term "Judeo-Marxism" to describe the innovative forms of Marxism associated with these Jewish socialists, ranging from strongly cosmopolitan positions hostile to all forms of nationalism to more sympathetic positions to cultural nationalism.

Radical Jews in Central and Western Europe, including the Jewish working class, began to explore radicalism in Jewish tradition. Some prominent figures included Martin Buber, Gershom Scholem, Walter Benjamin, Gustav Landauer, Jacob Israël de Haan, and Bernard Lazare. Walther Rathenau was a prominent figure of the Jewish left in Weimar Germany.

139

Socialist Zionism, first developed in Russia by Marxist Ber Borochov and non-Marxists Nachman Syrkin and A. D. Gordon, became a powerful force in the Yishuv, the Jewish settlement in Palestine. Poale Zion, the Histadrut labor union, and the Mapai party played a significant role in the campaign for an Israeli state. In the 1940s, many on the left advocated for a binational state in Israel/Palestine. Since 1948, there has been a lively Israeli left, both Zionist (the Labour Party) and anti-Zionist (the Palestinian Communist Party).

There are two worldwide left-wing Zionist organizations: the World Labor Zionist Movement and the World Union of Meretz. Both movements exist as factions within the World Zionist Organization and as regional or country-specific Zionist movements.

Jews' involvement in leftist causes has a long and complex history that spans centuries. From their participation in labor movements to their advocacy for civil rights and social justice, Jews have often been at the forefront of progressive and leftist movements. Here I explore the historical and current motivations for Jewish involvement in leftism, tracing it to its sources, examining its effect on the Jewish community as well as society at large, and looking into some of the challenges and ambiguities that it poses.

Another example, post-World-War II convergence for the Jewish working class became in England when the Arbeter Ring ended its activities during 1950s and also trade unionism after disappearance of Jewish. Despite that, Jewish working-class organizations retain some of their footprints today —Workmen's Circle and The Forward in New York, Jewish Labor Committee; International Jewish Labor Bund in Australia and United People's Order in Canada.

1960s—1990s

From the 1960s—1980s Western Jews began to get interested in Jewish working-class culture and radical traditions, which created space for growing of radicals who were interested in Yiddish culture, Jewish spirituality, and social justice. New Jewish Agenda was a national, multi-issue progressive membership organization during the period 1980-1992 in the US. In Britain, The Jewish Socialists' Group and Rabbi Michael Lerner's Tikkun have kept this tradition alive while groups such as Jewdas are eclectic about Jewishness.

Contemporary Jewish Engagement in Leftist Causes

A. Progressive Values

Jews still participate in leftwing advocacy because such appeals are based on progressive principles —social justice, equality and human rights.

1. Tikkun Olam: It should be noted that Jews are guided by the concept of "Tikkun Olam" (repairing the world). A lot of Jews see their participation in leftist causes as an exercise of this moral imperative to establish a fairer society.

2. Social Justice Judaism: Prophetic/Radical Judaism, Ordinary mystical Waters and Atlantic Religion Progressive all point to a growing preference for the social justice and inclusivity driven form of Jewish worship. It is this religious perspective that impels involvement in leftists struggles.

B. Holocaust Legacy

The cumulative remembrance of the Holocaust and Jews sufferings during World War II has had significant effect on Jewish involvement in leftist fights.

1. Never Again: "Never Again" is a slogan for many Jews, who stress the need to prevent atrocities and human right abuses. It is this commitment that normally causes their participation in genocide prevention and human rights related scenarios.

2. Refugee and Asylum Advocacy: Jews are often the pioneers of advocacy for refugees, owing to their historical experience as refugees; they address humanitarian crises.

1. Civil Rights Movement: One notable model was Jewish Americans who, especially through the American Jewish Congress and American Jewish Committee were very vocal in pushing for racial equality, as well as advocating for desegregation and voting rights.

2. Social Justice Organizations: For instance, Jews have played a major role in the establishment and leadership of social justice organizations such as NAACP and ACLU that seek possibly to improve civil rights.

21st century

During the 2000s, supporting Palestinian causes was a new additional component for diasporic Jewish left signaling the emergence of new wave organizations concerning Israeli-Palestinian conflict. After the 2014 Israel—Gaza conflict, Leftist Jewish organizations in the US and Canada chose to confront establishment Jewish organization face-to-face for backing up during that time of war.

The Jewish left is on the rise in United States since 2016, with new initiatives such as Never Again Action questioning the US government's increasing use of migrant detention.

In the 2000s, diasporic Jewish left was molded by an Israeli-Palestinian conflict culminating in new organizations such as Jewish Voice for Peace, Independent Jewish Voices and International Jewish Anti-Zionist Network advocating for Palestinian causes. Recently, this support has seen even establishment organizations like Jewish Federation, American Israel Public Affairs Committee (AIPAC), and Anti-defamation League (ADL) being challenged by leftist Jewish organizations in the US and Canada for supporting Israeli actions after the 2014 Israel-Gaza conflict. #JewishResistance formed within US to counter institutional Jewish support for Trump and white nationalism. Last election 71% of American Jews in the US voted Democrat, and Democrats have won the Jewish vote by at least

76-80% in each election over the past decade. The young Jews are growing more critical towards Israeli government and feel sorry for the Palestinians.

Conclusion

Jewish leftism is a complicated and historically based phenomenon directly linked to their values, historical narratives, as well as commitment to the ideals of social justice. Although their participation in labor movements, civil rights campaign and social justice projects has indeed helped to forward progressive causes, it has also introduced complexities triggering intra-communal disputes within Jewish community struggling with anti-Semitism and political splits.

Understanding why Jews became involved in leftist causes, and also what this involvement meant for both the Jewish community and the wider social arena, is crucial to a full understanding of Jewish fortunes. The decisiveness of Jews to these causes served as a testament of a deep connection between their identity and the struggle for justice and equality in the world.

THE PARADOX OF JEWRY ANTI-ZIONISM: A SINGULAR PHENOMENON

Introduction

The Israeli-Palestine conflict is one of the enduring issues in international politics that have stirred emotions globally. However, within the Jewish community, a unique phenomenon can be observed: Jews, who openly criticize the current state of affairs in Israel.

Understanding Jewish Anti-Israel Sentiment:

It is evident that in order to understand the causes of Jewish anti-Israel attitude, acknowledgment should be given to various dimensions that constitute identity of Jews- as a religion and culture. Establishment of a modern country inevitably leads to different understanding of Jewish identity and allegiance to their land that holds central place in the Jewish history.

The Complex Relationship between Judaism and Nationalism

Among the characteristics of Judaism distinct from others is its association with nationalism. While Christian and Muslim faiths have remained separate from any specific national identity, Judaism has traditionally linked closely with the idea of a particular country. These links have led to intra-Jewish debates on whether Jewishness is compatible with the notion of a modern nation-state.

The Influence of Jewish Intellectual Traditions

Critical thought and open debate are important aspects of Judaism, with a tradition full of rich intellectual thought. This intellectual heritage manifests itself through the anti-Israel sentiment among Jewish people who discuss the ethical issues surrounding Israel's policies and its effects on the Palestinians. Scruton's intellectual style creates an atmosphere where one can examine these debates with respect and acknowledging the variety of Jewish thought.

The Impact of Global Politics and Social Movements

It is impossible to sever anti-Israel sentiment among Jews from the wider political world. The style prompts a scrutiny to these external influences that shape it. For instance, the proliferation of the social justice movements with an emphasis on human rights sees many Jews condemn Israeli policies. Furthermore, the impacts of postcolonial ideas and considering Israel as a colonial force have added more fuel in the fire of Jewish anti-Israel sentiments. This demands critical examination of these external factors although the intricacy of the Israeli-Palestinian dilemma cannot be ignored.

The Role of Jewish Identity and Diaspora

The Jewish diaspora also plays a significant role in shaping Jewish anti-Israel sentiment. An examination of how one's intellectual style can shape personal identity with a bearing upon their politics is invited by Scruton's approach. This is because Jewish individuals who live outside of Israel might not understand why the government will enact certain policy changes; as a result, they could hold different views on those policy changes.

Conclusion

Critical Jews are an enigmatic anomaly of any religion community and the subject of this study. However, scrutinizing this phenomenon becomes feasible through intellectual style that features intricate analysis as well as courteous communication. The relationship between Judaism and nationalism should be recognized in order to understand Jewishness. This implies considering Jewish intellectual legacy, world politics and social movements in general, and Jewish identity and diaspora as well.

Overview

In the crucible of the Second World War, the operational dynamics of concentration camps relied heavily on the collaboration of carefully chosen overseers known as Kapos. Tasked with supervising inmates, these Kapos executed the directives of Nazi camp authorities with a brutality sometimes mirroring that of their SS counterparts. Strikingly, a considerable number of these enforcers were of Jewish origin. In extreme circumstances, where survival instincts override ethical considerations, certain individuals, ironically, surpassed the cruelty of the very guards they served alongside. These actions, driven by the primal instinct for self-preservation, have been regarded by many historians as a form of complicity, betraying both faith and the bonds they might have cherished under ordinary circumstances.

While the era of concentration camps has passed, prejudice and hatred persist in our contemporary world. Despite constituting a mere 0.0025% of the global population, the Jewish community has made substantial contributions to society, spanning literature, law, and science. Their enduring legacy includes foundational ideas shaping common legal systems and the tenets of strict monotheism from which both Islam and Christianity trace their roots. Despite these accomplishments, Jews have historically borne the weight of scapegoating, enduring massacres, inquisitions, ghettoization, expulsions, accusations of blood guilt, and the Holocaust. Regrettably, in the 21st century, Judeophobia or anti-Semitism continues to cast its shadow.

Dr. Gustavo Perednik, in his comprehensive overview of Judeophobia, offers insightful conclusions derived from a twelve-lecture Internet course prepared for "The Jewish University in Cyberspace." These conclusions shed light on the enduring question of "why the Jews?" in the context of ethnic, racial, and religious persecution. Perednik's conclusions are as follows:

1. Judeophobia provides an outlet for sadistic instincts, allowing individuals to harass, humiliate, and even kill, with an established ideological framework to justify such brutality.

2. In targeting Jews, a widely recognized group, the Judeophobe gains a sense of importance that surpasses what they might experience when targeting a less renowned group.

3. Jews, as a collective, often evoke guilt feelings among non-Jews, possibly due to their role in establishing moral principles encapsulated in the Jewish Bible or the historical persecution they endured.

4. Judeophobia represents an inherently anti-rational stance within generally rational societies. Attacks are directed specifically at Jews, and any response from the Jewish community is labeled as "egocentric." This irrationality, notably expressed by seemingly rational individuals, lends further credibility to the prejudice.

5. The sources of Judeophobia are characterized by profound hypocrisy, with Jews facing persecution by entities proclaiming love, enlightenment, fraternity, and equality.

6. Judeophobia operates on two levels: direct and aggressive actions, as well as a more subtle level that condones and supports the former. The stance toward Judeophobes themselves becomes a significant measure of the overall Judeophobic stance.

In summary, Dr. Perednik's analysis underscores the enduring and perplexing nature of Judeophobia, revealing its irrational foundations, historical paradoxes, and the subtle yet pervasive ways in which it persists in the contemporary world.

Why Kapos?

In the crucible of persecution, where Jews have historically borne the burden of being scapegoats for societal ills, enduring massacres, Inquisition, ghettoization, expulsions, accusations of blood guilt, and the

Holocaust, a phenomenon emerges wherein some individuals internalize this external hostility, leading to a form of self-hatred. In any community, particularly one marked by brotherhood, there inevitably arises a type of person willing to commit selfish acts, forsaking their deeply held convictions for acceptance by the majority and personal gain. This archetype, epitomized by the historical figure of the Kapo and, in contemporary terms, referred to as a self-hating Jew, remains notably prevalent today, inflicting considerable harm upon the Jewish people and Israel.

This thesis posits that the burgeoning discourse surrounding Jewish self-hatred can be traced back to three interwoven developments. Firstly, it attributes the phenomenon to the sway of psychological experts over American public life. Secondly, it points to the impact of German Jewish émigré intellectuals, exemplified by figures like Kurt Lewin, who lent social scientific legitimacy to the concept of Jewish self-hatred. Lastly, it underscores the polemical use of the notion of Jewish self-hatred and the concept of "the authoritarian personality" within the context of the Jewish Cold War—an acrimonious public dispute involving advocates of Jewish particularism and nationalism pitted against proponents of liberal universalism. This contentious debate, enlisting key figures such as Ludwig Lewisohn, David Riesman, Philip Roth, Clement Greenberg, and Harold Rosenberg, revolved around pivotal questions concerning Jewish group allegiance, survival, and affiliation.

In the United States and the United Kingdom, the label "self-hating Jew" is wielded to accuse an individual of Jewish descent of concealing, harboring shame about, or failing to comprehend their religious heritage. It is employed against those perceived to actively work against what the accuser deems the interests of the Jewish people. Notably, this term finds resonance in situations where a Jew is considered to be at odds with the collective aspirations of their community.

Comparatively, the scarcity of Germans publicly denouncing the Holocaust or the atrocities of the Second World War, the paucity of Japanese openly disavowing Japanese wartime actions, and the limited instances of English individuals publicly repudiating the deeds of the British

148

Empire underscore the rarity of such disavowals. Similarly, within the Muslim community, public denunciations of terrorism are infrequent. However, a distinct pattern emerges among Jewish individuals, where vocal dissent against Israel and its actions is not uncommon, often without due consideration for the existential struggle Israel faces. Furthermore, there exists a notable contingent of Jewish individuals who publicly repudiate Judaism itself, along with fellow Jews and their respective organizations. This distinctive posture of self-critique within the Jewish community stands in contrast to the patterns observed in other historical contexts.

Examples

In the realm of self-disparagement, a unique strain finds its manifestation in Israel, where leftists harbor a notable disdain for their own nation— a phenomenon seldom mirrored in other countries. Similarly, within the Jewish community, a contingent of the Left exhibits a palpable aversion toward the Jewish state. Notably, Israeli academics in Western institutions often spearhead anti-Israel demonstrations and movements, exemplified by figures like Professors Norman Finkelstein and Noam Chomsky, who dedicate substantial portions of their lives to undermining the singular Jewish homeland, expressing profound antipathy toward Jewish institutions.

Contemporary instances abound, showcasing individuals who, despite Israel's resilience and accomplishments in sciences, research, and maintaining a balanced democracy amid persistent hostilities, actively contribute to a narrative disparaging the nation. This is further compounded by economic pressures, with Israel consistently allocating more per capita for its own defense than any other nation on earth. Noteworthy is the disheartening commentary from the French ambassador in England, who dismissively labeled Israel as a "shitty little country" despite being of Jewish descent.

A topic that has stirred both historians and anti-Semites alike revolve around the question of the "13th tribe," positing that many Zionists, particularly Ashkenazi Jews, are not the descendants of the original Jews.

Some prominent Jewish leaders have propagated this idea, suggesting a racial distinction between the original Jews, who bore physical and genetic similarities to Arabs, and the later Ashkenazi Jews from Asia. However, DNA tests challenging this notion indicate that Jewish communities across Europe, North Africa, and the Middle East share a common Middle Eastern ancestral population. Notably, the Y chromosome study underscores the persistence of a distinct genetic signature among Ashkenazi Jews, even after centuries of residence in Europe.

Jews for Justice for Palestinians (JJP), a British-based group, positions itself as a proponent of human and civil rights, along with economic and political freedom, for the Palestinian people. Its core objective is to challenge Israel's existing policies concerning the Palestinian territories, with a particular focus on the West Bank and Gaza Strip, aiming for a transformation in their political status. The majority of its members are British Jews, who lack understanding of the political and security concerns of Israel

On the American front, Jewish Voice for Peace (JVP), known as Kol Yehudi la-Shalom in Hebrew, stands as an anti-Zionist left-wing Jewish activist organization. Operating in the United States, it lends support to the Boycott, Divestment, and Sanctions campaign against Israel. They were participants of Anti-Israel demonstrations following the Hamas Attack on Oct 07, 2023.

In a distinct category, we find the contentious Neturei Karta, a fringe religious faction within Haredi Judaism. Established in Jerusalem in 1938 following a split from Agudat Yisrael, this group vehemently opposes Zionism. Advocating for the "peaceful dismantling" of the State of Israel, Neturei Karta contends that the re-establishment of Jewish sovereignty in the Land of Israel is strictly forbidden until the advent of the Messiah. However, they do not mind the protection of Israeli soldiers and some do live in Israel.

Turning to prominent figures within the Jewish community, Rabbi Michael Lerner, while expressing objections to Israel's occupation of the West Bank and supporting the Geneva Accords for an independent

Palestinian State, perpetuates a distinction between Jews in Israel and those in the United States, particularly emphasizing the prevalence of Sephardic Jews in the former. On the other hand, Noam Chomsky, known for his significant critiques of Israel, including recent assertions of the nation heading for destruction due to warmongering policies, adds another layer to the complex landscape of internal dissent within the Jewish community.

And to The Lesser Extent

In my personal observations, the demeanor of "Modern Jews" toward their orthodox counterparts has struck me quite noticeably. A distinctive contrast emerges when comparing the interaction between Christians and the Amish to that of Jews and their Hasidic brethren. It's perplexing that both the Amish and the Hasidic community share similar appearances and attire, yet the sentiments expressed by Jews toward their Hasidic kin carry a palpable degree of visible and audible aversion.

What adds to the enigma is the distinct lack of mutual assistance among Jews in professional settings. Unlike the cohesive support seen among the Amish or the commonly held perception of the "Secret brethren of Jews" by Gentiles, there exists a tendency among Jews to actively avoid their perceived brethren in the workplace. This avoidance seems to stem from a desire to portray themselves as fully integrated Americans, steering clear of any display to the contrary and, paradoxically, fostering a sense of alienation among their own community members.

Conclusion

Self-hating Jews is a sensitive topic that has generated a lot of heat among Jews, as well as many non-Jews. This is a description for those who are classified as non-Jews, although they self-identify as Jews; they have negative opinions about their heritage, faith, and even the state of Israel. Although different views must be recognized, an appropriate and sensitive attitude toward this problem should also be observed. The purpose of this paper is to delve into the issue of self-hating Jews and the risks posed by this phenomenon for Israel.

151

The reasons that lead to self-hatred among Jews include. Such actions and the privilege felt by some people may cause them to have feelings of self-loathing or shame. Some others may have their own personal issues like discriminating experiences or religious clashes which influence them into having unfavorable opinion. Other external factors such as media bias and peer pressure can have some influence too.

Self-hating Jews pose an existential danger for intra-Jewish peace and solidarity. Various opinions represent a healthy democracy; however, if such thoughts become radicalized to an extent where they seek to invalidate Israel's raison d'être, then this will only erode the collective identity of Israel and its political stance in the international arena.

The need to distinguish between genuine criticisms of Israel practices and self-hate cannot be overemphasized. In any society, constructive criticism is an indispensable element; it provides space for introspection, growth and advancement in a nation like Israel. Although self-hatred could lead to demonizing Israel or the Jewish people; such hatred could have negative effects because it could re-invent stereotypes, fuel antisemitism, and offer assistance to people who aim in delegitimatizing the state of Israel.

There are many examples as Rabbi Michael Lerner and Noam Chomsky. They do not realize the damage they are causing to their own people and perhaps to the future of their children. During the Second World War the Germans relied on the co-operation of the Kapos, and today the Anti-Semites feast on the brilliant work of their modern Kapos.

Introduction

In the world of political speech, it is commonly presumed that there is one voice of unity among the Jewish community in support for the State of Israel. This however negates the fact that the diverse views that run through the Jewish community toward Israel and her policies. It is important to shed light on this important issue through discussing different reasons and ideologies that cause anti-Israel Jews.

However, it is important to point out that opposing Israel from a Jewish perspective is fundamentally different from negating one's ethnic background as well as origin. Contrarily, there are many Jews who oppose Israel because of a strong loyalty towards their religious and cultural beliefs. Such people challenge the actions and policies of the Israeli government as being contrary to Jewish ethics which include fairness, sympathy, and respect for human rights. They argue that genuine support of Judaism is based on demand for justice and fairness towards Israel just like another state should be treated in this matter.

The other idea that rises in the Jewish community concerns the welfare of Palestinians. Jews that disagree with Israel usually underscore respect for Palestinian human dignity and rights. According to them, it is the policies of the Israeli government like the expansion of settlements in the occupied territories for which Palestinians continue to suffer and are subjected to discrimination. They support an equal and fair solution for both Israeli and Palestine nationals on grounds that dialogue and compromise is what will settle the dispute once and for all.

Firstly, not all the Jewish opponents for Israel are motivated by political or geo-political issues. Some claim that Israel's action has intensified regional tension and destabilized the situation. They argue that a more even-handed approach, based on mutual understanding, could better promote security in the region. Instead of the old fashioned one size fits all approach to foreign policy that relies purely on power and the military, they promote a dialogue based foreign policy strategy.

However, it should be noted that these views lack homogeneity at large, with Israel being a very diverse topic in the Jewish society. The opposition is partly based on a long-rooted sense of disappointment and anger against the injustices perpetrated by the Israeli establishment among some Jews opposing Israel. For example, some may oppose on account of having individual experiences or lineages. However, irrespective of any particular motivation, there should be a civilized conversation which creates an opportunity for greater understanding of different perspectives as well as cultivates a broader discourse.

Historical Context

In 1948 Israel became an independent country and this was a major event in the history of Jews but at the same time Jews had different opinions. Even as Zionism, the political movement, which gave support to Israel gained broad support there were a number of Jewish voices within and outside this Zionist movement. Diaspora Jewish communities conducted diverse negotiations, with some apprehensive of the effect on their minority status. Palestinian-Israeli conflict has also remained a contentious issue, in which Jewish dissenters take different positions. These include some Jewish people and organizations who concentrate on human rights abuses, demanding for justice and fairness to all.

Forms of Dissent

The Jewish dissenters oppose Israel in public, through boycott, divestment and sanctions (BDS), as well as advocacy, & teaching. These often go to the streets, take part in protests and demonstrations expressing their opinions in public. The BDS movement is supported by Jewish organizations such as Jewish Voice for Peace, which seeks to pressurize Israel into changing its policy in the West Bank and Gaza.

The diverse opinions of Jews who oppose Israel led to an internal dialogue within the Jewish community on a number of issues. Intra-Community Debates Spur Internal Debates on the Complex Relationship Between Judaism, Jewish Identity, and Support for Israel. Views similar to those of Silberman and Peizer can introduce challenges and tensions into Jewish families and organizations—their perspectives mirror some of the larger complexities at stake in the current Israel-Palestine conflict.

Conversations with advocates of Israel may result in constructive dialogues and heated arguments, fostering understanding and mutual respect. A lot of challenges face the Jewish dissenters such as being accused of being self-hating Jews, political and social to mention a few.

Summary

In summary, the simplistic assertion of the unanimous solidarity of all Jews with Israel cannot be ignored in view of the existence of differing views among individual Jews. There are various reasons why Jewish opposed Israel, which can be religious, ethical, humanitarian and geopolitical considerations. It is imperative to carry out a constructive and considerate conversation with people who believe so, to understand the deeper aspect of the issues on Israel and the policies it pursues. Such dialogue will be the only way to shift to more accommodative and far-reaching solution in the sense of the Israeli-Palestinian conflict.

IRAN AND ITS TERRORIST PROXIES: UNPACKING A COMPLEX GEOPOLITICAL DYNAMIC

Introduction

Iran's engagement in terrorism through multiple proxies has come under heavy criticism worldwide. It goes without saying that such a country as Iran which has its multi-millennial history plays an important geopolitical role in the modern Middle East. The purpose of this article is to discuss how Iran supports terrorist proxies and examine why it does so; who these proxies include; as well as evaluate the impact of these activities on regional security.

Historical Context

It is important to consider the historical perspective in order to comprehend Iran's relationship with terrorists. Iran moved from being a monarchy ruled by the Shah after the 1979 Islamic Revolution that brought Ayatollah Khomeini into power. The change also saw a shift in Iran's objective of foreign policy and local governance systems. The country wanted to export its revolutionary ideas and counter the regional regimes that were considered to be supported by the western countries in general.

Motivations for Proxy Support

There are many reasons that Iran has the means and motives to utilize terrorism as foreign policy. Primarily, it is used for power projection as well as expansion of its sway in the area. Iran supports proxies in neighboring states like for instance, Hezbollah in Lebanon or the Houthis in Yemen in order for it to have an allied network that pushes its goals forward and thwarts their opponents.

Another reason is that Iran supports terrorist proxies and this is due to it counterbalancing regional rivals, mainly Saudi Arabia. Geopolitical, sectarian-theological, and ideological causes explain the enmity between Iran and Saudi Arabia. In order to challenge the Saudi Arabian influence,

Iran utilizes supporting proxies in conflicts like the Syrian Civil War and current Yemen conflict that will allow it to establish its supremacy over other countries presently existing within its borders or close proximity.

Key Proxies and Their Objectives

The support for various proxies by Iran is visible through its patronage of prominent ones among them. One of the world's best-known proxies, which comes from Lebanon, namely, Hezbollah. The primary goal of Hezbollah is to protect the interest of Iran in Lebanon and also counter Israeli power in the area. Politically, Hezbollah is one of the most powerful forces in Lebanon with large military capacities and influence over many aspects of the state apparatus.

Yet another important proxy is the Houthis of Yemen. Iran backs the Houthi in an effort to undermine the Saudi-Arabia's sway over Saudi-Arab pen. Hence, Iran seeks to bolster itself in Yemen as it tries to force Saudi Arabia by employing proxy warfare.

Implications for Regional Stability

Moreover, Iran's involvement and terrorism proxy affects the regional stability. It aggravates the ongoing conflicts which protract the pain suffered by civilians and frustrate any future chances towards peace. For instance, Iran's role in propping up of proxies in Syria's civil war has made the conflict longer than it should be, thereby thwarting diplomatic moves toward a political settlement.

Again, since Iran finances terrorist proxies the secondly issue aggravates sectarian crisis in which mainly the Shias opposed Sunnis. This aggravates already existing fault lines in the region with a potential risk of further destabilization. For example, the proxy war between Iran and Saudi Arabia in Yemen and its escalation into a sectarian divide leading to a humanitarian catastrophe.

Besides that, its terrorism alliance with proxy terrorists is also working on the relations between Iran and western countries like US. Finally, diplomatic ties between U.S.A and Iran are strained due to the labeling of Iran as a state sponsor of terrorism and placing of economic sanctions by the United States against Iran. Such a dynamic could lead to more tension that may even culminate in direct military encounter.

Conclusion

Iran's bond with terrorist proxies is one of these complicating political dynamics that carry far-ranging impacts. Iran's support for proxies is a matter of rivalry against Saudi Arabia; it also manifests itself as a tool for acquiring dominance in the region and showcasing strength. While these divisions are extended, the conflicts have continued to be drawn for longer periods with aggravated sectarian tensions as well as worsened global relations. This is a convoluted issue that needs multi-dimensional solution like diplomacy, regional integration and address of the root causes of such proxy wars. Such efforts are the only ways in which the region can become stable and peaceful.

Introduction

The Israeli-Palestinian conflict is one of the world's most enduring and contentious disputes. The pursuit of a lasting peace agreement between the two parties has been fraught with challenges, leading many to question the motivations and barriers to peace from both the Israeli and Palestinian sides. This essay examines the complex factors influencing the Palestinian perspective on peace with Israel, acknowledging that the situation is multifaceted and cannot be attributed to a single cause. While some Palestinians are indeed committed to peace, a range of historical, political, and social factors have contributed to the perception that peace remains elusive. It is essential to explore these factors to understand the dynamics of the conflict better.

Historical Perspective

A. Displacement and Refugees

The historical backdrop of the conflict is deeply ingrained in the Palestinian collective memory, with the Nakba (catastrophe) of 1948 being a pivotal event.

1. **Displacement:** The forced displacement of hundreds of thousands of Palestinians during the creation of Israel in 1948 continues to shape the Palestinian narrative and fuels the demand for the right of return.

2. **Refugee Issue:** The presence of millions of Palestinian refugees and their descendants in the Palestinian territories and neighboring countries has made the refugee issue a central component of the conflict.

3. **Nazi Influence:** The influence of Nazi Germany in the Palestin-
    ian cause can be described as one complicated and sensitive matter.
    Although there was no open support for the Nazis by the Pales-
    tinian leadership, there occurred some cases of collaboration with
    them as well as sympathies. Haj Amin al-Husseini was the Grand
    Mufti of Jerusalem and developed good relations with Nazi Ger-
    mans. In 1941, he had a meeting with Adolf Hitler and solicited
    help for the Palestinians. However, Al-Husseini was also working
    in unison with the Nazis in terms of providing them with Muslim
    soldiers for the SS and in propagating anti-Semitism.

B. Failed Peace Initiatives

A series of unsuccessful peace initiatives have left many Palestinians
disillusioned and skeptical about the prospects for a negotiated settlement.

1. **Oslo Accords:** The failure of the Oslo Accords, marked by ongo-
    ing Israeli settlements and a lack of progress on core issues, has
    eroded Palestinian trust in the peace process.

2. **Distrust of Mediation:** Mediation by international actors like the United States has not led to substantial progress, contributing to the belief that the process is biased.

Political Factors

A. Leadership Divisions

The division between the Palestinian Authority (Fatah) and Hamas has created political fractures and an inability to present a unified stance on peace negotiations.

1. **Political Rivalry:** The ongoing power struggle between Fatah, which governs the West Bank, and Hamas, which controls Gaza, hampers a cohesive approach to negotiations.

2. **Legitimacy Questions:** The lack of unity raises questions about the legitimacy of any agreement reached by one faction without the consent of the other.

B. Lack of a Viable Palestinian State

Many Palestinians believe that the reality on the ground, including Israeli settlements and control over territory, makes the establishment of a viable Palestinian state increasingly improbable.

1. **Settlement Expansion:** The continuous expansion of Israeli settlements in the West Bank and East Jerusalem has reduced the territorial contiguity of a future Palestinian state.

2. **Control and Restrictions:** Israeli control over borders, resources, and movement within the Palestinian territories has led to a perception of continued occupation.

Islam - religion and identity for Palestinians

Islam is more than just a religion for Palestinians; it is an indispensable component of their identity and culture. Although the Palestinian cause has majorly political aspect, it cannot undermine the role of religion especially that of Islam. It defines Palestinians' struggle for self-rule and their relationship with the land and their sacred sites. It is important for one to observe or understand the religious dimension of Palestinian cause, because it will reveal the depth of their aspiration and the meaning of their struggle.

Security and Violence

A. Impact of Conflict and Violence

Decades of conflict, violence, and security concerns have created an atmosphere of fear and mistrust.

1. **Casualties and Trauma:** Both Israelis and Palestinians have suffered casualties and trauma, leading to deep-seated grievances and a reluctance to engage in dialogue.

2. **Security Measures:** Stringent security measures, including checkpoints and border restrictions, contribute to feelings of oppression among Palestinians.

B. Extremist Elements

The presence of extremist groups within Palestinian society, such as Islamic Jihad and other militant factions, complicates the pursuit of peace.

1. **Militant Influence:** Extremist groups with a vested interest in perpetuating the conflict can undermine efforts toward a peaceful resolution.

2. **Threats to Moderates:** Moderates within Palestinian society may face threats and intimidation from extremist elements, making it difficult to advocate for peace.

Socio-Economic Challenges

A. Economic Disparities

Economic disparities between Israelis and Palestinians, including issues related to employment, poverty, and access to resources, exacerbate grievances and hamper prospects for peace.

1. **Unemployment:** High levels of unemployment in the Palestinian territories, exacerbated by Israeli restrictions, contribute to dissatisfaction and resentment.

2. **Economic Dependence:** The economic dependency of the Palestinian territories on Israel raises concerns about sovereignty and self-determination.

B. Humanitarian Conditions

The humanitarian situation in Gaza and parts of the West Bank has deteriorated, affecting the quality of life and contributing to frustration.

1. **Gaza Blockade:** The Israeli blockade on Gaza, along with internal Palestinian political divisions, has led to severe humanitarian conditions.

2. **Public Health Crisis:** The lack of access to clean water, electricity, and healthcare adds to the suffering of the Palestinian population.

International Dynamics

A. Geopolitical Considerations

The Israeli-Palestinian conflict is influenced by broader geopolitical dynamics, including regional tensions and the priorities of global powers.

1. **Regional Alliances:** The alignment of regional actors, such as Saudi Arabia and Iran, can impact the strategies and positions of Palestinian leaders.

2. **Global Superpowers:** The involvement of global powers, like the United States, in the conflict can introduce competing interests and priorities.

B. International Law and Resolutions

The application and enforcement of international law and United Nations resolutions in the Israeli-Palestinian context remains a contentious issue.

1. **Legal Framework:** Palestinians argue that the application of international law, including UN resolutions, is not effectively enforced, leading to continued Israeli actions seen as violations of Palestinian rights.

2. **Diplomatic Efforts:** Diplomatic efforts at the international level have yielded limited results, contributing to a sense of international indifference.

The Role of Public Opinion

The perceptions and sentiments of the Palestinian public play a crucial role in shaping the outlook on peace.

1. **Public Skepticism:** Many Palestinians view past negotiations and peace efforts with skepticism, given the lack of tangible improvements in their lives.

2. **Youth Perspective:** A younger generation of Palestinians, who have grown up amid conflict, may be more inclined to advocate for alternative approaches, including resistance.

Conclusion

The Palestinian perspective on peace with Israel is influenced by a complex web of historical, political, social, and economic factors. While it is essential to acknowledge that there are Palestinians who genuinely desire peace and coexistence with Israel, these challenges and grievances have contributed to the perception that peace remains elusive. Understanding these factors is crucial for any meaningful progress in resolving the Israeli-Palestinian conflict. Achieving a comprehensive and lasting peace will require addressing these core issues while considering the needs and aspirations of both Israelis and Palestinians

Overview

After the 1948 Arab-Israeli War and the 1967 Six-Day War, this created more complexities in terms of territory and politics thus resulting to Israeli occupation of West Bank, East Jerusalem and Gaza. Israeli-Palestinian peace is linked to regional dynamics that include Arab-Israeli Conflict and Iran's influence.

Israel, Palestinian Authority, Hamas, Muslim states and international mediation are key Innovations. Israel will always value its security, especially based on the historical context of conflict and close proximity to enemy forces. Growing Israeli settlements in the West Bank and East Jerusalem also cast doubts on the possibility of two-state resolution. Palestinian Authority seeks a sovereign Palestinian state, divided in twin by external pressures.

The division of Palestinians into West Bank and Gaza, and the Palestinian Authority's rivalry with Hamas make unified Palestinian leadership a challenge to realize. State of Palestine: Peace process and relations with Israel also suffers the peace with Israel because Hamas has political and military ambitions. The Palestinians and the international community are most concerned about the Gaza blockade and humanitarian crisis.

United States and United Nations as international mediators have tried to achieve balance on the interest side but it has brought about mixed outcomes with regards to lasting peace. The challenge has been on the implementation.

Some of the ongoing challenges include; settlements and territorial disputes, security concerns, militant factors and the humanitarian crisis in Gaza. The political divisions between the Palestinian factions persist to undermine chances for unified negotiations, with the Fatah-Hamas rift complicating efforts towards a united Palestinian front. Certainly, elections in Palestinian territories compound political tensions which in turn disturbs negotiation.

In the prospects of peace, public opinion matters much and younger generations from both sides have different visions of the future and attitudes. Trust and dialogue-building, however, need to be built by the grassroots movements and civil society organizations.

Historical Background

Israel-Palestinian conflict started with the formation of Israeli state in 1948. This resulted in resentment and hatred between Arabs and jews due to this uprooting of Palestinian population and construction of Jewish landmark. This has led to many wars, acts of terrorism and currently a lot of tension over the years.

Issues

Land is one of the major hindrances for peace that has been causing conflicts between the two countries. It is very hard to achieve a common ground. The problem is that both the Israeli and Palestinian people consider the land their own property. The creation of Israeli settlements in the West Bank and East Jerusalem further complicates the issue by making it difficult for Palestinians to establish a viable Palestinian state.

The other issue posed in relation to peace concerns the place of Jerusalem. Jerusalem is considered a capital of both Israelis and Palestinians which has become an issue in discussions between them. In 2017, when Trump recognized Jerusalem as the capital of Israel was a major event that brought additional protestations and condemnation from the Palestinian side.

Another problematic aspect of peace is the refugee question. As a result, there has been an explosive growth of the population of the refugees and currently millions of these refugees are staying in refugee camps in the West Bank, in the Gaza Strip as well as in surrounding countries. Though it has remained one of the main demands for Palestinians during

166

negotiations, the right of return for Palestinian refugees is an issue that many Israeli citizens find problematic as they are concerned that accepting such returnees might undermine the existing Jewish population majority in Israel.

While the Israeli-Palestinian conflict might be the most prominent reason, there are also other reasons as regards Israel's relationships with Muslim countries within the region. Traditionally, several Islamic governments have failed to acknowledge the existence of Israel. The major justification is the way the Palestinians are treated. Nevertheless, in the last few years things have generally improved in this respect.

The first Arab country to sign a peace treaty with Israel was Egypt in 1979 and then Jordan joined the list in 1994. These have served as a basis for diplomacy between Israel and all of its Arab neighbors. Most Muslim states also do not maintain diplomatic relations with Israel, and it is not only mistrust but also hatred, which need to be overcome.

However, the case for a peaceful coexistence of Israel and the Palestinians, as well as Muslim states, is not completely out of question. The different peace initiatives include Oslo Accords of the nineteen nineties among them. Such negotiations culminated in creation of the Palestinian Authority that allowed a moderate degree of self-governing functions in areas of the West Bank alongside the Gaza strip. Nevertheless, the Oslo process proved unable to bring definitive closure to this issue in question.

Certainly, during the last decades, progress was achieved here and there. In 2020 under the Abraham accords, diplomacy was normalized for Israel with Emirati of UAE, Bahrain, Saudi Arabia, Sudan, and Morocco. The signing of these agreements was viewed as a major milestone in the process of peaceful coexistence among the states of this region. Yet, such agreements do not tackle the main problems of Israeli-Palestinian dispute, and there is much to do until complete peace will be achieved.

As such, the prospect for peace is contingent upon the leadership from either side. The prime minister of Israel, Mr. Benjamin Netanyahu (served 2009 to 2021), was very tough on the Palestinians and concentrated on developing the Jewish colonies in the Western bank. The Palestinians and also the international community viewed these policies as being among the greatest hindrances to peace. Nevertheless, following the new political direction in Israel one could expect more reasonable and practical position about the peace process.

There should be unity and strong leadership among the Palestinians too. The Palestinian Authority under the leadership of President Mahmood has been disintegrated because it could not find a home among the people they were governing. The current separation of the Palestinian Authority in the west bank from Hamas in Gaza has only exacerbated this situation, making it virtually impossible for anyone to speak on behalf of all Palestinians in negotiations with Israelis.

Historical Efforts

Mostly, different peace agreements have been negotiated between the Israelis and Palestinians.

1. Oslo Accords: The Oslo Accords of the 1990s gave some autonomy to Palestine but did not achieve any final solution.

2. The Abraham Accords: However significant plans do soften progress though outside the Israel-Palestine framework in recent agreements between Israel and Arab states.

International Mediation Including peace negotiations that were mediated by international actors such as USA and UN.

1. U.S. Role: Historically, the United States has been a leading mediator, with efforts characterized by mixed success in reconciling interests and ensuring that peaceful coexistence is achieved.

2. United Nations: Resolutions have been passed in support of Palestinian statehood by international bodies including the UN but implementation has remained an issue.

Iran's efforts to undermine the progress of the Abraham of Abraham Accords

Invariably, Iran, the regional spoilsport has been striving to scuttle the peace wheels of Abraham Accords meant for normalizing Israel's relations with some Arab countries. Using covert strategy, Iran sees this as an opportunity to undermine the Accords through proxies that it influences in different parts of Middle East. This move, fits into the bigger Iranian geopolitical script to undermine emerging alliances that encroach upon Iran's dominance.

Iran disrupts through backing militant proxies such as Hezbollah, inciting regional conflicts and increasing sectarian feuds. Iran seeks to undermine the possibility for peaceful cohabitation by fueling instability as this will make it difficult for the countries involved in Abraham Accords. In addition, Tehran plays the game by anti-Israel rules using the betrayal of Palestinian right narrative to prepare support for those who stand against normalization.

Conclusion

The prospects of peace in Israel's relations with the Palestinian Muslims states is a delicate issue. This conflict has significant history, and several hurdles must be passed through. Recently, however, things have started looking up, most notably with regard to the Abraham Accords that are beginning to bring about fresh prospects for the region's cooperation. However, Iran's cunning and aggressive strategies, labeling it as a regional antagonist, have the potential to significantly impede the advancement of the Abraham Accords. There is still a chance of finding peace in this conflict through good leadership, political will, and assistance from international community.

THE FORGOTTEN EXODUS: EXPULSION OF JEWS FROM ARAB COUNTRIES

Introduction

Undoubtedly, it is the relevant historical episode refers to the expulsion of Jews from Arab countries during 1940s-50s based on which one can draw a parallel on how convoluted the situation in this part of world was throughout mid-twentieth century; characteristics and confusion similar to those observed in WWI. In the midst of a lot of attention that has been given to the Palestinian refugee crises as a result of creating their state in 1948, there is an aspect on this region's history during those times mostly not touched upon—the parallel expulsion or even more than hundreds of thousands of Jews from Arab countries.

Background

When the World War II was over, it gave birth to numerous geopolitical transformations and establishment of the State of Israel in 1948 became one of them. Tensions grew between Arab countries and the newly founded Jewish state, causing a major exodus of Jews across the Arab world. The expulsion of Jewish communities from nations like Iraq, Egypt, Yemen and Libya was a significant demographic and cultural shift.

Causes of the Forgotten Exodus

The expulsion of Jews from Arab countries was however influenced by several factors. Arab nationalism together with the Arab-Israeli conflict led to hate towards Jewish. Jews were declared culprits to violence, hence persecution and never-ending challenges. Further, the formation of Israel increased enmity against Jews in Arab countries who were viewed as enemies or conspirators.

Case Studies

Looking more into particular cases, it becomes evident that the experiences of Jewish communities in various Arab countries were different. For instance, in Iraq, Jews encountered more hostility and discrimination by the time of Farhud pogrom of 1941 that preceded later towing. It is the same case in Egypt where in 1956 after nationalizing their industries; Suez Canal Egyptian Jews were chased away thereby breaking ties with them from being part and puzzle of this country for many years.

Consequences and Displacement

The Forgotten Exodus is the event that caused hundreds of thousands of Jews to be displaced from their domestic business and cultural heritage. Their (Jewish) communities were abruptly uprooted, and a rich tapestry of Jewish life in Arab lands where Jews had lived for centuries—they not only suffered prohibitions under Islam—suffering subservity and humiliation—but contributed to the region's cultural diversity.

International Response

In this slam book, expelled Jewish communities received little notice from the international community concentrating on broader Middle East conflict. The focus on Palestinian refugees thwarts symmetrical suffering of Jewish refugees from Arab countries and hence the Forgotten Exodus.

Legacy and Reflection

The Forgotten Exodus is a lasting reminder of the continuing difficulties in the Middle East. Recognizing and comprehending this historical episode is pivotal to developing a complete understanding of the multifaceted past of the region, as well as appreciating how each side has been displaced in history over the Arab-Israeli conflict.

Conclusion

The Forgotten Exodus, therefore, emerges as a tragic tale to be included in the Middle-Eastern history and subject of research. Exploring the Reasons, Experiences and Implications of Arab Jews' Expulsion from Arab Countries Enables a More Sensitive Approach to Understanding the History of this Complicated Area. Remembering this neglected story is important to promote empathy, open dialogue and bring a broader perspective on the complex Middle East history.

Introduction

In the grand symphony of history, there exist two parallel narratives that resonate through the corridors of time. These narratives, although seemingly distinct, are intricately intertwined in the annals of the Middle East. The first pertains to the expulsion of Jews from Arab countries, while the second tells the story of the Palestinian Nakba. In the spirit of this writer, we embark on a journey of intellectual exploration, dissecting these narratives, their historical context, and the impact they've had on the complex tapestry of the Middle East.

A Prelude to the Exodus

To grasp the full scope of these parallel narratives, we must venture back in time to a region steeped in history. In the heart of the Middle East, Jewish communities flourished in Arab lands, their roots dating back centuries. These diverse communities, comprising an amalgamation of traditions and customs, coexisted harmoniously with their Arab neighbors. It was a mosaic of cultures, and for the most part, a testament to the age-old practice of harmonious coexistence.

Yet, the turning point came with the rise of political Zionism in the late 19th and early 20th centuries. This ideological movement, driven by the desire to establish a Jewish homeland in Palestine, injected a sense of purpose into the Jewish communities in Arab countries.

The Stirring of the Waters

The stage for our parallel narratives was set with the United Nations Partition Plan of 1947. The plan, a pivotal moment in the Israeli-Arab conflict, aimed to partition Palestine into separate Jewish and Arab states. Although it held promise, it also kindled resentment.

Jews living in Arab countries found themselves caught in a maelstrom of political tension. The partition plan brought about a surge in anti-Jewish sentiment, much like a tempest brewing in the distance. Economic discrimination and violence against Jewish communities escalated. As tensions mounted, the 1948 Arab-Israeli War erupted, unleashing a storm of change.

Exodus of Two Peoples

As the storm clouds gathered, the fate of two peoples, Jews in Arab countries and Palestinians in their ancestral homeland, hung in the balance. The tempest of the 1948 war led to the displacement of both Jewish and Palestinian communities.

For Arab Jews, the upheaval was swift and unforeseen. Their homes were taken from them, often with little warning. Precious property and assets were confiscated, and a life they had known for generations slipped through their fingers like desert sand.

Simultaneously, the Palestinian Nakba unfolded. Hundreds of thousands of Palestinians, deeply rooted in their ancestral lands, were torn from their homes. Their loss, much like a chasm in the desert, was immense.

Shared Struggles, Parallel Paths

The shared experiences of loss and displacement left deep scars on both Jews and Palestinians. Their homes, heritage, and possessions, the very essence of their existence, were ripped away. The trauma, akin to a relentless desert wind, continues to reverberate, etching its mark on the collective memory of both communities.

Their resettlement, too, mirrored each other's struggles. Arab Jews found refuge in Israel, a homeland still in its infancy, while Palestinians dispersed across the Middle East, many living in the shadow of dreams of return.

The Ripples of Change

The influx of Jewish refugees from Arab countries was akin to a rock thrown into a still pond. It transformed the demographic landscape of Israel. The challenges were immense, from housing and employment to the very integration of the newcomers.

Over time, Jewish refugees adapted to their new homeland, contributing substantially to Israel's economic growth. The ripples of their arrival had a profound effect on the nation's development.

Diaspora Communities and the Search for Identity

For both Jewish and Palestinian diaspora communities, the narrative didn't end with their displacement. Carrying the weight of their homelands, they embarked on a journey to preserve their cultural heritage and traditions.

The second and third generations grappled with questions of identity, much like explorers seeking an oasis in the desert. The quest for roots, the longing for belonging, and the pursuit of understanding became defining aspects of their journey.

Remembrance and Reconciliation

In the grand scheme of history, the expulsion of Jews from Arab countries and the Palestinian Nakba are not isolated tales. They are threads intricately woven into the complex fabric of the Israeli-Arab conflict. These parallel narratives, sharing profound experiences of loss and displacement, now stand acknowledged as significant historical events.

Commemoration efforts, much like intellectual oases in the desert, have emerged. Academic and educational programs aim to document and remember these events, ensuring that their memory endures.

In the spirit of reconciliation, initiatives fostering dialogue, interfaith understanding, and cultural exchange, are the bridge between historical divides, much like caravans crossing the desert.

Conclusion: Echoes in the Sands

We arrive at the conclusion of our exploration. The parallel narratives of the expulsion of Jews from Arab countries and the Palestinian Nakba, far from being unrelated tales, are intertwined threads in the grand tapestry of the Middle East.

In understanding the shared experiences of loss and displacement, we find a common thread, much like echoes in the vast desert. As we move forward, let us remember that these narratives are not divergent paths, but interwoven roads in the journey towards reconciliation and peace. The complexities of history, like the intricate patterns etched in the desert sand, may one day yield to a brighter future for all.

Introduction

We now embark on a journey to explore two parallel narratives etched deeply into the history of the Middle East. The first is the expulsion of Jews from Arab countries, followed by their absorption into the emerging state of Israel. The second narrative tells the heart-wrenching story of the Palestinian Nakba, where refugees have been held in a state of limbo for decades, with no Arab nation willing to grant them permanent sanctuary.

The Seeds of Displacement

Our journey through history commences in the heart of ancient Mesopotamia, where Jewish communities thrived alongside their Arab neighbors for centuries. These diverse communities were the living embodiment of coexistence, woven together by a tapestry of traditions and customs.

Now, imagine a time when the fervor of political Zionism began to sweep across the Jewish world, much like a desert wind. The movement sought to establish a Jewish homeland in Palestine, a vision that would significantly alter the fates of Jewish communities residing in Arab countries.

The Storm of Change

The stage for our parallel narratives was set with the United Nations Partition Plan of 1947. This plan, designed to carve out separate Jewish and Arab states in Palestine, held both the promise of hope and the seeds of discord.

Jewish communities living in Arab countries suddenly found themselves ensnared in the ever-intensifying web of political tension. The partition plan stirred a wave of anti-Jewish sentiment, much like an impending desert storm. Economic discrimination and violence began to punctuate the lives of these Jewish communities, their circumstances growing increasingly precarious. The tumultuous tempest that followed was the 1948 Arab-Israeli War.

The Exodus Unfolds

As the tempest of the 1948 war unleashed its fury, the fate of two peoples hung in the balance. Jewish communities in Arab countries and Palestinian families in their ancestral homeland became pawns in a geopolitical struggle.

Arab Jews were swiftly uprooted, often with scant warning. The homes they had known for generations were wrested from them. Property and assets, their cherished treasures, were confiscated as if by desert sands, leaving them in a state of utter despair.

Simultaneously, the Palestinian Nakba unfolded. Hundreds of thousands of Palestinians, deeply rooted in their ancestral lands, were displaced from their homes, their loss resembling a vast chasm in the desert landscape.

Shared Struggles, Divergent Paths

The shared experiences of loss and displacement left profound scars on both Jews and Palestinians. Their homes, heritage, and possessions, the essence of their very existence, were torn from them. The trauma, much like the relentless desert winds, lingers in the collective memory of both communities.

Resettlement brought its own set of challenges, with Arab Jews finding refuge in the nascent state of Israel and Palestinians dispersed across the Middle East, many living under the shadow of dreams of return.

A Demographic Transformation

The arrival of Jewish refugees from Arab countries in Israel reshaped the demographic landscape. Their presence, like a desert oasis, brought diversity and vitality. However, the challenges that accompanied this influx were formidable, from housing and employment to the very integration of these newcomers.

Over time, Jewish refugees not only adapted to their new homeland but also contributed substantially to Israel's economic growth. The ripples they created, like a life-giving oasis in the desert, had a profound and lasting impact.

Diaspora Communities and the Quest for Identity

For Jewish and Palestinian diaspora communities, the narrative did not conclude with their displacement. Carrying the weight of their homelands, they embarked on a journey to preserve their cultural heritage and traditions.

The second and third generations of these communities embarked on a quest for identity, much like nomads searching for an oasis in the vast desert. They grappled with questions of roots, belonging, and understanding.

The Echoes of Displacement

In the grand tapestry of history, the expulsion of Jews from Arab countries and the Palestinian Nakba are not isolated tales; they are interconnected threads in the rich fabric of the Middle East.

In recent times, these parallel narratives have gained recognition as significant historical events. Commemorative efforts, like intellectual oases in the desert, have emerged. Academic and educational programs aim to document and remember these events, ensuring that their memory endures.

In the spirit of reconciliation, initiatives fostering dialogue, interfaith understanding, and cultural exchange are the bridge between historical divides, like the trading caravans of old.

Conclusion: The Desert of Neglect

We conclude our exploration of these parallel narratives. The expulsion of Jews from Arab countries, their absorption into Israel, and the unending Palestinian Nakba constitute interconnected threads in the rich tapestry of Middle Eastern history.

The complexities and shared experiences of loss and displacement, like echoes in the vast desert, now resonate within these narratives. As we move forward, let us remember that these are not divergent paths, but interwoven roads in the journey towards reconciliation and peace. The desert of neglect can yet be transformed into an oasis of understanding and compassion, where the echoes of exile find solace.

Introduction

In the spirit of intellectual inquiry, we delve into the complex dynamics surrounding violence within some Muslim organizations. We will explore the factors contributing to violence, the varied motivations behind it, and the broader implications it has on both Muslim-majority countries and the global community.

Historical and Political Context

A. Colonialism and Its Legacy

The historical backdrop plays a significant role in understanding violence in Muslim organizations. The legacy of colonialism has left deep scars in many Muslim-majority countries. The arbitrary drawing of borders, economic exploitation, and political manipulation have sown the seeds of discontent, often fueling violence as a response to percceived injustices.

B. Geopolitical Factors

The involvement of powerful nations in the Muslim world has contributed to the perpetuation of violence. Whether through military interventions, support for autocratic regimes, or the pursuit of strategic interests, external factors have inflamed tensions and, in some cases, led to the radicalization of certain Muslim organizations.

Ideological Motivations

A. Religious Extremism

It is essential to recognize that the vast majority of Muslims do not support or condone violence. However, within certain Muslim organizations, a small minority subscribes to extremist interpretations of Islam. These individuals justify violence as a means to achieve religious or political goals.

B. Political and Social Marginalization

Many Muslim organizations that resort to violence often arise in regions where political and social marginalization is rampant. In such environments, some individuals may perceive violence as the only means to voice their grievances and fight for what they see as justice.

Socio-Economic Factors

A. Poverty and Lack of Opportunity

Socio-economic disparities often correlate with the prevalence of violence in Muslim-majority countries. Poverty, lack of access to education, and limited economic opportunities can push individuals toward extremist groups that promise a better future.

B. The Role of Unemployment

High levels of youth unemployment, in particular, have been identified as a contributing factor to violence within some Muslim organizations. Young people who lack job prospects may be more susceptible to recruitment by extremist groups offering them a sense of purpose and belonging.

Propaganda and Radicalization

A. Online Recruitment

The internet and social media have become powerful tools for the dissemination of extremist ideologies. Online recruitment and radicalization have played a significant role in the rise of violent Muslim organizations.

B. Propaganda Techniques

The persuasive tactics used by extremist organizations to recruit members cannot be underestimated. They often employ propaganda, drawing on religious texts and rhetoric to appeal to individuals searching for meaning or a sense of belonging.

Regional Conflicts

A. Conflicts in the Middle East

The Middle East, with its complex web of regional conflicts, has been a focal point for violence involving Muslim organizations. The ongoing conflicts in Syria, Yemen, and Iraq, among others, have created fertile ground for the emergence of extremist groups.

B. Sectarian Tensions

Sectarian divisions within Islam, particularly between Sunni and Shia Muslims, have fueled violence in some regions. Extremist groups exploit these tensions to further their own agendas.

The Global Impact of Violence

A. Terrorism and Global Security

The violence perpetrated by some Muslim organizations has global implications for security. Acts of terrorism, such as those carried out by Al-Qaeda or ISIS, have shaken the international community and necessitated collaborative counterterrorism efforts.

B. Refugee Crises

Conflict and violence in Muslim-majority countries have contributed to refugee crises, with millions of people forced to flee their homes. The global community faces the challenge of addressing the humanitarian needs of these displaced populations.

Counterterrorism and De-radicalization Efforts

A. Counterterrorism Strategies

Efforts to combat violence by Muslim organizations include intelligence sharing, military operations, and legal actions. International collaboration is often essential to track and neutralize threats.

B. De-radicalization Programs

Preventing and countering radicalization is equally crucial. Some countries have implemented de-radicalization programs aimed at rehabilitating individuals who have become involved with extremist organizations.

Conclusion

The question of why some Muslim organizations resort to violence is a complex and multifaceted issue. It is vital to distinguish between the actions of a small minority and the broader Muslim population. By examining the historical, political, ideological, socio-economic, and regional factors, we can gain a more nuanced understanding of the root causes of violence within certain Muslim organizations.

Addressing the issue of violence within these organizations requires a comprehensive and multi-dimensional approach, involving both the Muslim-majority countries affected and the international community.

THE IMPACT OF EMOTIONS AND A SENSE OF BELONGING ON NATIONAL PARTICIPATION AND DUTIES

Introduction

Emotions and a sense of belonging play a profound role in shaping individual attitudes toward national participation and fulfilling national duties. The complex interplay between personal feelings and one's connection to a larger collective, such as a nation, influences civic engagement, community involvement, and the fulfillment of responsibilities.

Emotional Connection and Civic Engagement

A strong emotional connection to one's nation often serves as a powerful motivator for civic engagement. Positive emotions, such as patriotism and pride, can inspire individuals to actively contribute to the well-being of their country. This can manifest in various forms, from participating in community service initiatives to actively engaging in political processes. Conversely, negative emotions, such as disillusionment or apathy, may hinder participation and create barriers to fulfilling national duties.

Sense of Belonging and Social Responsibility

A sense of belonging fosters a shared responsibility for the welfare of the nation. When individuals feel a deep connection to their fellow citizens and identify with a common national identity, they are more likely to recognize their role in contributing to the greater good. This sense of belonging can transcend individual interests, promoting cooperation and collaboration for the betterment of society. A cohesive and inclusive national identity, therefore, becomes a driving force behind the fulfillment of national duties.

National Duties as a Source of Fulfillment

Embracing a sense of duty toward one's nation can be inherently fulfilling. When individuals recognize their responsibilities as integral parts of a collective effort, they derive a sense of purpose and accomplishment. This positive emotional connection to fulfilling national duties reinforces a cycle of civic engagement, fostering a continuous loop of contribution and satisfaction.

Challenges and Barriers

However, challenges exist in cultivating a positive emotional connection and a sense of belonging for everyone. Societal divisions, economic disparities, and systemic injustices can create barriers that impede certain groups from fully participating in national affairs. Recognizing and addressing these challenges is essential to ensure that emotions and a sense of belonging are inclusive and accessible to all members of a society.

Education and Awareness

Education plays a pivotal role in shaping individuals' emotional connections to their nation and fostering a sense of belonging. By promoting an inclusive and accurate understanding of national history, values, and cultural diversity, education can contribute to a shared identity that transcends differences. This, in turn, enhances the likelihood of individuals actively participating in civic duties.

Emotions and a sense of belonging for Palestinians in Israel and other Western Minorities

Emotions and a sense of belonging in national participation and duties, especially for Palestinians in Israel and other Western Minorities. Emotions among Palestinians are usually compounded by historical and cultural links, which influence how they participate in national affairs. Their struggle for recognition and identity has an influence on their sense of belonging and subsequently, the desire to perform the national duties. Similarly,

Western countries' minorities can feel included or excluded in the society, thereby affecting their willingness to participate in civic activities. Creating such an inclusive environment where all the diverse communities will feel they are indeed part of the nation and are participating in its destiny, can only be achieved by acknowledging these feelings.

Conclusion

In conclusion, the effect of feelings and a sense of belonging on national participation and duties is a dynamic and influential aspect of civic life. Positive emotions and a deep connection to one's nation can serve as catalysts for active engagement, while a shared sense of belonging fosters a collective responsibility for the common good. Recognizing the reciprocal relationship between emotions, a sense of belonging, and national participation is crucial for cultivating a society where individuals willingly contribute to the well-being of their nation, creating a more cohesive and harmonious civic landscape.

187

Overview

Arab nations gained independence from colonists during turbulent times and twentieth century witnessed major political changes in the world. Nevertheless, the emergence of Israel in 1948 proved to be an exceptionally peculiar case which contrasted with the stories of Arab countries acquiring the right for independence.

Arab countries like Egypt, Iraq, Syria and Lebanon came out of their colonization era in the 20th century looking for a nationhood with self-rule. It should be noted that the latter nations emerged through separate historical paths and fought for their independence against imperial hegemony.

On the other hand, establishment of Israel was viewed by many Arab countries as a landgrab in Palestine. Thus, the juxtaposing of Israel establishment with the Arab countries fighting for their independence created that story inconsistency. The struggle for independence among Arab nations came in conjunction with the Palestinian plight and as such the Arab-Israeli conflict came to be a hotspot topic.

Contrary viewpoints about the independence of Israel is driven by opposing territorial claims about a singular territory. The creation of Israel for the majority of Arabs meant that they had lost their independence while at the same time were forced to be uprooted from their land, hence displaced and dispossessed of their possessions. Such a perception helped engender profound Arab resentment and Arab perception of Israel as a disputed entity.

Additionally, when the Arab countries got the impression that they were facing an outside power as their opponent —whether UK or more so USA —who came at the headline with Israel, it further fueled this feeling of injustice by the Arabs for them. For instance, the way some Arab countries viewed Israel's independence is unique as it emerged out of the complex interconnection of historical grievances, territorial disputes, and external influences.

Essentially, the Arab countries attained independence in the twentieth century as an issue related to "anti-colonial struggle" and "national liberation" while Israel was linked with the Palestinian story, leading to a special and problematical view of this issue, which still affects the Middle East geopolitics, **ignoring the fact that equal number of Jewish refugees migrated from Arab lands.** For better comprehension of the complications associated with the Arab-Israeli struggle, it is important to understand these historical aspects.

List of Arab Countries who gained Independence

1. Iraq: Iraq gained independence from British colonial rule in 1932.

2. Lebanon: Lebanon also achieved independence from French colonial rule in 1943.

3. Syria: Syria became independent from French colonial rule in 1946.

4. Jordan: The Hashemite Kingdom of Jordan, known as Transjordan at the time, gained independence from British administration in 1946.

5. Egypt: Egypt achieved independence from British occupation in 1952.

6. Libya: Libya gained independence from Italian colonial rule in 1951.

7. Sudan: Sudan achieved independence from joint British and Egyptian rule in 1956.

8. Morocco: Morocco became independent from French and Spanish colonial rule in 1956.

9. Tunisia: Tunisia also gained independence from French colonial rule in 1956.

10. Algeria: Algeria achieved independence from French colonial rule after a protracted war of independence, officially recognized in 1962.

11. Kuwait: Kuwait gained independence from British protection in 1961.

12. Yemen: North Yemen (the Yemen Arab Republic) and South Yemen (People's Democratic Republic of Yemen) both achieved independence in the 1960s. They later unified to form the Republic of Yemen in 1990.

13. United Arab Emirates: The United Arab Emirates, a federation of emirates, gained independence from British protection in 1971.

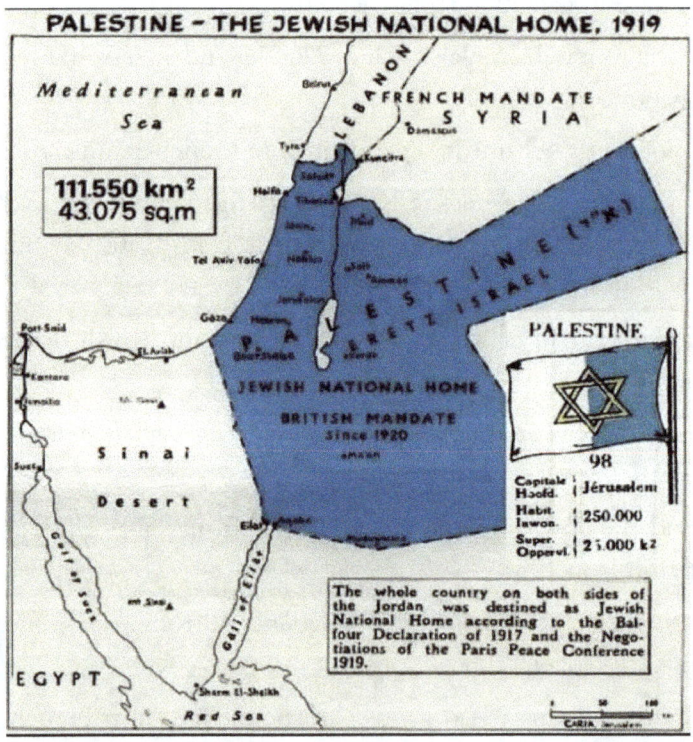

These are just some of the Arab countries that attained independence in the 20th century. The process of decolonization and independence varied in each nation and was often influenced by colonial powers, regional dynamics, and internal struggles.

In 1917, the British Balfour Declaration pledged to establish a Jewish national home in historical Israel/Judea, then a part of Ottoman-controlled Palestine, which also included Syria, Lebanon, Jordan, and Iraq. At that time, the region was known as Palestine, and the flag represented a Jewish identity. Interestingly, individuals from pre-1947 Jordan, 1958 Iraq, 1932 Saudi Arabia, 1943 Lebanon, 1979 UAE, or 1979 Iran (formerly Persia) are not commonly associated with the historical locations they stood on before political changes occurred.

The landscape of both Europe and the Middle East has transformed over time. Despite Israel's historical roots dating back 3500 years, as mentioned in the Quran, the new and old testaments, and historical records, some insist on emphasizing its re-founding in 1948. The Quran itself recognizes the Land of Israel as the ancestral home of the Jewish people, a heritage given to them by God, as documented in both religious scriptures. Notably, the mention of Palestine is absent in these ancient texts.

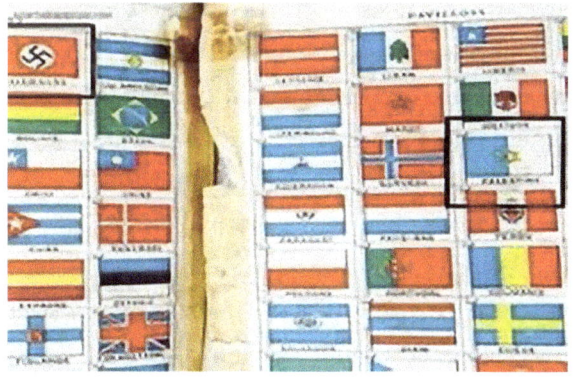

CLASHING WORLDS: PRINCIPLES OF WESTERN CIVILIZATION ARE ANTI-ISLAMIC PRINCIPLES

Overview

Divergent ideologies, beliefs, and principles have led to conflict among civilizations throughout history. Accordingly, there is a clash between Western civilization and Islamic principles. The tenets of Western civilization are inherently at odds with Islam, a religion that celebrates communalism, faith, and adherence to God's will. However, as a result of such an opposition, there exists tension, miscommunication, as well as conflict among the two worlds. This article seeks to discuss some of the major Western civilization values that go against Islamic beliefs.

The core pillar of Western society is based on this principle of individualism. Western societies prefer independence and liberty for each person, advocating for an open expression of self and one's choices. On the other hand, Islamic tenets attach more importance to society and collective responsibilities. By definition, Islam believes that people belong to a greater whole which they must use as guidance for their actions. It is often the case that the western world with its emphasis on personal liberties as opposed to communal interests, ends up in conflict within itself given the inherent contradiction between collectivism and individualism.

Secularism is another principle that differs with Islam and civilization of western cultures. There has been a growing trend of western societies adopting secularism through the separation of church and state affairs in society. The culture encourages different beliefs and is tolerant of people of various faiths. However, Islamic teachings urge on the synthesis of divine law with each sphere of activity, including politics or government. To Muslims, Islam is a complete way of life covering religion and secular affairs. However, the clash between secularism and incorporation of the religious matters in European communities always lead to such misconceptions and conflicts with Muslim nations.

These liberal issues include gender equality, the right of LGBTQ (lesbian, gay, bisexual, transgender, queer), etc., which have nothing to do with Islamic norms. The western society has come a long way, where it promotes gender equality, gives equal opportunities and rights to all. Likewise, the fundamental rights of other LGBTQ+ people have been established and acknowledged in contemporary Western societies. Nonetheless, Islamic principles view things differently in this regard. Islam defines specific gender roles and modesty by providing different privileges and duties for women and males. Just like that, such a thing is also forbidden in Islam because it is regarded as sinful. The disparities of values mostly give rise to controversies and arguments between western societies and Muslim societies.

There are other principles like the freedom of speech, which do not correspond with the ideals of Islamic tradition. Societies in the West value liberty especially the freedom to express one's thoughts, criticize authority and publicly debate. Although there are specific restrictions in Islam on the freedom of speech especially in the matters of religion and religious personalities. Some Islamic countries have blasphemy laws to guard against offenses on religious feelings. The debate for freedom of speech against blaspheming religions is a reason why western societal life often clashes with various Islamic groups.

Separating religious affairs from secular issues such as law is contrary to Islamic principles just like the principle of separation of church and state. In western society a line is drawn between religious bodies and political leadership which ensures that religious leaders are not in charge of government. The objective behind this principle is to eliminate discrimination based on religion and foster inclusiveness. Nonetheless, Islamic ideologies propose that religion should become part and parcel of politics and policy making with the clergy being key players. The conflict that arises between this principle and intertwining of religiosity among western states versus Muslim populations makes this a delicate subject.

Therefore, in this regard, the conflict between the western civilization and Islamic principles is rooted upon different philosophies in the world views, faiths as well as principles. Two worlds collide in the principles of individualism, secularism, liberal values, freedom of expression, and the separation of church and state. To ensure peaceful co-existence across the globe, understanding and embracing differences while creating common grounds between these opposing principles is important.

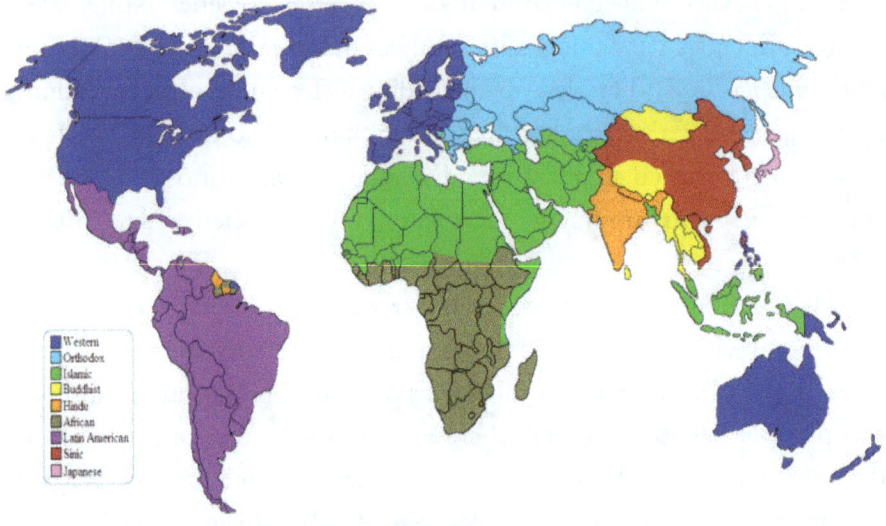

Summary

The conflict between Western civilization and Islamic principles stems from differing worldviews, faiths, and principles. Western civilization values democracy, while Islamic nations often exhibit authoritarian governance. Nationalism, a key component of Western civilization, often clashes with Islamic principles, which value the Islamic community. Recognizing these differences can foster peaceful coexistence in an interconnected world.

Western civilization is rooted in individualism and the autonomy of the self, while Islamic principles emphasize the collective responsibility of the ummah and the subordination of individuals to the greater good. Secularism advocates for the separation of religious and political authority, while Islamic societies aim to establish theocratic systems where religious principles and law intertwine. Both Western and Islamic principles share

194

the belief in monotheism, but their understandings differ. Personal redemption is attainable through faith, grace, and repentance, while Islamic principles emphasize submission to God's will. Ethical frameworks differ, with Western societies prioritizing individual freedom and liberty, while Islamic principles emphasize submission to God's will and adhering to religious law. Gender roles also differ, with Western societies advocating for women's autonomy, education, and professional opportunities, while Islamic principles emphasize honor and respect for women. Legal systems differ, with Islamic societies adhering to Sharia law, which regulates various aspects of life, often resulting in different legal standards and penalties.

Introduction

Jewish diaspora is one of the core elements in Jewish history that dates back several centuries. The essay is about diaspora Jewry experience and how they deal with safety and identity inability to be provided by Israel. The very idea of exploring a complicated link between the Jewish diaspora and the State of Israel implies acknowledging deeper philosophical and historical underpinnings.

The Significance of Diaspora Jewry

A. Historical Background

The roots of the Jewish diaspora can be traced to the Babylonian captivity, which resulted in the exile of the Jews from the land of Israel since 586 BCE. Jews have since spread around the world with different languages and cultures while remaining true to their religion and people's way of life.

B. Contributions to Host Societies

Jews, as they disperse, invariably make positive imprints on the sociocultural, scientific, artistic, and economic milieus. They made an indisputable dent in human civilization as far as their intellectual and art performances are concerned. In spite of that, the diaspora Jews have survived and assimilated well into their adoptive societies.

The Quest for Security

A. Historical Persecutions

Jews have suffered persecution, discrimination, and violence in different parts of the world for centuries. The Jewish diaspora has suffered very extreme adversity, from the Spanish Inquisition to the horrendous Holocaust.

B. The Holocaust and the foundation of Israel.

Diaspora Jewry was made vulnerable by the Holocaust, during which six million Jews were systematically murdered. it was on account of the collective trauma that Jews had developed an insatiable yearning for their own land, hence the establishment of the state of Israel in 1948.

The State of Israel

A. Birth of a Nation

Establishing Israel was a historical turning point for the Jews, as it served as their territorial home and offered them communal identity that traced back to Zionism. Since then, the State of Israel has always been very meaningful in the lives of diaspora Jews and their search for security.

B. Israel's Protection

To many diaspora Jews, Israel is a place of safety or refuge in case they fall victim to persecution or violence from their homelands. The strength and diplomatic support from Israel's military have given wide world Jews a feeling of being secure.

Diaspora Identity and Assimilation

A. The Dilemma of Identity

Identity is a fair complicated issue for Diaspora Jews. They are faced with the challenge of combining their Jewishness and assimilation in a multicultural society. The challenge of maintaining tradition while striving to extend to assimilating into host cultures remains.

B. Assimilation and Cultural Loss

Assimilation is important because it promotes co-existence within host societies but cultural and religious traditions are sometimes lost in assimilation. The dilution of Jewish identity is an issue to some, as intermarriage questions the unfolding of Jewish heritage.

Diaspora Jewry without Israel's Protection

A. Security Concerns

The increasing global anti-Semitism and/or incidents against Jews has created worries about the safety if diaspora Jewry. These concerns can be especially pronounced in areas with less Jewish population.

B. Identity and Continuity

In their search for an identity and assimilation, diaspora Jews might be vulnerable in the absence of Israel's protection. With this verse in consideration, the need of protecting Jewish values and meanings becomes vital while Israel itself is not being there as a guarantor.

Concluding Remarks

The relationship between the State of Israel and Diaspora Jewry is complex and deeply seated in a myriad of years. Israel is an essential sanctuary for the Jews across the world; however, it should be noted that diaspora Jewry has a great diversity of experience and challenges. Striking a balance between preserving the Jewish identity and heritage and assimilation presents an unending challenge.

The fact that the Jewish diaspora exists is testimony to resilience, adaptability and the abiding struggle for security and identity. While investigating the many variations of diaspora Jewry's experience, we must continue to develop a deeper appreciation for their struggles, mysteries and developed wisdom regarding the ongoing Jewish legacy worldwide.

Introduction

The concept of Jihad has garnered considerable attention and debate in recent times. Often misunderstood and misused, it is crucial to delve deeper into its philosophical and historical roots. In this essay, we will examine the concept of Jihad within the framework of Islamic philosophy, acknowledging the multifaceted interpretations and discussing the associations with terrorism that have emerged. It is essential to distinguish between the authentic meaning of Jihad as a profound spiritual struggle and the extremist interpretations that link it with acts of terror.

Overview

In modern discussions, these two terms (jihad and terror) seem almost synonymous. Historically, "jihad" is a term that means struggle or striving in Arabic. Terrorism by contrast refers to violence as well as terror in order for one to accomplish the same thing as politics or an ideology. The philosophy behind terror and jihad is what this book aims to analyze, covering their roots, meaning, and contemporary relevance.

Understanding the meaning of jihad requires a person to go back to where it came from historically. In the beginning, jihad meant a personal fight against one's inclinations towards immorality and striving for the advancement of one's soul and spirit. Each person considered it their private struggle with defects in themselves, vices. Nevertheless, this idea metamorphosed and incorporated other encounters like guarding of religion against oppressions or attacks.

Islamic writings usually tend to emphasize the interpretation of jihad as a defensive warfare. Justice is associated with protecting the innocent and oppressed and ensuring that everyone lives accordingly to his/her merit. Many have used this aspect of jihad to fight for their rights and oppose acts of foreign occupations or dictatorships.

Nevertheless, there is the issue of hijacking Jihad by extremists in order to perpetrate violent and terrorist acts. The members of these gangs use the idea of jihad, to lure recruits while also generating backing for their extremist notions. The terrorists assert that taking part on jihad is fighting in defense of Islam to establish a true Muslim state.

The literal translation of jihad as a holy war has resulted in tremendous controversy and disagreement within the Muslim community and between scholars. However, many Muslims insist that such extremist interpretations do not represent the true teaching of Islam. As they indicate jihad must be considered in the overall framework of peace, mercy, and justice.

Ethically speaking, linking Jihad and terrorism is problematic and can be argued on both religious and philosophical perspectives. Several philosophers posit that force should be the last option when there is no other amicable way to settle issues. Violence is an infringement on principles of justice and human right, it only breeds more damage than good.

Besides, it has raised very serious ethical questions by targeting civilian innocent people in the acts of terrorism. It flies in the face that violence ought to be proportional and distinguish between civilians and combatants. Terrorism is considered a breach of fundamental human values which makes it dangerous to world security.

One must note that jihad is not a synonym for terrorism. The correct meaning of such words like "Jihad" is a complex term covering personal improvement and struggle for justice. However, terror aims at inducing fear which leads to actions via violence.

There is also need for a comprehensive understanding of jihad and terrorism because they are complicated problems. Extremist ideologies are countered by education and dialogue, which helps to keep people away from radicalization. Only by creating an atmosphere of critical thinking and religious literacy in schools and mosques could we confront such a warped understanding of jihad and encourage a more peaceful perspective about Islam. Governments should also collaborate with international organization to deal with politico-sociological grievance which promotes violence. If we focus on resolving the fundamentals then people will not be forced to carry out acts of terrorism under the pretext of jihad.

Summary

The philosophical connection between jihad and terror is complex. Jihad, meaning "struggle" for personal or community development, has been twisted by terrorist organizations to justify violent acts like murder or suicide bombing. To create a better world, it is essential to appreciate diversity in terms of jihad and confront the underlying factors influencing violent extremism. The linkage of jihad with terrorism distorts Islamic principles and devalues the spiritual struggle it represents. Understanding the historical context and philosophical foundations of jihad can help dispel misconceptions and promote informed dialogue among different cultures and religions.

In the annals of history, around the year 1700, a young Dutchman by the name of Adrian Reland, or as his name is spelled in English - Adrian Reland (1676-1718), embarked on a fascinating expedition to the region known then as Palestine. This dauntless individual, possessed of a brilliant mind, was a polymath who had a command of at least five languages: Dutch, Latin, ancient Greek, Arabic, and Hebrew. His repertoire included skills in geography, cartography, linguistics, and, above all, a spirit of adventure. His sojourn in Israel spanned several months, during which he meticulously documented around 2,500 sites that held significance both biblically and in his contemporary era, encompassing demographic insights.

His monumental journey eventually found its culmination in a prodigious tome that sprawled across approximately 1,200 pages, published some years later. This magnum opus, titled "Palaestina Ex Monumentis Veteribus Illustrata," was predominantly composed in Latin but sprinkled generously with passages in Hebrew, Arabic, Greek, and more.

For those with proficiency in Latin, the book is available in its entirety online and can be accessed through sources like https://iiif.wellcomecollection.org/pdf/b30535062. While Latin may elude the grasp of most, there exist scholars who have delved into its contents. I have, in fact, cross-referenced several sources about this remarkable work and engaged with ChatGPT to glean further insights. A pertinent source can be found here: https://www.solonin.org/en/article_palestinian-issue.

Let us now focus on the demographic dimension of Reland's findings. At that juncture in history, Reland's observations painted a portrait of a land that was, by and large, sparsely populated, with a populace predominantly composed of Jews, followed closely by Christians. Minorities, including Muslims, made up the remainder. These Jews were not merely devout pilgrims who had journeyed to Israel for religious rites; rather, they were intricately involved in agricultural pursuits, deriving their sustenance from the land.

In Reland's meticulous records, major cities housed at most a few thousand inhabitants. According to his documentation, Jerusalem was home to approximately 5,000 residents, with nearly two-thirds being Jews, one-third Christians, and Muslims forming a nominal minority. Gaza counted 550 residents, evenly split between Jews and Christians, a stark contrast to today's statistics, where Gaza and its surrounding refugee camps are inhabited by over 1.2 million, the overwhelming majority being Muslims. In Nazareth, the population was exclusively Christian, numbering around 700. In Tiberias and Safed, the inhabitants were solely Jewish, while in Umm el-Fahm, there were ten Maronite Christian families. A similar demographic profile could be seen in other major cities like Acre, Jaffa, and Hebron, where Jews and Christians dominated the urban landscape. The only 'city' where Muslims constituted a majority was Nablus, with approximately 120 Muslims and an additional 70 Samaritans. It is noteworthy to acknowledge that the present-day Nablus is inhabited by over 150,000 people, with the predominant majority being Muslim. The Samaritan population in Israel today hovers around 700 individuals.

Apart from these urban centers, the majority of the Muslim residents in the region were Bedouins, leading a nomadic existence and occasionally seeking temporary employment as laborers in the cities, without any significant property ownership.

The Paradox

No Arab or Muslim State offered Permanent Entry of Palestinians

No Arab or Muslim State offered Permanent Entry of Palestinians while Israel absorbed all Jewish refugees from Arab lands and incorporated the residing Arabs as full citizens

Of the various contentious elements surrounding the current Israeli-Palestinian clash, Palestinian refugee claim to revert home has been a significant matter of contention. It should also be pointed out that none of the Muslim countries declared they would grant entry to Palestinians as a resolution for the refugee problem.

Indeed, the suffering of the Palestinian population, and especially those residing in refugee camps is of great concern to global nations. Many Muslim-majority nations also frequently criticize Israel in support of Palestinians. The solution of giving entrance to those displaced has never been officially declared by any Muslim country.

It brings into doubt the genuineness of the assurances made by certain states. Although these nations could support the cause of Palestine and condemn Israel's decisions, they have failed to do so in practical terms regarding the existence and settlement of Palestinian refugees. This may happen for a number of reasons that can include political considerations and the inability to handle economic issues that are likely linked with concerns over population change occurring in their home countries.

However, it should be noted that a number of Muslim-majority states are providing different humanitarian assistance to Palestinians. Such financial support extends to covering healthcare costs as well as funding education initiatives. Nevertheless, giving them a permanent settlement in their own territories has never been an option for now.

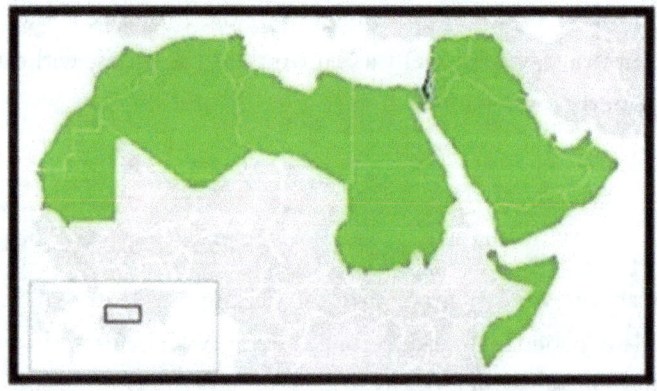

Israel appears as a diminutive blue dot when juxtaposed against the expansive Arab Lands.

The absence of a Muslim state allowing entrance into Palestine as a solution to the Palestinians displacements proves the Israel-Palestinian

conflict complexities and difficulty to search for fair and all-embracing solution. Moreover, it highlights the importance of further global initiatives
aimed at addressing the matter of Palestinian refugees and achieving long-
term resolution.

From the pages of 'The Last Empire," the Arab-Israeli conflict persists, concealing real facts, and its endurance and growth find root in one crucial factor: the active participation of the Western media and academia. In a myriad of publications, books, periodicals, and websites, Israel is often depicted as a state engaged in 'war crimes,' 'ethnic cleansing,' and 'systematic murder.' This portrayal sometimes stems from fashion, occasional misunderstanding, hypocrisy, double standards, or various forms of new and old antisemitism, emanating from both the left and the right, overt or covert. Despite the historical debunking of classic blood libels, the modern blood libel against the state of Israel continues to gain traction, with some Israelis and Jews unwittingly contributing to its perpetuation.

In examining the toll of wars on Muslim victims across the globe, a sobering picture emerges:

- Algeria: 500,000 to 1 million during the war of independence (mostly by the French); 100,000 in the civil war in the 90s.

- Sudan: 2.6 million to 3 million.

- Afghanistan: One million to one and a half million, a consequence of the Soviet invasion; about one million in the civil war.

- Somalia: 400,000 to 550,000 victims in the civil war.

- Bangladesh: 1.4 million to 2 million.

- Indonesia: 400,000 killed, with an additional 100,000 to 200,000 in East Timor.

- Iraq: 1.54 million to 2 million victims (war with Iran and during Saddam Hussein's reign).

- Iran: 450,000 to 970,000 victims (war with Iraq).

- Lebanon: 130,000 in the civil war.

206

- Yemen: 100,000 to 150,000 fatalities.

- Chechnya: 80,000 to 300,000 fatalities.

- Turkey, Syria, Kosovo, Jordan: 120,000-200,000.

In the context of the Israeli-Arab conflict spanning all wars from 1948 to the present, the total count reaches approximately 65,000 Arab fatalities and about 24,000 Israelis killed.

THE LEFT'S INFLUENCE ON THE DECLINE OF THE WEST

Introduction

One of the major worries in the present day talk about decline and fall of West is to what extent did Left have responsibility attributed for this. A respected conservative philosopher, Roger Scruton believes that the Left values and policies have succeeded in eroding the very basis of Western civilization. His perspectives were shaped by the ideas presented in Samuel Huntington's thesis, "Clash of Civilizations," as well as the works of Oswald Spengler, and to some extent, Arnold Toynbee's "Decline of the West."

Cultural Marxism and Identity Politics

Critiquing Scruton commences with the penetration of cultural Marxism into the Western culture, including academia and cultures such as institutions. In his view, the Left, with its identity politics culture war, has divided society into atomized individuals considered by their alleged immutable characteristics rather common values. According to Scruton, the focus on identity has undermined the common cultures that held Western societies in unity; this promotes bitterness and enmity.

Erosion of Traditional Institutions

Scruton adds that the Left has worked to challenge and tear down old institutions like family, religion, & civic organizations. He claims that the focus on individual freedom and liberation has depleted the social glue to hold Western civilization together. According to Scruton, this erosion of institutions has helped create a sense of 'homelessness', and disembodiments from some communal bonds that stabilized life.

Political Correctness and Free Speech

Scruton is an ardent opponent of political correctness that he contends the Left use to stifle differing opinions. He posits that censorship of free speech in college and public speaking deters the foundation principles on which western democracies were formed. According to Scruton, the failure of a society to undertake open and honest dialogue may deny it from the developments required for addressing major challenges while adapting new issues.

Immigration and National Identity

Scruton notes that western nations are in decline mainly because of the Left's approach towards immigration. Adverting to the humanitarianism of migration, he warns that blind enthusiasm for mass immigration and little regard for cultural assimilation undermines national self-knowledge. However, Scruton believes that the Left has been too absorbed in multi-culturalism, which prevents them for advocating and preserving the distinctive cultural identity of most Western nation.

Environmentalism and Anti-Capitalism

Scruton criticizes the Left's association with green campaigns and anti-capitalist moods. He acknowledges the necessity for bared management of environment, but rebukes the left's demonization of capitalism as culprits in ecological complexities. According to him, the abandonment of the free-market in preference for centralized control places individual freedoms, and economic prosperity in jeopardy.

Globalism and Sovereignty

Scruton also interrogates the Left's support for globalism and the erosion of national sovereignty. He claims that dissolving of border lines and power transfer to supranational entities undermine ability of the countries to govern themselves in line with their unique beliefs and customs. Scruton believes that the left has sought a world without borders thereby ignoring the fact that different people ought to maintain their cultural identity in separate countries.

Conclusion

The Scrutonian view associates the decline of the West to Leftist influence on cultural, social and political aspects. Scruton's observations will serve as a limiting principle against full adoption of ideologies that erode the very basis of Western civilization. Despite noting that the challenges faced by the West are complex, Scruton recommends a reconsideration of how the Left steers Western societies. Ultimately, this perspective allows the reader to reflect on the dilemma concerning development vis-à-vis maintaining core principles of culture that define Western heritage.

Note: This chapter is based on teachings of Shaykh Prof. Abdul Hadi Palazzi who holds a Ph.D. in Islamic Sciences by decree of the Grand Mufti of the Kingdom of Saudi Arabia. He served as an Imam for the Italian Islamic community, and as a lecturer in the Department of the History of Religion at the University of Velletri in Rome, Italy.

In exploring the issue of sovereignty over Jerusalem, a Muslim professor and cleric provides a perspective on Muslim support for the city as Judaism's holiest. Delving into political, cultural, psychological, and religious dimensions, he attempts to discern whether, from an Islamic standpoint, there exists a valid theological reason preventing Muslims from recognizing Jerusalem as both an Islamic holy place and the capital of Israel.

O God, King of the kingdom, Thou givest the kingdom to whom Thou pleasest, and Thou strippest off the kingdom from whom Thou pleasest. Thou endurest with honor whom Thou pleasest, and Thou bringest low whom Thou pleasest. All the best is in Thy hand. Verily, Thou hast power over all things. (Koran, Sura 3:26, "The Imrans")

The professor emphasizes a crucial principle derived from the Koran, asserting that no individual, people, or religious community can claim a permanent right of possession over a specific territory. According to Islamic belief, the earth belongs exclusively to God, who has the authority to entrust sovereign rights as He deems fit. This notion rejects the idea that any group can assert an eternal claim over a particular land.

And [remember] when Moses said to his people: O my people, call in remembrance the favor of God unto you, when he produced prophets among you, made you kings, and gave to you what He had not given to any other among the people. O my people, enter the Holy Land which God has assigned unto you, and turn not back ignominiously, for then will ye be overthrown, to your own ruin. (Koran, Sura 5:22-23, "The Table")

211

He rejects the notion that Muslims cannot accept Israeli sovereignty over Jerusalem due to Islam, contending that such an argument is a recent development and is not rooted in classical Islamic sources. He traces this perspective back to figures like Mufti Amin al-Husseini and later, Jamal el-Din Abd el-Nasser, who incorporated anti-Zionism into their ideologies.

And thereafter We said to the Children of Israel: Dwell securely in the Promised Land. And when the last warning will come to pass, we will gather you together in a mingled crowd. (Koran, Sura 17:104, "The Night Journey")

The professor argues that the relationship between the Children of Israel and the Land of Canaan is not tied to any colonization project but is directly linked to the will of God, as outlined in both the Koran and Torah. He cites specific Koranic verses that indicate God's command to Moses for the Israelites to conquer the Promised Land.

Examining the Islamic acknowledgment of Israeli sovereignty over Jerusalem, he contends that, based on the Koran's recognition of Jerusalem as the Jewish direction of prayer, there is no theological reason to deny Jews the same right over the city. He emphasizes the need for fairness and equal treatment of Jews, Christians, and Muslims, asserting that Israelis and Jews should have their political and ethnic capital, even if certain places within it are considered sacred by other faiths.

Moreover, the professor criticizes the denial of Jewish prayer on the Temple Mount, arguing that it contradicts Islamic principles and displays a pseudo-religious stance that interferes with the relationship between believers and God.

In conclusion, he calls for an understanding that respects the rights of all religions, promoting dialogue and cooperation for a common future of peace and prosperity. The professor emphasizes the need for a new attitude, encouraging mutual respect and recognizing common roots to foster a shared understanding among diverse religious communities.

by Shaykh Prof. Abdul Hadi Palazzi

THE QUR'AN SAYS THAT ALLAH GAVE THE LAND OF ISRAEL TO THE JEWS AND WILL RESTORE THEM TO IT AT THE END OF DAYS

THE QUR'AN SAYS

"To Moses We [Allah] gave nine clear signs. Ask the Israelites how he [Moses] first appeared amongst them. Pharoah said to him: 'Moses, I can see that you are bewitched.' 'You know full well,' he [Moses] replied, 'that none but the Lord of the heavens and the earth has revealed these visible signs. Pharoah, you are doomed.'"

"Pharoah sought to scare them [the Israelites] out of the land [of Israel]: but We [Allah] drowned him [Pharoah] together with all who were with him. Then We [Allah] said to the Israelites: 'Dwell in this land [the Land of Israel]. When the promise of the hereafter [End of Days] comes to be fulfilled, we [Allah] shall assemble you [the Israelites] all together [in the Land of Israel]."

"We [Allah] have revealed the Qur'an with the truth, and with the truth it has come down. We have sent you [Muhammed] forth only to proclaim good news and to give warning."

[Qur'an, "Night Journey," chapter 17:100-104]

Shaykh Prof. Palazzi Comments

God wanted to give Avraham a double blessing, through Ishmael and through Isaac, and ordered that Ishmael's descendants should live in the desert of Arabia and Isaac's in Canaan.

The Qur'an recognizes the Land of Israel as the heritage of the Jews and it explains that, before the Last Judgment, Jews will return to dwell there. This prophecy has already been fulfilled.

213

Is there any fundamental reason which prohibits Muslims from recognizing Israel as a friendly State?

I realize that a negative answer to the above question is taken for granted by popular opinion. My approach, however, is not based on popular opinion or the current political situation, but on a theological analysis of authentic Islamic sources.

Viewing the Jewish return to Israel as a Western invasion and Zionists as recent colonizers is new. It has no basis in authentic Islamic faith. According to the Qur'an, no person, people or religious community can claim a permanent right of possession over any territory. The Earth belongs exclusively to God, and He is free to entrust sovereignty over land to whomever He likes for whatever time period that He chooses.

"Say: 'O God, King of the kingdom (1), Thou givest the kingdom to whom Thou pleasest, and Thou strippest off the kingdom from whom Thou pleasest; Thou endowest with honour whom Thou pleasest, and Thou bringest low whom Thou pleasest: all the best is in Thy hand. Verily, Thou hast power over all things.'"(2) [Qur'an 3:26]

From the above Qur'anic verse we deduce a basic principle of the Monotheistic philosophy of history: God chooses as He likes in the relationship between peoples and countries. Sometimes He gives a land to a people, and sometimes He takes His possession back and gives it to another people.

In general, we can say that He gives as a reward for faithfulness and takes back as a punishment for wickedness, but this rule does not permit us to say that God's ways are always plain and clear to our eyes, since His secrets are inaccessible to the human intellect.

Using Islam as a basis for preventing Arabs from recognizing any sovereign right of Jews over the Land of Israel is new. Such beliefs are not found in classical Islamic sources.

Concluding that anti-Zionism is the logical outgrowth of Islamic faith is wrong. This conclusion represents the false transformation of Islam from a religion into a secularized ideology.

Such a false transformation of Islam was in fact made by the late Mufti of Jerusalem, Haj Amin el-Husseini. He is the one person most responsible, both morally and materially, for the repeated Arab defeats in their conflict with the Jews in Israel.

Husseni not only incited Arabs against Jews. He also encouraged the torture and murder of all Arabs who correctly understood that Arab cooperation with Jews was a precious opportunity for the development of the Land of Israel. Husseini ended his woeful life by putting his perverted religious teachings at the service of the evil and pagan Nazis.

After Husseini came Jamal al-Din 'Abd al-Nasser. Nasser based his policy on Pan-Arabism, hatred and contempt for Jews, and an alliance with the atheistic Soviet Union. Nasser's terrible choices were critical factors in maintaining Arab backwardness. Fortunately, most of Nasser's mistakes were afterward corrected by the martyr Anwar Sadat. (3)

After the defeat of Nasserianism, Islamic fundamentalist movements made anti-Zionism the primary feature of their propaganda. They presented the negation of any Jewish rights to the Land of Israel as rooted in authentic Islam and derived from authentic Islamic religious principles.

The Land of Israel in Qur'anic Exegesis

The fundamentalist Muslim program to use Islam as an instrument for political warfare against Jews finds a major obstacle in the Qur'an itself. Both the Bible and the Qur'an state quite clearly that the right of the Israelites to the Land of Israel does not depend on conquest and colonization. This right flows from the will of almighty God Himself.

Both the Jewish and Islamic Scriptures teach that God, through His chosen servant Moses, decided to free the offspring of Jacob from slavery in Egypt and to constitute them as heirs of the Promised Land. Whoever claims that Jewish sovereignty over the Land of Israel is something new and rooted in human politics denies divine revelation and divine prophecy as explicitly expressed in our Holy Books (the Bible and Koran).

The Qur'an relates the words by which Moses ordered the Israelites to conquer the Land:

"And [remember] when Moses said to his people: 'O my people, call in remembrance the favor of God unto you, when he produced prophets among you, made you kings, and gave to you what He had not given to any other among the peoples. O my people, enter the Holy Land which God has assigned unto you, and turn not back ignominiously, for then will ye be overthrown, to your own ruin.'" [Qur'an 5:20-21]

Moreover - and those who try to use Islam as a weapon against Israel always conveniently ignore this point - the Holy Qur'an explicitly refers to the return of the Jews to the Land of Israel before the Last Judgment - where it says: "And thereafter We [Allah] said to the Children of Israel: 'Dwell securely in the Promised Land. And when the last warning will come to pass, we will gather you together in a mingled crowd.'" [Qur'an 17:104]

Therefore, from an Islamic point of view, there is NO fundamental reason which prohibits Muslims from recognizing Israel as a friendly State.

Islam And Normalization of Relationships Between Islamic States and The Jewish State

PLO documents can in no way be regarded as Islamic. The PLO leaders are a gang of criminals and thieves, and Arabs will be the main victims of any supposed "Palestinian State" under their leadership.

I do not believe that Islam is the factor preventing normalization between Arabs and the State of Israel. The real problem is that members of the ruling classes in Arab countries believe their authority and power would be threatened by democracy, modernization, and education in the Arab world. They use a distorted interpretation of Islam as a political tool, and unfortunately the majority of uneducated Arabs believe their poisonous propaganda.

I believe that we must return to the time when Islam was in the vanguard of scientific progress and interfaith dialogue. Instead of false "leaders" such as Qadhafi, Saddam Hussein, Arafat [el-Husseini] or Yasin, we Muslims again need true leaders such as al-Ghazali, Ibn Rushd and Ibn Khaldum.

King Faysal of Iraq said: "The Arabs, and particularly the educated ones among them, must look at the Zionist movement with the deepest sympathy."

Tragically, true leaders such as Faysal were silenced, and fanatics such as Haj Amin al-Husseini prevailed.

The evil consequences of the victory of fanaticism are clear for all to see: Jews expelled from Arab countries where they lived in peace for over one thousand years, "Palestinian" refugees, terrorism, etc. To avoid future mistakes, we must learn from our past ones.

Unfortunately, there are Arabs who believe that they must fight against Israel until they completely destroy it (a tragedy which I do not believe the God of Israel will ever permit to happen - Never again!).

Unfortunately, there are also naive and foolish Israelis who believe, incredibly to me, that they will achieve "peace" with their Arab neighbors by giving the murderer "Arafat" [el-Husseini] a State, an army, etc. This is insane. You Jews are supposedly famous for your intelligence. How can some of your "leaders" be so stupid?

From the perspective of the natural world, I am not optimistic about what the future holds. However, from the supernatural perspective of faith, we who believe in God must face the future with a positive attitude.

We must have faith that we will see the day when real peace and prosperity—which can only be based on true faith in God and His Word (the Bible and Rabbinic Tradition for you; the Bible, Qur'an and Authentic Islamic Tradition for us)—±will spread throughout the world. Meanwhile, we must work together to prepare for a better future.

From an Islamic point of view, is there any fundamental reason which prohibits Muslims from recognizing Jerusalem both as an Islamic Holy Place and as the capital of the State of Israel?

I realize that a negative answer to the above question is taken for granted by popular opinion. My approach, however, is not based on popular opinion or the current political situation, but on a theological analysis of authentic Islamic sources.

Jerusalem in the Qur'an

The most common argument against Muslim acknowledgment of Israeli sovereignty over Jerusalem is that, since al-Quds [Jerusalem] (4) is a Holy Place for Muslims, Muslims cannot accept that it is ruled by non-Muslims, because such acceptance amounts to a betrayal of Islam.

Before expressing our point of view on this question, we must reflect upon the reason for which Jerusalem and Masjid al-Aqsa [the Al Aksa Mosque] hold such a sacred position in Islamic faith.

As is well known, the inclusion of Jerusalem among Islamic holy places derives from al-Mi'raj, the Ascension of the Prophet Muhammed to heaven. The Ascension began at the Rock, usually identified by Muslim scholars as the Foundation Stone of the Jewish Temple in Jerusalem referred to in Jewish sources.

Recalling this link requires us to admit that there is no connection between al-Miraj [the Ascension] and Muslim sovereign rights over Jerusalem since, in the time that al-Miraj took place, the City was not under Islamic, but under Byzantine administration. Moreover, the Qur'an expressly recognizes that Jerusalem plays for Jews the same role that Mecca does for Muslims.

We read:

> "...They would not follow thy direction of prayer (qiblah), nor art thou to follow their direction of prayer;

nor indeed will they follow each other's direction of prayer..." (5)

All Qur'anic commentators explain that "thy qiblah" [direction of prayer for Muslims] is clearly the Ka'bah of Mecca, while "their qiblah" [direction of prayer for Jews] refers to the Temple Mount in Jerusalem.

To quote only one of the most important Muslim commentators, we read in Qadn Baydawn's Commentary:

"Verily, in their prayers Jews orientate themselves toward the Rock (sakhrah), while Christians orientate themselves eastwards..." (6)

In complete opposition to what "Islamic" fundamentalists continuously claim, the Book of Islam [the Qur'an] - as we have just now seen - recognizes Jerusalem as the Jewish direction of prayer.

Some Muslim commentators also quote the Book of Daniel (7) as a proof for this.

After reviewing the relevant Qur'anic passages concerning this matter, I conclude that, as no one denies Muslims complete sovereignty over Mecca, from an Islamic point of view - despite opposing, groundless claims—there is no reason for Muslims to deny the State of Israel—which is a JEWISH state—complete sovereignty over Jerusalem.

Islamic Holy Places

Anti-Jewish sentiments expressed by Islamic leaders throughout the Middle East are, in fact, not religious in nature, but, rather, political. The best proof of this is in the fact that Islamic anti-Judaism is quite recent.

Omar ended the Roman ban that prevented Jews to enter Jerusalem, the Ummayad caliphs in Cordoba built a synagogue for Maimonides, and Salahu-d-Din, after defeating the Crusaders, wrote to the Jewish leaders, "Your exile is over. Whoever wants to come back is welcome."

The late King Faysal of Iraq openly expressed his sympathy for the Zionist movement, while King Abdullah of Jordan was compelled to wage war against Israel by the other Arab leaders.

Recently, the Resident Arab ["Palestinian"] Wakf has made pronouncements, such as that the Western Wall (Kotel) is not a Jewish shrine, but, rather, the wall to which the Prophet's [steed] was tethered, or, at best, the wall surrounding the Muslim Mosque. The Wakf has also stated that all of Hebron should be turned over to the Resident Arab ["Palestinian"] Authority, and that Jews would be forbidden to pray in the Cave of the Patriarchs. These kinds of declarations by the PLO gangsters are ridiculous and absurd.

The Kotel was effectively, according to the Islamic tradition, the place where al-Buraq [the Prophet's steed] was tethered, but it was already an existing part of the Herodian structure. Muslims have never prayed close to it, and it has never had a special relevance in Islam. On the contrary, everyone knows how important it is for Jewish worshippers.

Apart from Mecca, no Islamic holy place is off-limits for non-Muslims. Historical sources say that the Prophet Muhammad entertained a delegation of Christians from Najran in the Mosque of Medina, and permitted them to celebrate a mass inside the Mosque, notwithstanding the fact that Christian rites can include words that are against Islam [such as stating that Jesus is God].

There is nothing in Jewish worship that can be offensive for Muslims, and nothing in Islamic Law prevents Jews to pray on Haram al-Sharif/Har Habayyit (the Temple Mount), in the Cave of Machpela or in any other place that is regarded as holy by Muslims.

Every time I meet those who say otherwise, I ask them to identify a single authoritative Islamic source as legal proof of their claim. None of them has ever answered such a request of mine.

Shaykh Prof. Abdul Hadi Palazzi Notes

1. The original Arabic word we translated as "kingdom" is mulk, from a Semitic root m-l-k, that is common to both Arabic and Hebrew. According to Islamic theological terminology, the three synonyms for "kingdom" are mulk, malakut and jabarut. They refer

respectively to the physical, psychic and spiritual levels of existence. Of course, G-d can be called King of all of them; if here only mulk is quoted, it depends on the fact that this verse directly concerns the earthly domain. To denote a kingdom in the secular and political sense, Arabic commonly uses another derived form, that is mamlakah.

2. Koran 3:26. For typographical reasons, it is not possible to reproduce here the original Arabic text of the Koran, which must nevertheless be understood as quoted. As well here as in other Koranic quotations, the English translation of the meaning of Koranic words from Arabic is my own, but based on the most authoritative English commentaries, such as M. Marmaduke Pickthall's "The Meaning of The Glorious Koran" (Beirut 1973), 'A. Yusuf 'Ali, "The Holy Koran - Text, Translation and Commentary" (Maryland 1983) and A. 'A. Maududi "The Holy Koran - Text, Translation and Brief Notes" (Lahore 1986).

3. In using the term "martyr" I do not simply refer to one who lost his life for a good cause. I give a precise translation of the Arabic word "shahid," which identifies a "martyr" in the strictly religious sense; that is to say, someone who spent his life serving the cause of G-d. Since making peace with former enemies is an explicit Koranic order (see Koran 8:61), and since, according to Islam, Peace is G-d Himself, any believer who is killed because of his search for Peace must be understood as a religious martyr. The same considerations clearly apply to Yitzhak Rabin.

4. Arabic name of Jerusalem, from the root q-d-s, meaning "holiness". It is an abridged form of Bayt al-maqdis, "the sanctified House" or "the House of the Sanctuary", an exact equivalent of the Hebrew Beth ha-mikdash. The name originally referred only to the Temple Mount, and was afterward extended to the City as a whole. This extension of meaning became common among Arabs

from the tenth century C.E. onwards. Earlier Islamic sources use the name Iliyia, an adaptation to Arabic pronunciation of the Roman name Aelia.

5. Koran 2:145.

6. M. Shaykh Zadeh Hashiyaah 'ali Tafsir al-Qadn al-Baydawn (Istanbul 1979), Vol. 1, p. 456.

7. Daniel 6:10.

Overview

Note: Based on Analysis of the Center for Strategic and International Studies

The analysis of the links between Islam and violent extremism faces challenges due to the lack of reliable data and compartmentalization of analysis. It is easy for analysts to focus on the small part of the extremist threat Muslim extremists pose to non-Muslims in the West and demonize one of the world's great religions, leading to Islamophobia. It is also easy to avoid analyzing the links between extremist violence and Islam for political correctness or to provoke Muslims and governments of largely Muslim states. The overwhelming majority of extremist and violent terrorist incidents occur in largely Muslim states, with a small minority of Muslims seeking power primarily in their areas of operation. Most governments in these countries are actively fighting extremism and terrorism, and the vast majority of Muslims oppose violent extremism and terrorism. Religion is only one of many factors that lead to instability and violence in largely Muslim states, not representing the core values of Islam.

The analysis reveals that global patterns of terrorism are dominated by extremist violence in largely Muslim states and extremist movements that claim to represent Islamic values. The START database counts 70,767 terrorist incidents between 2011 and 2016, with 85% occurring in largely Islamic states and 73% in the Middle East and North Africa region. Only a small portion of these incidents can be attributed to ISIS, and key organized extremist groups like Al Qaida, Al Nusra, ISIS,

and the Taliban account for 17% of the total. The report also shows that the vast majority of Muslims do not support extremist violence, with their primary concerns being jobs, governance, security, and practical values shared by non-Muslims. **Only 17%** of Muslims see religion as the key factor in recruiting fighters for ISIS, and interpretations of Islam rank seventh in Arab views of defeating extremism.

The analysis highlights the ongoing threat of extremism and instability to the Islamic world and the state outside it. It reveals that current threats include ISIS, Al Qaida, and the Taliban, but they are only a small part of a broader problem that will persist for decades. Even total victories in Syria and Iraq could have limited impact, as most ISIS "affiliates" outside the current range of major military efforts are not closely linked to ISIS "caliphates." The analysis also highlights the lack of a clear grand strategy to bring security and stability to these regions. The analysis also highlights the uncertainty in Afghanistan and Pakistan, where even tactical success is uncertain. The report also warns that the cost of failing to create effective strategic partnerships can be greater and more destabilizing, as seen in Yemen, Libya, Somalia, the Sudan's, and Sub-Saharan African countries.

The West Bank and Gaza

The Palestinian Authority (PA) continued its counterterrorism and law enforcement efforts in the West Bank, where Hamas, PIJ, and the Popular Front for the Liberation of Palestine (PFLP) remained active. The PA exercised varying degrees of authority over the West Bank due to the presence of the IDF in certain areas and frequent Israeli entry into PA-controlled areas for counterterrorism operations. The United States coordinated with PA security forces in counterterrorism efforts, and the PA developed professional security forces capable of some but not all counterterrorism functions. The number of Palestinian terrorist attacks against Israelis in the West Bank in 2019 was in line with recent years and lower than rates during the heightened period of violence from October 2015 to April 2016. Hamas maintained control of Gaza in 2019, and several militant groups launched rocket attacks against Israel from Gaza. The total damage in 2019 was estimated at $3.46 million.

The Palestinian Authority (PA) lacks comprehensive legislation for counterterrorism, despite existing Palestinian laws criminalizing terrorist acts. The dissolved Palestinian Legislative Council has limited power to pass new laws, and NGOs have accused the PA of making arbitrary arrests based on political affiliations. The Preventive Security Organization and General Intelligence Organization play crucial roles in preventing West Bank terrorist attacks. Israel retains control of border security across the West Bank and Area C. The PA is a member of MENAFATF and has launched a new banking system, Know Your Customer, to track financial transactions. However, official PA media and social media have shown content supporting terrorism, and Palestinian leaders have not consistently condemned individual terrorist attacks. Despite these challenges, PA justice, security leaders, and security force personnel continue to participate in regional conferences and meetings to combat terrorism.

Sources:

    Israel and the Ayatollahs —Amir Taheri —NY *Daily News*

    Foreign Policy Focus —The United States, Israel, and the Possible Attack on Iran

    CIA —The work Factbook —Iran / Israel

    Israel Newspapers —*Maariv* and *Haaretz*

    Wikipedia —History of Iran, Politics of Iran

Terrorist Groups

Beyond Al Qaeda and its influential Yemen and Arabian Peninsula affiliate, numerous other terrorist organizations, including several domestically rooted groups, pose significant threats. Alongside Middle Eastern entities, Hezbollah demands attention, exercising dominance in Lebanon's government and possessing an extensive arsenal, including tens of thousands of missiles and precision-guided weaponry capable of reaching Tel Aviv. These groups exhibit substantial transnational capabilities, and while the absence of a 9/11-scale event might not forecast future failure, it remains essential to acknowledge the potential risks. Historical cooperation between Al Qaeda and Hezbollah suggests a likelihood of collaboration in the future, emphasizing the intricate and interconnected nature of contemporary terrorist networks.

Nuclear Weapons Proliferation

While North Korea and Iran often dominate discussions on nuclear weapons proliferation, there are additional nations receiving less frequent media attention. Pakistan presently possesses an arsenal exceeding 200 nuclear weapons, and there are reports suggesting Burma's involvement in a nuclear weapons program. Syria, having had a nuclear weapons program in the past, continues to deny access to the International Atomic Energy Agency. The potential acquisition of nuclear capabilities by Iran raises concerns, with widespread skepticism regarding the ability of Saudi Arabia,

Turkey, Egypt, and other nations to resist following suit. The effectiveness of the Nuclear Non-proliferation Treaty's safeguards and the commitment of these governments to prevent the transfer of nuclear weapons to other entities remain uncertain.

Cyber

Moreover, cyber warfare has dominated the 21st century. This caused the Obama administration order the creation of a military cyber command and allocating major finances from both the military, intel community, and government proper towards cyber defense. Beyond the numerous systems depending on a huge and fragile cyber infrastructure, the danger is much bigger. The potential for serious impacts, however, not as widely discussed is no less important especially with respect to industrial sector. The threat goes beyond the protection of intellectual property to even include the basic functioning process of today's economy. Cyber warfare is an area that many countries including Russia, China, and North Korea are committed to developing.

China

China's ascendance is also among unmatched events that have taken place on earth, liberating millions from poverty and projecting Chinese companies onto world economy arena. The cash flow from growth of the China, however, is not merely been employed for reducing poverty of it, but on the contrary, China's budget for defense during the last 20 year's period was being steadily boosting up. Since 1949, China's People's Republic under the rule of the Chinese Communist Party (CPC) has developed its military capacity, namely the acquisition of a naval vessel named Liaoning, which is classified as an aircraft carrier, along with nuclear powered ballistic missile.

The Obama administration shifted away from the Middle East towards Asia, where China poses one of the biggest challenges to the US. Nevertheless, the change is more symbolic, seeing the US lacks sufficient capacity to tip such balance of forces. The US would have a lesser number of ships and planes if the expenditure on the defense dropped further. However, some think that the emerging Chinese economy will put brackets on its geopolitical aspirations, and others consider the growing wealth of China as a solid background for its domination in the Paci However, evidence seems to support this latter view.

As per the statement by a former US director of national intelligence James Clapper's, China remains the biggest enemy of US. For instance, the US has a treaty with Russia while China is expanding its strategic and nuclear forces, denying dialogue with the US over numerous matters. Clapper was convinced that Gaddafi will win the fight with the rebels and possibly divide Libya into three republics or a stateless state similar to Somalia. This goes against what the White House has demanded that Gadhafi leaves office.

Some Senate members criticized Clapper's statements on China and Libya calling for his resignation/termination. Later, Clapper explained that this kind of threat of China referred to capabilities and not intentions. US defense officials concede that they had underrated China's military potential while experts in the US intelligence community are beginning to worry over China's covert arms construction project. An enhanced Chinese power projection, centered on a strategic objective of Taiwan, but with wider, regional and global aims. This includes China inserting cyber probes into US classified computer networks, which according to Clapper should be a major worry.

With the largest population worldwide as well as ranking as the second biggest economy, China constitutes a leading global power whose role in the world can hardly be overestimated. China's rise has provided many opportunities but it is important not to ignore the risks that may arise from these behaviors.

The main concern is the way that China is getting more and more aggressive in disputed territories. The country has been engaged in disputes relating to territorial issues in the South and East China Seas, which have strained relations with neighboring states. China's militaristic measures like building camps on unowned isles might turn out as dangerous to peace with time.

It is also dangerous because it involves human rights records of China. It is apparent that China's regime stands accused of repressing political opposition, censoring media and internet and maltreating some nationalities including minority tribes like the Uyghurs. In addition, such human rights abuses in China also work against attempts at democratization and the free world as a whole.

In addition, the development of high economic growth in China was not cheap and it paid a heavy price on environment. It is the biggest polluter in the world, leading to changes in the earth's climate. It has relied heavily on coal as source of power with minimal environmental regulations leading to massive destruction of air, pollution of water bodies, and deforestation. The environmental problems that China suffers are felt beyond its borders; they become global problems.

To sum up, there is no denying that the expansion of China offers economic benefits and technological progress; however, it is important to bear in mind the possible threats that it entails. These include territorial disputes, human rights abuses and environment, it is imperative in ensuring a stable and sustainable global future.

Iran Is the Current Greatest Threat to the West and The Arab Countries (Not Particularly to Israel)

Iran is not Israel's real problem. Iran is a greater threat to the West and then the Arab Nations around her.

Preview and History

The history of the Persian Jews has been uninterrupted for over 2,500 years. It is a Mizrahi Jewish community in the territory of today's Iran, the historical core of the former Persian Empire, which began as early as the 8th century BCE, at the time of captivity of the ancient Israelites in Khorassan (eastern Iran).

As of 2005, Iran had the largest Jewish population in the Middle East outside of Israel. A larger population of Iranian Jews reside in Israel with the former President of Israel Moshe Katsav, the defense minister, former Chief of Staff Shaul Mofaz, Ex Air-Force commander Dan Halutz and Israeli Hip-Hop star Kobi Shimoni being the most famous of this group.

Relations between Iran and Israel have alternated from close political alliances between the two states during the era of the Shah to hostility following the rise to power of Ayatollah Ruhollah Khomeini. Upon its establishment in 1948 and until the Iranian Revolution in 1979, Israel and Iran (ruled by the Pahlavi dynasty) enjoyed cordial relations. Iran was one of the first nations to internationally recognize Israel, and was considered Israel's closest Muslim friend.

After the second phase of the 1979 Iranian Revolution which witnessed the establishment of the Islamic Republic, Iran withdrew its recognition of the state of Israel and cut off all official relations. However, Iran is said to have purchased weapons valued at $2.5 billion from Israel through third party intermediaries during the Iran-Iraq war during the 1980s and the 1990s. This has been alleged to have been part of the Iran-Contra scandal. In 1998, Israeli businessman Nahum Manbar was sentenced to 16 years in prison in Israel for doing business with Teheran, and in the course of the investigation, "hundreds of companies" were found to have illegal business dealings with Iran.

Israel also had dealing with Hizzboulah for exchanging their kidnapped officer and other missing soldiers. Dealing with Hizzboulah may also initiate indirect channels of communication with Iran.

Iran's History —Successive Empires:

The **Persian Empire** was a series of historical empires that ruled over the Iranian plateau. The political entity which was ruled by these kingdoms is the country now known as Iran (literally "Land of Aryans"). Generally, the earliest entity considered a part of the Persian Empire is Persia. Some of the important periods of the Persians empires are listed below:

Achaemenid dynasty (648—330 BC): United Aryan-indigenous kingdom that originated in the region now known as Fars and was formed under Cyrus the Great.

Sassanid Empire (AD 226—650): The Sassanid (or Sassanian) dynasty was the first dynasty native to the Pars province since the Achaemenids; thus, they saw themselves as the successors of Darius and Cyrus. They pursued an aggressive expansionist policy. They recovered much of the eastern lands that the Kushans had taken in the Parthian period. The Sassanids continued to make war against Rome; a Persian army even captured the Roman Emperor Valerian in 260. The Sassanid Empire, unlike Parthia, was a highly centralized state. The people were rigidly organized into a caste system: Priests, Soldiers, Scribes, and Commoners. Zoroastrianism was finally made the official state religion.

The Safavid dynasty (15-18 Century): links medieval with modern Iran. The Safavids witnessed wide-ranging developments in politics, warfare, science, philosophy, religion, art and architecture. But how did this dynasty manage to produce the longest lasting and most glorious of Iran's Islamic-period eras?

Qajar dynasty, ruling from 1779 to 1925: Persia found relative stability in the Qajar dynasty, ruling from 1779 to 1925, but lost hope to compete with the new industrial powers of Europe; Persia found itself sandwiched between the growing Russian Empire in Central Asia and the expanding British Empire in India. Each carved out pieces from the Persian Empire that became Bahrain, Azerbaijan, Turkmenistan, Uzbekistan, and parts of Afghanistan.

Iran was left unprepared for the worldwide expansion of European colonial empires in the late 18th century and throughout the 19th century.

Period after World War I: By World War I, Iran was not the world power it had once been. It had become a tool in the political battles of other empires. In 1919, northern Persia was occupied by the British General William Edmund Ironside to enforce the Turkish Armistice conditions and assist General Dunsterville and Colonel Bicherakhov contain Bolshevik influence in the north. Britain also took tighter control over the increasingly lucrative oil fields. In 1925, Reza Shah Pahlavi seized power from the Qajars and established the new Pahlavi dynasty. However, Britain and the Soviet Union remained the influential powers in Iran into the early years of the Cold War. United States helped the Shah to stay in power until his dynasty demise in 1979, after the Iranian revolution and the creation of the Islamic Republic of Iran-Islamic republic, theoretically, is a state under a particular theocratic form of government advocated by some Muslim religious leaders. In an Islamic republic, the laws of the state are required to be compatible with the laws of Sharia, Islamic law, while the state remains a republic.

In summary we can say that the successive states in Iran prior to 1935 can be collectively called the *Persian Empire*. From 1979 it became the Islamic Republic of Iran, practically speaking, a historical empire stripped out of its original glory and it historical past.

The new Islamic regime objectives:

1. Rebirth of the Persian Empire which will control the whole Moslem world and perhaps the west in the future.

2. Abolition of the monarchies of the Middle East regimes.

3. The regime's desire to hide its Shiite identity so that it can claim the leadership of radical Islam.

4. The regime's desire to hide its non-Arab identity so that it can claim leadership of the Middle East.

5. Re-direction of pan-Arab nationalism movement and pan-Arab Sunni Islamism.

In the Islamic Republic of Iran (established in 1979), the president and members of the legislature are elected by direct vote of the citizens (although many westernized and pro-monarchy Iranians object to these elections as a means of legitimately choosing leaders). Iran's Islamic republic is in contrast to the constitutionally democratic and partially secular state of the Islamic Republic of Pakistan (proclaimed as an Islamic Republic in 1956) where Islamic laws are technically considered to override laws of the state, though in reality they rarely do.

Today, the creation of an Islamic Republic is the rallying achievement for Islamists all over the world. However, the term itself has different meanings among various people. Many proponents of Islamic Republics advocate the abolition of the monarchies of the Middle East, regimes which they believe to be overly secular or otherwise destructive to Islam.

If Israel was not in the middle-east, the energy of pan-Arab nationalism movement, which dominated Arab politics in the post-war era, would have been directed against two other neighbors: Turkey and Iran. Even today, the Arab League claims that the Turkish province of Iskanderun is "usurped Arab territory". Both pan-Arab nationalism and pan-Arab Sunni Islamism are as much mortal foes for Iran as they are for Israel. If Israel will not exist the Arabs objective will be to get rid of Iran (non-Arab Shiites who are not "real Moslems").

Iranians Ethnic Groups:

Persian 51%

Azeri 24%

Gilaki and Mazandarani 8%

Kurd 7%

Arab 3%

Lur 2%

Baloch 2%

Turkmen 2%

Religions:

Shi'a Muslim 89%

Sunni Muslim 9%

Zoroastrian, Jewish, Christian, and Baha'i 2%

Iranian society is composed of only 51% ethnic Persians. The Shi'a Islam is the only common denominator that exists in Iran. Without Islam they have a great chance of instability due to ethnic composition of Iranian society.

Most Arabs are Sunni who do not like Shiites because they believe they are not true Moslems. Iranians are mostly Shiites, non-Arab (not considered real true Moslems by the Sunni Moslems, which are about 85-90% of Moslems). Iran is interested in having Israel as a cause to unite its own people and then unite the Moslem world while redirecting their anger toward Israel.

(Source: Wikipedia, the free encyclopedia)

Why Does Iran Now Have A Face-Off War Of Words and Proxy Terrorism With Israel?

Recent Declarations of Iranian Leadership:

- Iran's supreme leader, Ayatollah Ali Khamenai, explained in Jan. 2001 that "**the foundation of the Islamic regime is opposition to Israel**, and the perpetual subject of Iran is the **elimination of Israel** from the region."

- Khamenai said in a recent sermon that "the cancerous tumor called Israel **must be uprooted from the region.**"

- In Dec. 2001, former Iranian President, Hashemi Rafsanjani, called the establishment of the Jewish state 'the worst event in history,' and declared his intention to decimate Israel, clarifying that **'one [nuclear] bomb is enough to destroy all Israel,'** and that "in due time, the Islamic world will have a military nuclear device."

- Iran's President, Mahmoud Ahmadinejad, has challenged the reality of the Holocaust and said that Israel must be "wiped off the map."

Israel is the easiest target to direct the energy of pan-Arab nationalism and anti-west sentiments. Israel is also a subject that unifies the Arabs. Arabs see Israel as a western entity planted in the Middle East with western support. The Arabs see Israel as a western plot, an idea of which interpreted differently, is in essence anti-west sentiment redirected toward Israel.

Iran in realty does not want the destruction of Israel or its removal from the middle-east. Israel's existence is important for Iran's goals and, in truth, Iran does not want Israel to be annihilated. According to Iran's President, Mahmoud Ahmadinejad, the Jews have to return to their original countries. Iran does not want the several hundred thousand of Iranians Jews returning to Iran. Iran knows exactly what the composition of Israel's population is. Iran has about 25,000-35,000 Jews living in its borders. Bringing more Jews to Iran and then the rest of Mizrachi Jews to the Arab world is not a real objective neither perceived by the Iranians nor accepted by the Arab countries of the middle-east. Furthermore, Iran's President understands that without Israel, Arab anger would have been directed against Iran (and Turkey). Also, tough rhetoric against Israel (sub-consciously against the west), will present Iran as a leader of the Moslems while causing the Moslem world to forget that Iranians are non-Arabs Shiites. In other words, Iranians are neither Arabs nor 'real Moslems.' What he says in public is just "show business."

As a main motive to unite the Moslem world and as a theocracy with a fundamental lack of accountability, Iran's nuclear program brings the free world's several great nightmares; WMDs falling into the hands of Islamic terrorists and a loose extremist state with nukes hoping to achieve its past glory as an Empire.

Israel's Past Actions

The West's interest was always to keep the flame in the Middle East so the Moslem's anger will be focused on Israel. In fact, part of Israel's problems now and in the past, stem from the failure of its successive leaders to steer the country clear of other middle-eastern quarrels, and the lack of understanding of western objectives in the Middle East.

In successive wars during the Cold War, Israel destroyed the Soviet-built arsenals of several Arab countries. That helped protect Washington's Arab allies against aggression by pro-Soviet Arab powers—and thus kept the Soviets from gaining indirect control of the region's vital oil resources. Israel also taught Washington ways to build new weaponry to fight soviet hardware. In addition, Israel taught the Pentagon generals strategic modern fighting schemes against Soviet made hardware and fighting schemes against middle-east powers.

In 1981, Israel knocked out the French-made Iraqi nuclear-weapons center, even though Saddam Hussein was making that bomb to drop on Teheran. The Israeli action helped the major powers avoid catastrophe in a region vital to their interests. Israel's reward? Being described by Jacques Chirac, then mayor of Paris, as "a criminal state." Washington, Israel's ally joined the nations condemning Israel.

Possible Actions by Israel

Patrick Clawson, an Iran expert who is the deputy director for research at the Washington Institute for Near East Policy and who has been a supporter of President Bush. "So long as Iran has an Islamic republic, it will have a nuclear-weapons program, at least clandestinely," Clawson told the Senate Foreign Relations Committee on March 2nd. The key issue, therefore, is: "How long will the present Iranian regime last?"

Some claim they've found the perfect solution to Iran's nuclear ambitions. It's simple: Israel attacks the Islamic Republic to destroy much of its nuclear infrastructure, setting the bomb project back by a decade, time for a more responsible regime to emerge in Teheran. This would please the Europeans, because it would remove the spotlight from their appeasement policy, which is partly responsible for the crisis. They could shake their heads in a "told you so" gesture at the mullahs, and feel glum about their ability to stand above dirty games played by "immature powers" such as the Islamic Republic and Israel. The Americans, who clearly lack a policy on Iran, will also be happy. The Arab states also will be happy because Israel took care of the prospect of a nuclear-armed Iran. Russia will also be happy. Hostility to its neighbor is deep-felt in Iran, which lost territory to Russia in bitter wars with the Czars. By the middle of this century, Iran's population will outnumber Russia's. A nuclear-armed Islamic Iran would emerge as an even stronger player.

Former members of the Russian military have been secretly helping Iran to acquire technology needed to produce missiles capable of striking European capitals. The Russians are acting as go-betweens with North Korea as part of a multi-million-pound deal they negotiated between Teheran and Pyongyang in 2003. It has enabled Teheran to receive regular clandestine shipments of top-secret missile technology, believed to be channeled through Russia. As in 1981, when Israel knocked out the French-made Iraqi nuclear-weapons center, and then was scolded by the French, so it may be the same that when Israel knocks down the Russians hardware, it will be scolded by Russia. Behind the curtains, France was very happy, as will be Russia.

The EU-3 nations of Britain, France and Germany —which have negotiated with Iran in hopes of reaching a resolution —together with the United States must work to persuade other nations to join their stance, said Merkel. "And we will certainly not be intimidated by a country such as Iran," she said. However, these nations will not do anything. They will wait for the US or Israel to do their job.

Implications of Israel's Attack

The implication of this analysis is an emerging picture of Israeli raids on Iranian nuclear facilities resulting in three advantageous outcomes: damage to Iranian nuclear ambitions, the possibility of taking politically popular military action in southern Lebanon, and the involvement of U.S. forces in weakening Iranian military capabilities.

An Israeli attack could well drag the United States in, with consequences for longer-term U.S./Israeli relations. Furthermore, Israeli planners would recognize that any major raids on Iran would be seen from Teheran as being done in conjunction with the United States, and there would most likely be Iranian retaliation against U.S. forces in Iraq, or against oil-supply routes from the region. Either eventuality would necessitate a strong U.S. military reaction that might weaken Iran.

237

Should America attack or Israel? Even a basic description of what will be entailed in a United States military operation against Iran is enough to sound a note of caution in Washington, and this might be what is prompting the back-channel talks that seem to be underway. Moreover, this brief litany omits other possible Iranian responses such as withdrawal from the nuclear Non-Proliferation Treaty; redevelopment of the damaged nuclear facilities to include a clear-cut weapons program, perhaps located in deep underground shelters; and encouragement of paramilitary actions against Saudi, Kuwait or United Arab Emirates oil facilities, potentially producing chaotic activities on world oil markets. Iran could also make life in Iraq even more difficult for United States forces.

If America does not strike, Mofaz is saying, Israel will. Yet, as that could produce the same results as an American attack, without the same assurance of success, Obama may have to restrain Israel, if he does not want a wider war.

Michel Samaha, a veteran Lebanese Christian politician and former cabinet minister in Beirut, said that the Iranian retaliation might be focused on exposed oil and gas fields in Saudi Arabia, Qatar, Kuwait, and the United Arab Emirates. "They would be at risk," he said, "and this could begin the real Jihad of Iran versus the West. You will have a messy world."

To be sure, Israel should make it clear that it would retaliate with double force against any attack. But it should also remind those urging it to act that the Islamic Republic's policies, including its quest for nuclear weapons, represent a threat not only to Israel, but to many other nations in the Middle East and beyond.

Iran's Threats Summary

Iran serves as the primary orchestrator and financial supporter of Hizballah, Palestinian terrorist groups in Gaza (such as Hamas and Islamic Jihad), and various other militant organizations in Iraq, Syria, Bahrain, Yemen, and across the Middle East. It poses a substantial threat not only to Western nations but also to Sunni Arab countries in the region, including Saudi Arabia. The primary concern with Iran lies in the proliferation of nuclear weapons and the potential supply of such weapons to terrorist groups. If Iran acquires the necessary capabilities, there is a significant fear that they might deploy these weapons.

Conclusion —National Security of the USA.

The greatest threats to the national security of the United States and the Western world emanate from the proliferation of nuclear weapons, with the possibility of North Korea and Iran supplying these arms to terrorist groups. China, in particular, poses a significant menace to the national security of the USA.

Hamas Attack on Oct 07, 2023 and the Western World Response

Individuals with limited knowledge, presuming a deep understanding, can often be the most outspoken and, unfortunately, potentially hazardous, particularly in the context of the Israel-Palestinian conflict. It is crucial to note that Israel withdrew from Gaza in 2005 displacing 9,500 of its cit-

izens. Currently, Gaza is under the control of Hamas, an organization designated as a terrorist entity by Israel, the United States, and the European Union.

Following Hamas's brutal barbarian attack on Oct 07, 2023, the question arises: What kind of individuals endorse horrific acts such as beheading children, kidnapping innocent individuals, including children, women, and grandmothers, and committing acts of rape and murder against young girls? Who supports the murder of innocent civil-

ians within Western nations? An institution that tolerates and accepts such behavior deviates from its moral compass, heading towards self-destruction and alienation from a rational society. As Israel responded, there was an inevitable display of images portraying the tragic toll on innocent bystanders. All of a sudden, Palestinian protesters are holding effigies of dead babies, calling for cease fire. They didn't have a problem when Israeli babies were being beheaded by Hamas. It is a disturbing reality that Hamas, much like ISIS and other terrorist organizations, deliberately places their own children and women in harm's way, using them as human shields. In some instances, Hamas stages scenes with victims in the streets, even using those who were not killed as human shields. Given these tactics, it becomes a challenge for people in the West to equate the actions of the two sides morally.

The New World Hamas Hero

Hamas calls for the end of Israel, while also accusing Israel of committing genocide. They demand selective airborne targeting of Hamas killers, who use civilians as shields. Gazans are put in more danger by Hamas than by the Israel Defense Forces, but the world accepts that Israel would never employ such a ruse. Hamas' apologists insist that Israel warns civilians to stay clear of Israeli bombs, yet daily Hamas launches rockets into Israel. The real issue is not about the principle of civilian deaths, but the efficacy of the Israeli response and the impotence of Hamas rocketry. Israel is being blamed for being too effective in its bombing, while Hamas is rewarded for being too ineffective in its rocketing.

The global elite community siding with the murderous aggressors rather than seeking justice for the murdered is due to factors such as the large number of Arabs and Muslims, the Muslim Middle East, and the romanticization of non-Westerners as blameless and victimized underdogs. The best way to understand this sick war is that Israelis are Jews and the ancient plague of

antisemitism is again sweeping the globe. Did any country call upon Hamas and/or Hezbollah to end launching of rockets as well as mortars into Israel before killing, harassing and torturing Israeli families?

Middle East immigrants, students, and radical leftists chant "Free Palestine from the River to the Sea" and "Israel, you can't hide, we caught you in genocide." Hamas and its supporters call for the genocidal end of Israel, but also claim it is Israel committing genocide. Hamas blasts Israel daily for retaliating for the October 7 butchery of 1,400 Israeli infants, children, women, and the elderly. Gazans are put in more danger by Hamas than by the Israel Defense Forces. The world accepts that Israel would never employ such a ruse, and civilian shields would attract Hamas rockets.

Withdrawing fully from Gaza under "land for peace" plan, Israel should have been given peace when they trusted the "peacemakers". The world donated billions of dollars to Gaza to help better their living standards. Nevertheless, the top three leaders in Hamas stole much money, while underground concrete tunnels spanning to 300 miles were built for importing missiles to destroy Israel. Hamas does not help the Palestinians and cannot be viewed as a partner for peace towards Israel.

242

The population that once supported Hamas in power claims no connection to the group, yet the world assumes they are inseparable from Israel's military. Hamas killed over 30 American citizens in a mass murdering spree, with 13 still unaccounted for. The Biden administration has not forced Hamas to return kidnapped Americans or responded to their killings. The US is pressuring Israel to be measured in its retaliation against Hamas, indirectly aiding Hamas.

God and Religion

The concept of God is a complex and inseparable one, with no universally accepted answer. Monotheistic faiths view God as one all-powerful, personal god, while polytheistic belief systems invoke multiple gods with unique features. Deism presents a distant Creator without intervention, while pantheism and panentheism emphasize interconnectedness. Atheists argue for insufficient proof, while agnostics are more hesitant. Theistic philosophy and process theology offer reasonable perspectives on understanding God. Monotheistic Gods are deeply influenced by transcendence, omnipotence, omniscience, omnibenevolence, and immanence. The implications of monotheism are felt in morality, ethics, worship, theology, and interfaith relations.

Jewish monotheism, a fundamental component of Christianity and Islam, has significantly influenced the development of morality, ethics, and spirituality, shaping the moral governing of mankind.

The United States is transitioning from a predominantly Christian nation to one characterized by religious diversity and a growing atheist/agnostic presence. Critics argue that religion serves as a more robust foundation for morality, while others argue that religious-based morality carries greater weight. Atheist figures like Richard Dawkins propose an evolutionary, socio-biological origin for human morality, emphasizing the dynamic nature of moral imperatives shaped by biological and cultural factors. Critics like Cardinal Cormac Murphy-O'Connor view atheism as a significant societal evil, attributing war and destruction to its influence.

However, historical examples like Soviet Russia show that atheism can lead to religious persecution and mass murders. Critics like Robert Wright and Mark Chaves challenge the New Atheists' criticism of religion as the sole cause of conflicts, highlighting the need to address deeper root causes and the evolving nature of religious beliefs. **Islam has the potential to gain acceptance due to its teachings, emphasizing ethical conduct and unity against racial or ethnic discrimination.**

Anti-Semitism and Hate

Anti-Semitism is a complex social issue that has persisted for centuries. Despite being a small percentage of the global population, Jews have made significant contributions to literature, jurisprudence, and scientific advancements. They have also influenced the development of legal systems and monotheistic beliefs, impacting Islam and Christianity. Despite facing societal ills, Jews have refrained from seeking vengeance and continue to excel in productive activities. Anti-Semitism is the oldest and most persistent form of hatred, with negative stereotypes about Jews often leading to physical violence.

Multiculturalism and supremacy can promote social cohesion and understanding, but when they coincide, they can lead to dangerous consequences. Multiculturalism can create feelings of "them" against "us," leading to discrimination, prejudice, and violence. It can also result in the dilapidation of personal liberties, perpetuating stereotypes and prejudices. These ideologies can inhibit social harmony and progress. To address these threats, promoting inclusiveness and equality involves educating people about different cultures, acknowledging their worth, and fostering authentic interaction between cultures.

Human migration, particularly Osmosis Migration, significantly influences societies, economies, and cultures. It can harmonize societies but also presents challenges like economic disparities and cultural clashes. The migration of people from nations with prevalent antisemitic sentiments through osmosis, poses a potential for substantial future issues in Western countries. To mitigate these challenges, there needs to be proactive intervention aimed at assimilating and educating these migrants. Addressing these requires a multifaceted approach involving governments, international cooperation, and policies. Recognizing and understanding these dynamics is crucial for a more inclusive and prosperous world.

ADL surveys show that around 12% of Americans have deeply rooted anti-Semitic sentiments, with over 30% of African Americans and Latinos holding such views. However, only 3% of the 70% population not comprising these groups maintain such beliefs. This contrasts with the over 30% prevalence among African Americans and Latinos. Concerns about hypothetical anti-Semitism from white evangelical Christians appear to preoccupy Jewish communities more than anti-Semitism within core Democratic constituencies. Factors contributing to anti-Semitism among minority communities include social and economic factors, political beliefs, propaganda, historical narratives, religious beliefs, social networks, and lack of education and awareness. The influx of antisemitism among Muslim immigrants presents a challenge, as the American Muslim community generally does not align with antisemitism. As economic security and education levels rise, the study suggests a potential moderation of antisemitic tendencies among Muslim immigrants, advocating vigilance in addressing such issues while recognizing the heterogeneity within American Muslim attitudes toward Jews.

Self-hating Jews is a sensitive issue that affects both Jews and non-Jews. It stems from personal issues, discrimination, religious clashes, media bias, and peer pressure. This can lead to feelings of shame, self-loathing, and erode Israel's collective identity. Self-hatred can re-invent stereotypes, fuel antisemitism, and support those aiming to delegitimize Israel. Examples like Rabbi Michael Lerner and Noam Chomsky illustrate the damage they can cause to their own people and their future.

Just like in any other setting, old and hazardous prejudice against the Jews is even springing up at Cornell University in New York next to the green grass and smooth stream. Since October 7, Jewish students have experienced death threats, plots against "Jewish control," and a lecturer's celebration of the "Hamas massacre was exciting." Although this was disguised as a criticism, it promoted false beliefs that created a sense of fear and animosity among students. Recently, there have been some shocking incidences of people acting as their own inner Nazis and making unfounded "Zionist conspiracy theories". Such tendencies are usually encountered in education contexts where information is highly susceptible to falsehoods and discrimination.

This word "Zionist control" is often a euphemism for attacking Jews. The age-old hate stereotypes are often the foundations of such conspiracies. The Cornell events underline that there are still anti-Semitic feelings among respectable institutions.

I had never encountered antisemitism until I attended a divorce court in NJ. The judge initially displayed fairness until my ex, in her first court action, being familiar with the Judge and the legal system, disclosed that I am Jewish. Subsequently, the judge exhibited the most prejudiced behavior I have ever faced. Despite being born in India to a Jewish family that never experienced antisemitism, I encountered full-blown prejudice here in the US. Consequently, I lost my pre-marital house, custody of my children, and received a restraining order without any supporting evidence. Over time, I managed to gain access to my children, and now they spend all their free time with me.

To combat these aspects of bias, there must be united actions aimed at fostering knowledge, sensitivity, and comprehension. Societies and campuses should be engaged in the demolition of stereotypes where they celebrate differences among people and one is judged for being him/herself. Societies become inclusive through open dialogues as well as by fighting against antisemitism.

The Islamic World and the West

The Islamic world, spanning from the Atlantic to the Pacific, is characterized by its unique identity and commitment to coexisting with the West. It seeks peaceful coexistence, avoiding subjugation and directing resources towards improving life for its people. The term "Islamic fundamentalism" is often criticized for its association with political activism, extremism, fanaticism, terrorism, and anti-Americanism. However, scholars like Bernard Lewis argue that all Muslims are fundamentalists in their reverence for the Qur'an, drawing from the Prophet's Traditions and theological and legal knowledge. The Fundamentalism Project, initiated by the University of Chicago, defines fundamentalism as an approach to preserve a religion's distinctive identity through selective retrieval of doctrines, beliefs, and practices from a sacred past. Muslim scholars Sadiq Jalal al-Azm and Hassan Hanafi defend the term, describing it as suitable for new Islamic movements and capturing the essence of Islamic awakening or revival in the West.

The Western world has been significantly influenced by historical movements like the Renaissance, Ages of Discovery, Enlightenment, Industrial and Scientific Revolutions, and the ancient world of Greece and Rome. The United States' government was influenced by Enlightenment philosophy and ancient Greek and Roman thought. The Enlightenment era, spanning the 18th century, influenced Western political thought, with philosophers like Montesquieu, Rousseau, and Locke contributing significant ideas. The late 18th and early 19th centuries saw revolutions, new ideologies, and societal changes. Western and Muslim government systems differ in philosophical underpinnings, organizational structures, and authority sources. Both aim to provide governance and uphold societal order, but their foundations and guiding principles shape diverse political landscapes.

Religion and nationality in Islamic countries' politics are complex issues influenced by history, culture, and religion. The future of these countries depends on their ability to negotiate these conflicting forces.

Western civilization's individualism, secularism, and freedom of speech are fundamentally at odds with Islamic principles. Western societies prioritize individualism, while Islamic values emphasize society and collective responsibilities. Western societies adopt secularism, while Islamic teachings emphasize divine law and religious synthesis. Liberal issues like gender equality and LGBTQ rights are not in line with Islamic norms. Freedom of speech, particularly in religious matters, is restricted in Islamic countries, leading to conflicts with various Islamic groups.

Violence has risen in Europe as a result of opening its doors to several million uninspected immigrants whose core beliefs and goals are entirely diverse from those of Europeans. While many individuals integrate successfully, those who do not contribute to the worsening situation as their children resist assimilation and exhibit higher birth rates.

The conflict between Western civilization and Islamic extremist principles arises from differing worldviews, faiths, and principles. Western civilization values democracy, while Islamic nations often exhibit authoritarian governance. Recognizing these differences can foster peaceful coexistence in an interconnected world.

Is it possible for Muslim communities in the West to embrace and peacefully coexist within its secular democratic systems? Probably not without full integration, as such an adaptation would require true Muslims to compromise the sacred Quranic principles of their revered canon, considered eternal and unalterable truth. Ethnic separation poses a perpetual threat to secular democracies, as it invites the potential disintegration or societal fragmentation of the state and its institutions through non-assimilation and cultural upheaval. A cult of repentance manifests as a suicidal syndrome of cultural self-destruction, where the majority willingly grants special privileges and rights to these radical groups.

The term "Palestine" has evolved over time due to its historical, political, and cultural significance. It has been associated with various empires and peoples, including the Philistines, Babylonians, Assyrians, Persians, Greeks, Romans, Byzantines, Arabs, Mamluks, and Ottomans. The origins of the name "Palestine" remain a mystery, and it's unclear whether names like Ammonites, Moabites, or Nabateans would elicit more empathy from the Jewish population in Israel.

Israel's political landscape is shaped by its complex relationship with nationality and religion. As a hub for diverse ethnic and spiritual communities, Israel is also the epicenter of world Abrahamic faiths. Understanding this interplay is crucial for Israel's future as a democratic and inclusive nation, addressing the challenges that define its political landscape.

The Israeli-Palestinian conflict is primarily due to land ownership, religious issues and Jerusalem's status as the capital of both countries. Despite progress in diplomacy with Arab countries under the Abraham Accords, the main issues remain. Iran, a regional spoilsport, has been using covert strategies to undermine the peace process, fueling instability and sectarian feuds. Despite these challenges, there is a chance of finding peace through good leadership, political will, and international assistance. The Abraham Accords have shown promise in normalizing relations, but Iran's aggressive strategies could impede their progress.

Iran is using covert strategies to undermine the Abraham Accords, aiming to normalize Israel's relations with Arab countries. This includes supporting militant proxies like Hezbollah, fueling regional conflicts, and supporting those against normalization. Despite the challenges, there is hope for peace through good leadership and international assistance.

The Forgotten Exodus, a historical event in the 1940s-50s, is a significant aspect of Middle East history that has been overlooked. It encompasses the forced displacement of hundreds of thousands of Jews from Arab countries, a situation reminiscent of the wartime dispersion of Jews during WWII. This event is crucial for understanding the complex history of the region and promoting empathy and open dialogue. Recognizing and understanding this tragic tale is essential for a broader perspective on the Middle East's history. The expulsion of Jews from Arab countries and the Palestinian Nakba are two interconnected narratives in the Middle East's history. The expulsion transformed Israel's demographic landscape, affecting economic growth. The diaspora communities struggled with identity and longing for belonging.

The Israeli-Palestinian conflict is a contentious issue, with Palestinian refugee claims being a significant concern. No Muslim country has officially declared entry for Palestinians, raising doubts about the genuineness of assurances made by certain states. While some Muslim-majority states provide humanitarian assistance, permanent settlement is not yet an option.

Many Arab nations gained independence from colonists in the 20th century, but the emergence of Israel in 1948 was a unique case. Arab countries like Egypt, Iraq, Syria, and Lebanon fought for independence against imperial hegemony. The Arab-Israeli conflict was a hotspot topic, with opposing territorial claims and the perception of Israel as a disputed entity. The Arab-Israeli struggle is influenced by historical grievances, territorial disputes, and external influences. The landscape of Europe and the Middle East has undergone changes over time. Nevertheless, Arab nations continue to center their attention on Israel and Palestine, using these issues as a means to channel and deflect the frustration stemming from the helplessness of the impoverished masses.

The Arab-Israeli conflict persists due to the active participation of Western media and academia, which often portray Israel as a state involved in war crimes, ethnic cleansing, and systematic murder. This portrayal can stem from misunderstandings, hypocrisy, double standards, and antisemitism. Despite historical debunking of classic blood libels, modern blood libel against Israel continues to gain traction. The toll of wars on Muslim victims worldwide is sobering, with Algeria, Sudan, Afghanistan, Somalia, Bangladesh, Indonesia, Iraq, Iran, Lebanon, Yemen, Chechnya, Turkey, Syria, Kosovo, and Jordan having the most fatalities (about 12 million in total). Nevertheless, news coverage consistently centers on the relatively small percentage of Muslim victims in the Palestinian conflict compared to other Muslim related wars.

Feelings and a sense of belonging play a crucial role in shaping individual perspectives on national participation and the fulfillment of duties. Among the assimilated Arab population residing in Israel (constituting 20% of the total), positive emotions such as patriotism serve as motivating factors for active involvement in various sectors, including the military, medical fields, and the Israeli Parliament. Additionally, a deep sense of belonging cultivates a shared responsibility for the well-being of the nation. This connection to national duties inherently brings fulfillment, creating a cycle of civic engagement that contributes to a more unified and harmonious civic environment.

The Jewish World and Israel

The Jewish left refers to Jews who support left-wing or left-liberal causes, either individually or through organizations. Originating from the Jewish Enlightenment and European Jews like Ludwig Börne, Jewish leftism has been significant in various movements, including labor, women's rights, and anti-racist, anti-colonialist, and anti-fascist movements. The movement has led to complexities and intra-communal disputes within the Jewish community, highlighting the deep connection between Jewish identity and the struggle for justice and equality.

The Jewish community's support for Israel is often based on unity, but this overlooks the diverse views and ideologies that contribute to this opposition. Some Jews oppose Israel due to their religious and cultural beliefs, challenging the Israeli government's actions as contrary to Jewish ethics. Others support justice and fairness for Palestinians, arguing for equal and fair solutions. The Israeli-Palestinian conflict is influenced by religious, ethical, humanitarian, and geopolitical considerations. Recently many individuals have revealed their latent anti-Semitic sentiments, and recent occurrences underscore the vulnerability of Jews without the protection of Israel. Nevertheless, there might be a perceived contradiction when Jews in the West advocate for a homeland safeguarded of the Palestinians by the sacrifice of their compatriots in Israel.

Israel's relationship with Diaspora Jewry is complex, balancing heritage preservation and assimilation. Their resilience and adaptability demonstrate the ongoing struggle for security and identity.

Global Terrorism

Iran's involvement in terrorism through multiple proxies has been criticized globally, affecting regional security. Iran's support for proxies is a political dynamic, fueled by rivalry against Saudi Arabia and gaining dominance in the region. This has led to prolonged conflicts, aggravated sectarian tensions, and worsened global relations. A multi-dimensional solution, including diplomacy, regional integration, and addressing root causes of proxy wars, is needed for regional stability and peace.

The root causes of violence within Muslim organizations are complex and require a comprehensive approach involving both Muslim-majority countries and the international community.

Jihad, a term in Islamic philosophy, has been a subject of debate and misinterpretation. Historically, it meant a personal struggle against immorality and spiritual advancement. However, it has also been linked to acts of terror, often used by extremists to gain support for their ideologies. This has led to controversy and disagreement within the Muslim community. The ethical implications of linking jihad to terrorism are complex, with some arguing that violence is a breach of human rights and a threat to world security. Jihad, a spiritual struggle, has been twisted by terrorists to justify violent acts, highlighting the need for understanding and addressing the historical context and philosophical foundations of jihad.

Adrian Reland, a Dutchman, embarked on an expedition to Palestine during the 17th century, documenting around 2,500 sites and revealing a sparsely populated land. He found that Jerusalem had 5,000 residents, with two-thirds being Jews, one-third Christians, and Muslims forming a nominal minority. Major cities had a few thousand inhabitants, with Jerusalem, Gaza, Nazareth, Tiberias, Safed, and Nablus having varying populations. Most Muslim residents were Bedouins, leading a nomadic existence without significant property ownership. Presently, Israel has emerged as a primary target for terrorism, with a growing inclination among the Arabs in the region to expel them.

The analysis of the link between Islam and violent extremism is challenging due to lack of reliable data and compartmentalization. The majority of extremist and violent terrorist incidents occur in largely Muslim states, with a small minority of Muslims seeking power. Most governments in these countries are actively fighting extremism and terrorism, and the vast majority of Muslims oppose violent extremism and terrorism. The analysis highlights the ongoing threat of extremism and instability to the Islamic world and the state outside it, with current threats including ISIS, Al Qaida, Hamas, Hezbollah and the Taliban.

Islam and the Jews

A Muslim professor discusses the issue of Jerusalem's sovereignty, arguing that it is a holy place and the capital of Israel. He cites the Koran's principle that no group can claim permanent possession over a specific territory. The professor also criticizes the denial of Jewish prayer on the Temple Mount, arguing it contradicts Islamic principles. He calls for a new attitude that respects the rights of all religions. The Qur'an explains that Allah gave the Land of Israel to the Jews and will restore them to it at the end of days. The Qur'an recognizes Israel as the heritage of the Jews and explains that before the Last Judgment, Jews will return to dwell there. Using Islam as a basis for preventing Arabs from recognizing Jewish sovereignty over the Land of Israel is recent and unfounded.

The fundamentalist Muslim program to use Islam as a political weapon against Jews faces a major obstacle in the Qur'an. Both the Bible and Qur'an state that the right of the Israelites to the Land of Israel does not depend on conquest and colonization, but on divine revelation and prophecy. From an Islamic point of view, there is no fundamental reason that prohibits Muslims from recognizing Israel as a friendly State. The real problem is the distorted interpretation of Islam as a political tool, which has led to the expulsion of Jews from Arab countries.

The Greatest Threats to the United States

The greatest threats to the national security of the United States and the Western world emanate from the proliferation of nuclear weapons, with the possibility of North Korea and Iran supplying these arms to terrorist groups. China, in particular, poses a significant menace to the national security of the USA. Based on AI latest knowledge update in January 2022, the following are key obstacles and potential threats:

1. **Cybersecurity Threats:** The increasing dependence on digital infrastructure makes the U.S. vulnerable to cyberattacks from state-sponsored actors, criminals, and hacktivists.

2. **Terrorism:** Despite successes in counterterrorism, the threat persists from both domestic and international terrorist groups.

3. **Geopolitical Rivalries:** Relations with major powers like China and Russia pose challenges, including competition in economic, technological, and military domains.

4. **Pandemics:** The COVID-19 pandemic highlighted the vulnerability of public health infrastructure, emphasizing the need to address global health challenges.

5. **Climate Change:** Environmental factors, such as extreme weather events and rising sea levels, pose threats to infrastructure, agriculture, and overall national security.

6. **Nuclear Proliferation:** The spread of nuclear weapons, especially in regions of geopolitical tension, remains a concern.

7. **Economic Challenges:** Economic instability, trade imbalances, and disruptions can impact the country's financial health.

8. **Domestic Extremism:** Internal threats from extremist ideologies and movements can lead to violence and social unrest.

9. **Infrastructure Vulnerability:** Aging infrastructure and susceptibility to cyber or physical attacks on critical systems pose risks.

10. **Mass Migration:** Global instability and conflicts may contribute to large-scale migrations, impacting domestic and international stability.

The Decline of the West per Roger Scruton

Roger Scruton, a conservative philosopher, argues that the Left's values and policies have eroded the foundation of Western civilization. He criticizes cultural Marxism, identity politics, and the erosion of traditional institutions, such as family, religion, and civic organizations. Scruton also opposes political correctness and free speech, and argues that the Left's approach towards immigration and environmentalism has led to the decline of Western nations. He also questions the Left's support for globalism and the erosion of national sovereignty.